1969

AUGUSTUS AND NERO

AUGUSTUS
and
NERO

THE SECRET OF EMPIRE

⤞⤞⤞⤞⤞⤞⤞⤞⤞⤞ by ⤝⤝⤝⤝⤝⤝⤝⤝⤝⤝

GILBERT
CHARLES-PICARD

TRANSLATED FROM THE FRENCH BY
LEN ORTZEN

THOMAS Y. CROWELL COMPANY
NEW YORK · ESTABLISHED 1834

This translation © J. M. Dent & Sons Ltd, 1965
Original: *Auguste et Néron*, Hachette, 1962

Printed in Great Britain

Library of Congress Catalog Card No. 65–12832

CONTENTS

v

INTRODUCTION

'When people hailed him as King, Julius Caesar answered: "I am Caesar. not King".'

SUETONIUS, *The Life of Caesar.*

'The constitution of Augustus is not founded either on royalty or dictatorship, but on the title of "Prince".'

TACITUS, *Annals*, Book I, chapter 9.

WHAT is an emperor? Why was this title born and when? In what does it differ from royalty and dictatorship? Such are the questions which this book attempts to answer by analysing the personality and the achievements of the first Caesars.

In a moment we shall justify our choice of Augustus and Nero from among some sixty Roman emperors. Let us bear in mind first that the only genuine emperors were those of Rome, whereas all nations at some time have been ruled by kings. The title 'Imperator' exists only in Latin. In other languages some paraphrase has to be found and, when it is translated, it is never exactly rendered. (In many languages, on the other hand, the word for 'emperor' is some adaptation of the proper name Caesar—e.g. in German, Russian and Urdu.)

The Greeks, who were subject to emperors for five centuries, and eventually provided their own emperor for a thousand years, never managed to give him a name: instead they changed the meaning of their original word 'Basileus', which had meant 'king' and which ceased after this semantic change to be applied as a description to ordinary kings.

Imperium and *imperator*, which have become, in modern English, empire and emperor, were born with Rome and express from the beginning peculiarly Latin conceptions of power, but these ideas remain until 31 B.C. widely removed from what they will become hereafter; they are bound up with war, with violent conquest, just like our 'imperialism' which in the nineteenth century recovered the primary sense of its root for historical reasons which will be immediately apparent. The Roman Empire of the first centuries of our era is, on the contrary, that 'common fatherland of various nations' which was invoked by the Gallic poet Rutilius Namatianus at the moment of its dissolution. The head of it is the temporal and spiritual guide of the entire human race. The transition from one form to the other took place at a time when the civilized world as the nations knew it, that is to say the Mediterranean and the fertile lands surrounding it, was threatened with extinction in default of an organization which should ensure peace there. Greece had created a civilization founded upon humanism, the superiority of which was acknowledged by all the peoples who had come in contact with it except for the Jews and a few other oriental nations, and all had attempted to practise some imitation of it; but Alexander had not managed to establish a political unity corresponding to the cultural unity so achieved.

Thereafter Rome had managed to subordinate all the other peoples, at the very time when she had adopted, in a scarcely modified form, that Hellenic humanism to which she had always been joined by a profound affinity. Thus the Empire was born; but the system in that early form was founded and remained based on the inequality of victors and vanquished, and the exploitation of the latter by the former; on the other hand, republican institutions, thought out to cater for the needs of a citizen body only a few thousand strong, were outmoded by the demands made by governing a territory as extensive as that of the largest modern states and populated by tens of millions of people. This imbalance had given birth to civil wars which raged for one hundred years, and produced a devastation comparable on the scale of what was technically possible then and now with that caused by the world wars that we in our generation have witnessed.

Then as now men saw salvation only in the establishment of a world government, which should be able to give authority to an order acceptable to individuals, almost all of whom aspired and turned to the same ideal, but were separated from each other by profound differences in their standards of living and subject to very diverse political régimes. This is the world government that Augustus created,[1] making it depend entirely on his personality. He was able to inspire, not only in the Romans, but in almost all the inhabitants of the Empire, no matter what their social or political status, that absolute confidence and almost mystic devotion which, at various times, among various peoples, the great leaders of men have evoked. It is the universal breadth of that

[1] Bear in mind that his world was a highly exclusive one, and that it took no account, for instance, of the Chinese Empire, which was technically and intellectually somewhat more advanced, though separated by a thousand miles of nomad-haunted steppe from the Mediterranean world and owing absolutely nothing to it. (Trans. note.)

spiritual conquest which endows that success with an exceptional and
almost miraculous character.

It has often happened in the course of history that a Man of Destiny
should carry his whole nation with him: often enough also the dictator
then uses the enthusiasm which he has called to life to throw his
faithful followers against neighbouring states and overpower them.
But we believe that Augustus is the only one who successfully secured
the voluntary adherence of all the peoples with whom he came in
contact almost unanimously. Very probably too he saved the Roman
Empire in guiding it across that dreary stretch in the career of great
power groupings, which is generally fatal to them and is nowadays
known as 'decolonization'. In him and his successor those who were
formerly the vanquished recognized a master who was their property;
and, led on by the example of their head, the whole Roman people
progressively denationalized itself to become not just another race
among the rest but that common *élite* of the universe, defined in the
second century A.D. by a Greek sophist from Asia Minor called Aelius
Aristides.

This first 'Augustan miracle' indelibly marked the function which he
created. All the time that there have been emperors they have been at
once Roman and universal, and that is essentially where they differ
from kings who are the heads of only one people. The extraordinary
thing is that this spiritual universality of the imperial function survived
even the material destruction and fragmentation of the Empire; when,
from the third century onwards, practical necessity obliged the emperors
to set up colleagues, it was understood that even when each of the
Augusti or Caesars was ruling a separate territory he remained bound
to his colleagues by unity of spirit. The rulers of the later Empire were
one Emperor incarnate in several individuals at once, just as the God
of the Christians—whose nature, as defined by theologians, took shape
at precisely this time—is one God in three persons. Beginning from the
close of the fourth century, it is true the eastern and western Empire
began to go their separate ways; but the fiction of unity persisted, and,
when there is at length no emperor, except at Byzantium, this character
'Basileus' continued to proclaim himself 'Autocrat of the Romans' and
to count himself the suzerain of those barbarian kings who had divided
the West between them. Moreover the latter continued to recognize his
sovereignty for a long time. In the year 800 Pope Leo re-established
the imperial dignity in the West, for the benefit of Charlemagne; when

*

the Roman populace acclaimed him in the basilica of St Peter it was as a Roman emperor and not as an emperor of the Franks, and his apologists were charged to justify this act in particular, considered as it was by Byzantium as an usurpation, by the default of the eastern Empire, which had fallen into the hands of a woman. After the Carolingians, the Ottonians and all the kaisers of Middle Ages and of modern times have considered themselves effectively Roman emperors; several of them wasted their strength in maintaining Italy as a dependency and in wrangling with the Pope for the primacy of Christendom. Among the Italians themselves a numerous party recognized in the German ruler the legitimate successor in title to Caesar; this is the mystique which leads Dante to represent Brutus and Cassius as the greatest criminals in history, and to join them with Judas in one punishment which he makes Satan inflict.

The effects of the extraordinary success of Augustus went on being felt right down to the time of the French Revolution and Napoleon, who, thinking to revive the Empire, succeeded only in destroying its fundamental principle, which was anyway obscured by the thought of the period. The four or five European emperors of the nineteenth century are nothing but tribal chieftains, or a superior type of king; all that they retain of the ancient and noble universal tradition is 'imperialism', that is the claim to subjugate to their own other nations whom they considered inferior 'racially'. The last and most ridiculous consequence of this nationalist-inspired nonsense was the proclamation of the King of Italy as Emperor of Ethiopia in 1937. In imagining that he had thus resuscitated the Roman Empire, Mussolini was in fact demonstrating that he had not the slightest grasp of the fundamental idea which had been its great strength.

This mistake on the part of the Duce serves to remind us to what a great extent Augustus differs from the dictators of our day, and in general from those tyrants, both great and little, ancient or modern, of whom Herodotus and Plato painted lifelike archetypal portraits that are still valid. Since there is not an infinite number or variety of ways of playing on the emotions of the crowd, it often happens that we shall discover close relationships between the methods they employ and the methods of Augustus. But these resemblances must not be allowed to veil a fundamental difference which we shall endeavour to make clear in the first part of the present book: whereas the tyrant at once inflates and prostitutes his own personality, the founder of the Roman Empire accomplished his task only by sacrificing his personality. The man originally known as Octavius began by abandoning his name to take that of a spiritual father. Then the name and personality of Caesar were swallowed up in Augustus, which signifies not so much an individual but a moral and religious entity. These changes of name, reminiscent of those made by the religious on entering an Order, are the outward and visible sign of a great and noble effort by which a founder of the Empire tried to blot out, or at least to disguise, his passionate and carnal nature, to become the exemplary type of man defined by Greek wisdom and Roman morality, and to make himself worthy of leading the nations by example as much as by authority. To be sure, this ideal of reason and policy is on quite another plane from Christian renunciation or Buddhist asceticism; no doubt because it was not founded on any sort of mysticism, which indeed it rejected having first been tempted by it; for the 'conversion' of Augustus undertaken in hypocrisy did not bring him peace. We shall see on the contrary that it caused the Master of the World, who was a demi-god and not a saint, the most shattering suffering, and it destroyed those around him who were unable to understand him or to follow him, plunging them into disorder and crime. The labour, however, was not in vain, and in the end it brought forth its fruits. If the whole Roman people at length succeeded in the centuries which followed in forgetting their national egoism, in transcending humanity to become its *élite* after having once been its oppressor, the cause was the personal example of the Emperor continued by the better of his successors.

If Augustus succeeded in his task the reason is substantially because his work was continued over more than three centuries after his death. Here is another 'miracle' no less admirable than the first: the ancients were fully aware of it, revering as they had the eternity of Rome as well as her universality. Nevertheless when we read the history of the Empire as written down by the authors of the time we find in it a long series of violent and often atrocious deeds, *coups d'état* and usurpations punctuated by sanguinary repression. The moderns have concluded that the system never succeeded in working out a law of succession which could ensure its stability. If we look closer at things we discover that this shortcoming is the direct result of the emergency which gave rise to the mission of Augustus, that he seemed to have been sent by providence. His contemporaries, convinced that he could never be replaced, were seized with terror when his sickness gave them reason to believe that their saviour might be eliminated, allowing chaos to return. When in the fullness of time Augustus died, each of his successors was obliged to become himself a new Augustus. Here again the choice of names is significant: all the princes adopted in their turn, not only the titles of the founder, but his proper names. So each of them is forced to the same sacrifice of personality which he himself performed: as they could not possess all the authorities necessary to this renunciation, which had been so powerful to Octavius in his time, it is not surprising that few of them withstood the terrible ordeal, while it should have produced in some of them, like Caligula, unmistakable symptoms of insanity.

Nevertheless it is observable that exactly a hundred years after the foundation of the Empire (from A.D. 69 onwards) the gravity of the crisis diminishes materially. From Vespasian to Commodus seven princes succeeded each other legally on the throne over a period of 110 years. During this time one only, i.e. Domitian, fell victim to a revolution. The calm of this period is the more remarkable in that it coincided with the extinction of the family of Augustus. Besides, of all these eight emperors, three only were legitimate sons of their predecessor; and of these three, two (Domitian and Commodus) were overthrown by force. How are we to explain the apparent paradox of this stabilization? Down to the end of the nineteenth century it was considered sufficient to blame chance and individual psychology; there were good emperors and bad emperors, naturally, because, so the argument went, human heredity is unlikely to throw up a constant series of good princes, and the best system was that of adoption which permitted the reigning monarch to choose the most worthy successor.

Now over the last hundred years or so the learned have become dissatisfied with this traditional but over-simplified view. Deeper explanations have been looked for in the study of institutions and of society. The most effective aid for this research has been provided by inscriptions which reveal facts which the classical historians had not perceived, or had judged to be of little interest. Thus it has been possible to establish that the imperial function, at first almost isolated, had in some degree secreted round it new organisms which had hastened to establish contact between the sovereign and his subjects, filling the place of the old republican magistrature which was now stripped of all royal importance. Of these forces the most important are the palace, the regular army and the civil service. Their advent is a capital event in the

history of western man, for the framework which they constitute is
without precedent in Mediterranean society: having disappeared in the
crisis of the high Middle Ages [1] it will rematerialize, having borrowed
much from the Roman model, around the European dynasties, and will
form the basis of modern states. It was formerly imagined that these
instruments of the imperial power had all been fashioned throughout
by Augustus, but nowadays we know that they were continually being
developed throughout the duration of the Empire, and that the moment
when they arrived at a true efficacy, and acquired an official character,
corresponds roughly to the first century A.D., when the imperial function became stabilized. By this fact the crushing weight that bore on the
person of the sovereign was greatly relieved: the Emperor was able to
break out of this terrible isolation, and the occupant of the throne was
no longer required to sustain by himself like Atlas the whole burden of
the habitable world; in place of a supernatural being he became the
principal wheel in a skilfully geared machine. This point of evolution
will form a natural limit for our inquiry, which we will not pursue
beyond the year A.D. 70.

On the other hand we had no wish to study in the same detail the
four emperors of the Julio-Claudian dynasty: Tiberius, son-in-law of
Augustus, who reigned from A.D. 14 to 37; Caius, whom we call
Caligula, son of Germanicus and great-grandson of Augustus through
his mother Agrippina the Elder, who was assassinated in 41; Claudius,
brother of Germanicus, nephew of Tiberius and grand-nephew of
Augustus, who died in 54; and finally Nero, whose mother Agrippina
II linked him directly with the blood of the founder and who was overthrown in 68. All doubtless very interesting characters; but all did not
play an equal part in the evolution of the imperial office which is our
subject. Tiberius wished only to be a sort of earthly deputy to the
divine Augustus, whose apotheosis was held to have perpetuated his
providential function. But despite his very great personal qualities, he
did not succeed in obtaining undisputed recognition for the legitimacy
of his mandate which Agrippina the Elder repudiated in favour of
descent by blood from the founder: this claim brought in its train
atrocious scandals related by the sombre genius of Tacitus, who has an
evident prejudice against the sovereign. Claudius also tried to follow

---

[1] I do not agree that all of these forces disappeared even at the peak of
medieval feudalism. All the time they were recognizable by some vestige that
represented them. (Trans. note.)

as closely as possible the rules laid down by Augustus: but he could not keep up the balance between the new institutions—palace and civil service—where henceforward the springs of power were to reside, and the constitutional façade represented by the Senate: nor was he able to integrate them into a coherent whole, so that his reign was dominated by dark forces held in leash by men and women whose moral character was not of the same calibre as their ability. In fact these two princes, who would have been perfectly capable of administrating a stable and regularized Empire, were quite unable to transform themselves into providential saviours of the universe. Caligula met spectacular failure for a quite different reason: convinced that he possessed supernatural powers, he took himself for a god, and became insane almost immediately:[1] the absurdity of his conduct, which so fascinated Albert Camus, is more curious than instructive for the historian.

There remains Nero, who also may appear mentally deranged to us and in addition a second-rate character at once ridiculous and odious. But this strange personality, although totally unable to interpret political facts, nevertheless had a perfectly adequate grasp of the spiritual role which was expected of an emperor. He even took account of the shortcomings of the Augustan theory of sovereignty in that respect and attempted to give it some of the dash and spiritual warmth which it lacked. It shall be our task to discover the devious ways which brought him to this source of renewal, not in religion, nor in philosophy, but in aesthetics. The figure of Nero is not, therefore, merely grotesque and monstrous: it helps us to understand what the paradox of the Empire was in the first century of its life: the obligation under which a man found himself to ensure the happiness of the world and to rise above the human condition without being able to let himself be carried away by some grand spiritual force. It is this paradox which we are trying to convey to the reader by demonstrating in our conclusion how it was resolved by the reintegration of the imperial function in the new order which had slowly been worked out almost unknown to the people who contrived it. The year of great crisis which followed the death of Nero is very revealing in that respect: in the shock of suddenly released forces the illusions which blind men to the realities of their own time melt away, exposing to view the facts of a new social life.

[1] It would be more in line with modern clinical observation to say that the conviction of his own divinity was a symptom of his insanity, rather than that it was followed by insanity. (Trans. note.)

Perhaps it will be considered over-bold to attempt an essay, having as its subject men so different from us, and attempting to rectify judgments which have been formed about them in their own time, or not long afterwards, and so handed down to us over so many centuries. However, we are not daunted in this attempt, and recent progress in historical method offers us resources which were lacking to our predecessors. Up to the present the principal source for writing the history of that day has been the critical study of texts which enables us to correct the errors, voluntary or not, of contemporary witnesses to a certain degree; epigraphy has brought to light some new documents, not twisted by copyists or adaptors; public law which determines the formation of new institutions, and finally, the science of religions. We have drawn relatively little on one other discipline: that of archaeology. Now excavations at Rome have revealed the setting in which Augustus and Nero lived, and, in our opinion, this is a particularly interesting means of comprehending not only the exterior manifestation of their personality, but also the intimate thoughts which they were unwilling to reveal and on which Suetonius alone throws some light. To be sure, the interpretation of these documents remains in great measure subjective and disputable, but the technique of interpreting sculptured monuments has been elaborately enough worked out in our time by scholars such as F. Cumont and K. Schefold, among others, so that one can try to extend their field of application. It is currently admitted, thanks to their researches, that the decoration of tombs reveals the beliefs of those who were laid to rest in them, and that the frescoes of Pompeian houses reflect the spiritual preoccupations of those who lived in them quite as much as literature does. That much is true of princes, who are not hampered by economic consideration when it comes to choosing the artists to decorate their palaces, and who are the setters of fashion and not its followers. In any case we have the feeling that we can better understand maligned princes in this way, and sometimes find the explanation, if not the excuse, for some deed regarded as monstrous. Perhaps too we are better placed today than the man of more placid centuries to understand the stresses and strains imposed on the leaders of a fluid world, where all traditional values were thrown back into the melting-pot, and if we cannot grant them our approbation at least we can now spare a certain sympathy.

SUMMARY OF
HISTORICAL BACKGROUND

AUGUSTUS (OCTAVIAN)

Watches struggle for power between Mark Antony and Lepidus, after death of Julius Caesar, *1*; given special powers by the Senate (January, 43 B.C.), but turns against that body in July–August, and forms, with Antony and Lepidus, Second Triumvirate, *1*; marries Scribonia, 39 B.C., but divorces her, in following year, to marry Livia, *1*. Master of Mediterranean world after final defeat of joint navies of Antony and Cleopatra off Actium, 31 B.C., and capture of Alexandria in following year, *2*; restores order and organizes administration, 30–27 B.C.; gives up extraordinary powers, conferred at start of war with Antony, and is made governor of most of the frontier provinces, with command of all armed forces, 27 B.C., *2*; 'Augustus', *2*.

Pacifies Gaul and Spain, 24 B.C.; twice seriously ill, and escapes plot against his life; refuses offer of dictatorship by the people, and also rejects perpetual consulship, but accepts tribunician power, renewed yearly, 22 B.C., *2*; gives his daughter Julia in marriage to Agrippa, 21 B.C.; adopts their two sons, Caius Caesar and Lucius Caesar, 17 B.C., *3*.

Inspects and reorganizes provinces in the East, 21–20 B.C., and Gaul and Spain, 16–13 B.C.; returns to Rome, *3*; scandal of Julia and Julius Antonius, 2 B.C., *4*, *70–3*; turns to Caius and Lucius for affection, *73*; need for friendship, *81*; 'Father of the Country', 2 B.C., *4*; dies, A.D. 14, *5*.

NERO

Adopted by Claudius, A.D. 50, as successor to the throne, *10*; assumes *toga virilis*, marries Octavia and receives proconsular imperium, *11*.

Governs, A.D. 54–9, under guidance of Seneca and Burrhus, *11*; allows Senate to control home affairs, while himself retaining provinces, army and diplomacy, *11*; takes Poppaea Sabina for his mistress, *11*;

has his aunt Domitia poisoned, *11*; the Juvenalia, A.D. 59, *138–9*; repudiates Octavia, has her killed, and marries Poppaea, A.D. 62, *12*.

Performs at the theatre in Naples, A.D. 64, *12*; orders the rebuilding of Rome on improved plan, after the great fire, *12, 98–100*; starts Christian persecution, *12*.

Subdues conspiracies, A.D. 65–6, *12*; leaves for Greece, and has successes in the Games, *12, 146*; returns to Rome as fresh conspiracy breaks out, *13, 147–8*; flees in terror and commits suicide, *13*.

HISTORICAL BACKGROUND

AUGUSTUS

On 15th March 44 B.C. Julius Caesar, dictator of Rome after his victory over Pompey and the conservatives barely a year before, was assassinated by a group of republicans led by Brutus and Cassius. A majority of the Senate supported the murderers, but the people and the army remained loyal to Caesar's memory. The succession was claimed by Mark Antony and Lepidus. Octavian, Caesar's great-nephew by female descent and his adoptive son, then aged nineteen, cleverly manœuvred between the two parties. Antony and Lepidus were hoping to get rid of him, but he was given special powers by the Senate (January 43 B.C.); he then turned against that body (July–August) and formed with Antony and Lepidus a coalition known as the Second Triumvirate (October) which, unlike the first, was legalized by vote. Proscriptions followed, and the republican party in Rome was destroyed; it was crushed in the East, where Brutus and Cassius had taken refuge, by defeat at the battle of Philippi (23rd October 42 B.C.). Sextus Pompeius, younger son of Pompey the Great, held out in Sicily until 36 B.C.

For ten years a state of 'cold war' interspersed with open conflict existed between Octavian (officially named Julius Caesar Octavianus until 27 B.C.) and Antony; Lepidus had soon been relegated to a secondary role. Antony, who was master in the East yet still had strong support in Italy, revived Caesar's policy in its boldest form. In 41 B.C., although married to Octavian's sister Octavia, he began an association with Cleopatra, the Macedonian Queen of Egypt who had been Caesar's mistress; and he endeavoured to transform the Roman Empire into a federation of kingdoms on the Hellenic model. Octavian, on the other hand, had become reconciled with the conservative party and established his own group of faithful supporters. He married Scribonia in 39 B.C., but divorced her the following year to marry Livia, who already had two children, Tiberius and Drusus.

By the beginning of 32 B.C. the break between the triumvirs was complete. The final civil war, like the others, was waged chiefly in the

Balkans. On 2nd September 31 B.C. the combined navies of Antony and Cleopatra were defeated off Actium. Octavian captured Alexandria on 1st August 30 B.C., when Antony and Cleopatra committed suicide.

Octavian was master of the Mediterranean world, whose richest and most civilized regions—notably Italy and Greece—had been ravaged and ruined by twenty-eight years of almost continuous warfare. During the years 30–27 B.C. he restored order and organized his administration. The Triumvirate had expired on 1st January 32 B.C., so that Octavian's authority officially rested in the consulship that he had again accepted on 1st January 30 B.C. and which he retained until 23 B.C.; but his authority actually came from the special powers conferred on him when war was declared against Antony, and which had been sanctioned by an oath of loyalty to Octavian by the Italian people and the western provinces. On 13th January 27 B.C. Octavian gave up his extraordinary prerogatives to the Senate; that assembly then conferred on him the general governorship of most of the frontier provinces, which implied command of all the armed forces stationed there. The Senate showed its gratitude for 'restoring the Republic' by bestowing on him the title of Augustus and other honours. The temple of Apollo on the Palatine was dedicated.

Augustus spent the years to the end of 24 B.C. pacifying Gaul and Spain; he fell gravely ill in the latter country in 25 B.C. Agrippa remained in Rome, where he carried out a considerable building programme. Maecenas was in charge of intellectual propaganda (Virgil had published the *Georgics* in 29 B.C. and was working on the *Aeneid*; Horace had completed his *Epodes*). In 23 B.C. Julia, Augustus's daughter by his first wife Scribonia, married her cousin Marcellus, Octavia's son. The years 23 and 22 B.C. were critical. Agrippa retired to Mitylene to make way for Marcellus, but the latter died that year. Social unrest due to economic causes broke out in Rome; Augustus was again seriously ill, and a plot against his life was made by Caepio and Murena; he was offered the dictatorship by the people, but refused it. He also rejected the perpetual consulship, but received in compensation the tribunician power, which was renewed for him every year.

Early in 21 B.C. Augustus gave Julia in marriage to Agrippa, then left his new son-in-law to act for him in Rome while he set off to inspect and reorganize the provinces in the East. In Asia he put military and diplomatic pressure upon the Parthians and compelled their king,

Phraates, to return to Tiberius the Roman standards lost by Crassus (20 B.C.). This event was celebrated at Rome with great rejoicing, and the propaganda services represented it as bringing about a universal empire; many monuments were erected to commemorate it, in particular a triumphal arch on the Forum. A son was born to Julia and Agrippa at the end of 20 B.C. Virgil died on 21st September 19 B.C. without having completed the *Aeneid*, but the work was nevertheless published. Augustus returned to Rome on 12th October. In 18 B.C. Agrippa, who had carried out another mission in Gaul, was associated with the tribunician power for five years. Laws were passed punishing debauchery, but the marriage law was rejected by the people's assembly.

A second son was born to Agrippa in 17 B.C. Augustus adopted both children, who were given the names Caius and Lucius Caesar. Horace composed the official hymn to Apollo and Diana (the *Carmen Saeculare*) for the Secular Games, which marked the beginning of a 'golden century'.

Augustus was again absent in Gaul and Spain from 16 to 13 B.C., completing the organization of those provinces and establishing new colonies (Aix and Nîmes among others). Tiberius and Drusus conducted campaigns against the Alpine and Germanic tribes. Agrippa, accompanied by his wife, went to supervise affairs in the East.

The Emperor's return to Rome on 4th July 13 B.C. seemed to usher in a period of general pacification. An altar dedicated to the Peace of Augustus was set up in the Field of Mars, but was not completed until 9 B.C. Lepidus died, and Augustus succeeded him as grand pontiff. Horace published the fourth book of the *Odes*.

Agrippa died in 12 B.C., and at the end of the year Julia was married a third time, to Tiberius. Drusus was victorious in Germany, subduing the country as far as the Weser. His wife, Antonia, the younger daughter of Octavia and Mark Antony, had borne him a son, Germanicus; she gave birth to another son, Claudius, in 10 B.C. at Lyons. Augustus went there on 1st August from his field headquarters in northern Italy, for the dedication of the temple of Rome and Augustus (its great altar had been consecrated in 12 B.C.). Drusus died in 9 B.C., by which time Tiberius had conquered Pannonia as far as the Danube.

Horace and Maecenas, who had withdrawn from public life, both died in 8 B.C. Tiberius took over his brother's command in Germany, where Marbod had founded the powerful kingdom of the Marcomanni, in Bohemia, and was giving refuge to Gauls fleeing from Roman domination. Augustus made a fourth journey into Gaul, granted a triumph to Tiberius, and closed the temple of Janus for the third time. The municipal administration of Rome was reorganized, and this was an opportunity for dedicating many monuments of the imperial cult. In 6 B.C. Tiberius was given tribunician power, but soon afterwards retired to Rhodes in semi-disgrace, leaving behind Julia—with whom he was most unhappy. In 5 B.C. Caius Caesar assumed the garb of manhood, the *toga virilis*; he was given the title of 'prince of youth', and was elected consul-designate.

Herod, King of the Jews since 30 B.C., died in 4 B.C. Quirinus, legate of Syria, ordered a census that year, which was probably the year of Our Lord's birth.

On 5th February 2 B.C. the Senate and the people voted Augustus the title of 'Father of the Country'. In July the scandal over Julia broke, and she was exiled; her lover and accomplice, Julius Antonius, a son of Mark Antony, was executed. In August the temple of Mars Ultor was dedicated by Augustus in his Forum, which he also inaugurated. Lucius Caesar, like his elder brother, received the title of 'prince of youth' and was designated for the consulship. In 1 B.C. Caius Caesar was sent to Asia to try to recover Armenia, which had revolted against the Roman protectorate. He was badly wounded in a skirmish in A.D. 3, and died on 21st February A.D. 4. His brother Lucius had died at Marseilles on 20th August A.D. 2. In that year Tiberius returned to Rome, and in A.D. 4 was again given the tribunician power; Augustus adopted him as his son, and also Agrippa Postumus, the last son of Agrippa and Julia. Tiberius was given command of the army in northern Germany, where Domitius Ahenobarbus had in the meantime advanced to the Elbe.

A critical situation developed in the year 6, when the Dalmatian and Pannonian peoples rose in revolt, which prevented Tiberius from carrying out a major expedition against Marbod. Rome's food supplies and finances were jeopardized. The Pannonian war lasted until A.D. 9. It no sooner ended than, in Westphalia, Arminius led the Cherusci tribe in an attack on the troops commanded by Varus and wiped out three legions (a tenth of the whole Roman army). However, Tiberius managed to restore the situation. He was again victorious in A.D. 12, and handed over his command to Germanicus.

The younger Julia had been banished in A.D. 9, like her mother; and so had Agrippa Postumus, to Planasia, an island near Corsica. Their disgrace involved Ovid, who was exiled to Tomis (Constanza). The only grandchild remaining to Augustus was Agrippina, married to Germanicus.

Augustus died at Nola on 19th August A.D. 14.

TIBERIUS

Tiberius seems to have been reluctant to assume all the powers possessed by Augustus, although already invested with the tribunician power and the proconsular *imperium*. It was not until 17th September A.D. 14 that the Senate acknowledged him as emperor. He had saved the Empire at the critical time of the Pannonian and the German revolts, and was—as Augustus himself had said—the only defender of the Roman people. But many feared his restless and untrustworthy character. A strong party supported Germanicus, the heir presumptive and holder of the tribunician power.

At the beginning of the new reign a grave situation developed, when the legions in Pannonia and Germany mutinied; but Germanicus and Drusus (Tiberius's son) restored order. Germanicus then undertook to avenge the defeat of Varus, and in 15 and 16 devastated Westphalia as far as the Weser. But at the end of 16 Germanicus was recalled by Tiberius, who decided to establish the Empire's frontier on the Rhine.

At home the Emperor adopted a conservative policy, giving control of the government to the Senate and the magistrates. The powers of the people's committees, however, were transferred to a limited assembly and finally to the Senate.

In 17 Germanicus, having celebrated his triumph, was appointed commander-in-chief in the East; a revolution among the Parthians had brought to power a new dynasty, hostile to the Romans. Germanicus succeeded in restoring Armenia to the Roman protectorate. But he behaved as though he were a sovereign, accepting divine honours, governing the East without reference to Rome; and he visited Egypt without permission from Tiberius, that country being forbidden to senators. Germanicus probably gathered support there for himself, which would explain the persecution of the Egyptian cults that Tiberius ordered in Rome directly after the death of Germanicus.

He had returned to Syria, where he died on 10th October 19, commonly believed to have been poisoned by Piso, the legate of Syria, who had reported his disloyal conduct. Piso was recalled to Rome and brought to trial, but committed suicide. Tiberius tried to transfer Germanicus's popularity to his own son, Drusus junior. But the widow, Agrippina the Elder, led an active campaign for their sons, Nero and Drusus tertius.

Meanwhile serious trouble had broken out in the West. From 17 to 24 the tribes of southern Tunisia were in revolt against the extension of agriculture to their grazing areas. In the year 21 the tribes that had settled between the Ardennes and the Rhine tried to throw off the Roman yoke; the triumphal arch at Orange was built to commemorate their submission.

Tiberius was induced by these difficulties to increase his effective powers. He was urged to do so by Sejanus, who had been commander of the praetorian guards for several years. In 23 the latter concentrated the nine cohorts of the guard in a camp on the Viminal hill, not far from the present-day ultra-modern Termini railway station. Sejanus obtained juridical and administrative powers, in addition to his military command, so that he became a kind of prime minister. His power increased still more when, later in the year, Drusus junior died; report had it that the young prince was poisoned by his wife, Claudia Livilla (Germanicus's sister), at the instigation of Sejanus, who had seduced her. Tiberius was obliged, in any case, to name as his heirs the two eldest sons of Germanicus, Nero and Drusus tertius, which caused him to fear the intrigues of Agrippina more than ever. He had been living mainly in Campania since 21; in 27 he moved to the island of Capri, and never returned to Rome.

In 24 Tiberius refrained from asking the Senate to renew his *imperium*; Augustus had had it renewed every ten years. This omission, together with the expanding powers of the praetorian prefect, and the permanent institution of a *praefectus urbi* whose title-holder became the absent Emperor's representative in Rome and carried out the functions of president of the Senate, all indicated the authoritarian nature of the régime. Sejanus, moreover, was persecuting senators with republican opinions and the friends of Agrippina. She herself was accused in 29, together with her two eldest sons. Banished to Pantellaria, she was so badly treated by the centurion guarding her that she lost an eye. Nero was sent to the island of Pontia, and Drusus tertius was kept in prison in Rome. However, the opposition was not beaten, and spread many infamous tales about the debauchery and cruelty of

Tiberius, which were later repeated by Tacitus and Suetonius in their writings; most were certainly exaggeration or pure invention.

Sejanus, although only of knightly origin, had in the meantime received many honours, in particular a consulship shared with the Emperor; this gave him hopes of acceding to the imperial throne. But Tiberius began to suspect his designs; and on 18th October A.D. 31 he was suddenly arrested and killed, together with his family, in particularly horrible circumstances. Agrippina, Nero and Drusus all died in 33. Their supporters suffered from the terror as much as did those of Sejanus. Yet Tiberius showed some goodwill towards the remaining children of Agrippina and Germanicus—Caius, Agrippina the Younger, Livilla and Drusilla. In 35 he named as his joint heirs Caius and his own grandson, Tiberius Gemellus, the son of Drusus junior.

There was more unrest in the East after 35. The kingdom of Herod had been split up at his death in 4 B.C., and Judea had been annexed by the Empire in A.D. 6. Political and religious strife spread throughout Palestine. In 34 Tiberius annexed the tetrarchy of Philippos, son of Herod. This was the background to the message of Christ and to His Passion, which according to St Jerome occurred in the year 29. The invasion of the Alani south of the Caucasus in 35 caused disorders in Parthia, which were adequately dealt with by the legate of Syria, Lucius Vitellius.

Tiberius died at Cape Misenum on 16th March A.D. 37.

CALIGULA

Caius Caesar, nicknamed Caligula ('little boots') by his father's soldiers, was enthusiastically greeted as emperor by the Senate and by people everywhere. But this popular recognition was based on an ambiguity: the conservative party had made approaches to Germanicus's family, then in opposition, and had pretended they had 'republican' opinions. It is probable, though, that Agrippina the Elder was even then turning her thoughts towards a monarchy on oriental lines. Caligula's tyranny is traditionally explained by a serious illness in September 37 A.D. which impaired his mental powers. There is no doubt of his subsequent madness. A result of this was the application of a policy prompted by Egyptian influences and the memory of Antony, Caligula's maternal great-grandfather, and which had far-reaching, grave consequences.

Suetonius says explicitly that Caligula's intention was to change the principate into an absolute monarchy, but that he then decided it was not a sufficiently high dignity, and wanted to be a living god. His desire was to establish a theocratic monarchy similar to that of the Pharaohs. He behaved as a sovereign who was a magician and worker of miracles; hence his extravagant dress and his apparently absurd mystical practices —for instance, his invented triumphs over imaginary enemies or the forces of nature; and, too, his debauchery—his alleged incest with his sisters—and the honours given to his horse (obviously based on Egyptian practices). He built a temple of Isis in the Field of Mars and dedicated a chapel to her in his palace.

Few outstanding events occurred during his short reign, which was a very prosperous period for the Empire. In 37 Caligula removed the proconsul of Carthage from command of the army in Africa, and gave independence to Commagene, a district of Syria, and also to a small Jewish territory held by Herod Agrippa. In the following year Caligula lost his favourite sister Drusilla, with whom he has been accused of incest. He revived the people's assemblies, doubtless to gain the support of the plebs against the Senate. The early months of 39 saw the persecution of many senators; and Herod Antipas, tetrarch of Galilee, was deposed. Caligula went to Gaul in September, fought the German tribes, and made a hostile demonstration of his intention to cross to Britain. He suppressed an army conspiracy against him, in which his surviving sisters Agrippina the Younger and Livilla were implicated. Early in 40 he had King Ptolemy of Mauretania put to death at Lyons, probably because he was Cleopatra's grandson and might become a rival. Serious disorders between Greeks and Jews had broken out at Alexandria in 38; Caligula forced the Jews to participate in the Imperial cult, and ordered a statue of himself to be erected in the temple at Jerusalem. He returned to Rome on 31st August 40. In January 41 he imposed a new taxation system copied from Egypt, and prepared to leave for Alexandria. On 24th January he was assassinated by an officer with republican views: Chaerea, tribune of a praetorian cohort.

CLAUDIUS

The accession of Claudius was entirely due to chance. This brother of Germanicus, born at Lyons in 10 B.C., had always been considered a booby. He had led a quiet life, devoting himself to literary pursuits and keeping apart from the dramas that caused the destruction of his family. Tiberius had kept him out of political affairs. Caligula made him consul and conferred on him other honours appropriate to his birth, but made him pay for them by pestering and annoying him. After the murder of his nephew, the praetorians found him hiding in fear behind a curtain; as they had little liking for Chaerea's proposal for a return to the Republic, they proclaimed Claudius emperor in spite of his unwillingness.

As Emperor he had the defects and qualities of his intellectual character. His contemporaries wrote chiefly of his unfitness for practical matters, which made him appear artless and complaisant, with sudden bursts of anger. They disregarded the political shrewdness, resulting from his studies, which is evident in his speech on the admission of Gauls to the Senate; in it the Emperor expressed the need for the assimilation of provincials and denounced the reactionary conservatism that had always been systematically opposed to reforms. Claudius recognized the importance, too, of the administrative services created by Augustus, and he expanded them by increasing the number of procurators and by having a single exchequer for all the revenues in his charge. He took wise measures in economic and social matters. Italy was beginning to feel the adverse effects of competition from the provinces and of the transfer of wealth from the old aristocracy to the self-made men, who came chiefly from the ranks of freedmen of Eastern origin. Claudius caused these people to contribute to the financial needs of the State by granting them certain political rights. But at the same time he endeavoured to maintain the essentials of Roman traditions; he respected the prerogatives of the Senate, harshly punished any usurpation of citizenship, and demanded complete Romanization of those who were granted honours. He was, however, blamed by the opposition for giving too much power to the freedmen who were in charge of the imperial administration.

The last months of 41 were used to put affairs of state in order: Caligula's murderers were executed, but his decrees were abolished and the people he had exiled were recalled. The kingdom of Commagene was restored, and that of Judea was given to Herod Agrippa; the Jews were allowed freedom of worship. In 42 Suetonius Paulinus subdued Mauretania, which was then formed into two provinces. Furius Camillus tried unsuccessfully to get the army in Dalmatia to rebel. The impoverishment of Italy was affecting food supplies to Rome, and

to improve matters a large harbour was built at Ostia. In the following
year an army commanded for a time by the Emperor had little difficulty in subduing southern Britain. Claudius celebrated his triumph in
44, reorganized the financial administration and the food supply, and
merged Judea into the Empire again on the death of Herod Agrippa.
Thrace was annexed in 46. From 46 to 47 Claudius, having assumed the
functions of censor with Lucius Vitellius (father of the future Emperor)
as his colleague, pursued a progressive social policy; it was then that he
proposed the Senate should admit Gauls as members, and he restricted
for the first time the right of life or death that masters had over their
slaves. Meanwhile his third wife Messalina, who had given him a son,
Britannicus, soon after his accession, and then a daughter, Octavia,
was using her influence in favour of various unsavoury rackets and to
bring down her enemies; several members of the aristocracy had been
condemned to death. Messalina, whose private life was wild and
wicked, caused a terrible scandal in the autumn of 48: she 'married'
one of her lovers during a Bacchanalia. Claudius had her put to death
at the instigation of Narcissus, the freedman who was his principal
private secretary. Several young women belonging to the aristocracy
tried to seduce Claudius, each being prompted by one of the freedmen
who had become the Emperor's ministers. Early in 49 Pallas, the
financial secretary, persuaded Claudius to marry Agrippina the
Younger, Germanicus's daughter and his own niece. Seneca, who had
been banished to Corsica at the beginning of the reign, was recalled
through the influence of Agrippina; he was made praetor and appointed
tutor to her son Nero. Agrippina prevailed upon the Emperor to set
aside his own son Britannicus in favour of Nero. On 25th February
A.D. 50 Claudius adopted Nero as successor to the throne.

In the East the situation was still confused. Rome tried to take
advantage of internal disorders in Parthia to place a pretender on the
throne, but was unsuccessful. In 51 Armenia became part of the Iranian
Empire, which had been re-established. Political and religious agitation
increased among the Jews; the followers of Christ, who had seemed to
be no more than a Judaic sect, began from 44 onwards to spread the
gospel throughout the Roman Empire, under the leadership of St Paul.
In 51 the Roman authorities expelled from the capital 'the Jews who
were stirring up trouble at the instigation of Christ' (Suetonius).
Agrippina became all-powerful after 51. She had Burrhus, who was
devoted to her, made praetorian prefect. Nero assumed the *toga virilis*,

married Octavia (in 52), and received the proconsular *imperium*. But Narcissus warned the Emperor against the intrigues of his wife. She, however, apparently decided to get rid of him; Claudius died during the night of 12th October A.D. 54, poisoned, so it was said, by Agrippina.

NERO, GALBA, OTHO, VITELLIUS

Under the guidance of Seneca and Burrhus, Nero governed from 54 to 59 A.D. according to the desires of the conservative party. Agrippina—having put an end to her chief enemies, Narcissus and the proconsul of Asia, Silanus—was herself discreetly excluded from power early in 55; Pallas had to give up control of the fiscal services. Britannicus was poisoned (February 55) to prevent a reconciliation between Agrippina and Claudius's children. In that year Seneca dedicated to Nero his *De Clementia*, which was a declaration of the Emperor's policy. Nero allowed the Senate to control home affairs, and retained the provinces, the army and diplomacy for himself. Limited campaigns were undertaken in Lower Germany. In Asia, Corbulo began an offensive against the King of Armenia, Tiridates, who had been placed on the throne by his brother Vologaeses, King of the Parthians. In 58 St Paul was arrested in Jerusalem. Nero took Poppaea Sabina for his mistress and sent her husband Otho to govern Lusitania (Portugal). A great fire devastated Lyons. Agrippina was murdered at Baiae in March 59. Nero had his aunt Domitia poisoned. Corbulo captured Artaxata and Tigranocerta, the chief towns of Armenia. In September Nero drove chariots and played the lyre at the theatre.

St Paul was sent to Rome in August 60, but did not reach there until the following March. Corbulo established a Roman nominee, Tigranes, on the Armenian throne. Nero instituted the Quinquennial Games. The currency was debased. Rubellius Plautus, a descendant of Augustus, was banished to Asia. In 61 Corbulo drove back a counter-offensive by the Parthians. Vologaeses sent an embassy to Rome, but negotiations broke down. Towards the end of the year Boudicca led an insurrection and seized several towns, including London; but Suetonius Paulinus defeated her forces and crushed all resistance. The prefect of Rome, Pedanius Secundus, was killed by one of his slaves, and all those in the house were executed by order of the Senate, in spite of public protests. Galba was appointed legate of northern Spain, where there was unrest.

In 62 Vologaeses invaded Armenia, defeated the forces of Caesennius Paetus, and concluded an armistice with him. Burrhus was put to death. Tigellinus succeeded him as praetorian prefect, with Faenius Rufus as colleague. Seneca tried to withdraw from public life. Cornelius Sylla, in exile in Gaul, and Rubellius Plautus, still in Asia, were put to death. Nero repudiated Octavia, had her killed, and married Poppaea. Pallas was poisoned.

In 63 Corbulo attacked Armenia, negotiations having failed. A treaty gave the Armenian crown to Tiridates, on condition that he went to accept it from the hands of Nero. Poppaea gave birth to Claudia, but the baby died after four months.

In 64 Nero performed at the theatre in Naples, planned a journey to Greece and another to Egypt, then gave up both projects. In the early summer Tigellinus gave an entertainment for Nero on Agrippa's lake in the Field of Mars. The great fire (19th–28th July) destroyed much of Rome; Nero ordered the rebuilding on an improved plan, began his own Golden House, and started persecuting the Christians, who were given the blame for the fire damage.

Piso formed a conspiracy early in 65, but it was discovered on 12th April. In the repressions that followed Seneca, the poet Lucan and the praetorian prefect Faenius Rufus were executed. Nymphidius Sabinus was appointed to the vacant place of colleague to Tigellinus. Poppaea died in late summer.

Many more prominent people were put to death early in 66, including Petronius, Thrasea Paetus, Barea Soranus and his daughter, the leaders of the conservative party. Helvidius Priscus was sent into exile. The great Jewish rebellion broke out (and continued until 70, only ending with the recapture and destruction of Jerusalem). During the summer Tiridates came to Rome, did homage to Nero and received the Armenian crown from him. The temple of Janus was closed. The revolt in Judea spread to the entire country, and the last Roman positions in Jerusalem fell at the end of September. Vespasian was given command of the Jewish war. Nero left for Greece at the end of the year, and took part in the Games. He spent all of 67 in Greece, having more successes at the Games; he gave freedom to the Hellenes, and tried to have a canal dug through the Isthmus of Corinth. He summoned Corbulo, who was implicated in a conspiracy by Vicinius, and ordered him to commit suicide. Vespasian and his son Titus reconquered Galilee and the coastal area of Palestine. In 68 they laid siege to Jerusalem.

Nero was informed by his freedman Helius of new plots, and at the beginning of 68 returned to Rome, where he celebrated a triumph of a novel kind. In March Vindex raised the standard of revolt at Lyons, and in April Galba followed suit in Spain. Vindex was defeated and killed at Besançon, in May, by the army from Upper Germany commanded by Verginius Rufus. Nevertheless several other provinces joined the insurrection. In June the praetorian prefect Nymphidius Sabinus succeeded in neutralizing the praetorian guard; Nero fled in terror from Rome, and committed suicide on 9th June.

On receiving news of Nero's death Galba assumed the title of Caesar instead of that of Senatorial Legate which he had held until then. He spent the summer in Gaul, rewarding the cities that had supported him and penalizing those that had not; he removed Verginius Rufus from command of the legions of Germany and appointed Hordeonius Flaccus in his place. Meanwhile Nymphidius Sabinus tried to have himself proclaimed emperor, but was killed. Galba entered Rome in mid October. He heard of the death of Macer, who had raised a revolt in Africa. Cornelius Laco became praetorian prefect, Vitellius legate of Lower Germany.

On 1st January 69 the legions of Upper Germany refused to take the oath to Galba, and on the 3rd all the troops in Germany proclaimed Vitellius emperor. Galba adopted Piso Licinianus in Rome on the 10th. Otho seized control of the capital on the 15th, Galba was killed in the Forum and his supporters massacred. The Senate granted Otho the tribunician power and the title of Augustus. But Vitellius obtained the support of Gaul and Britain, and the legions of Germany marched into Italy in two groups commanded by Vitellius's generals, Valens and Caecina Alienus, one down the Rhône valley and the other through the Alps. Otho ordered Tigellinus to commit suicide. In March Otho's forces commanded by Suetonius Paulinus held up Valens's advance and inflicted several defeats on Caecina Alienus in Cisalpine Gaul. But Valens succeeded in reaching Italy, and on 14th April the army of Vitellius won a decisive victory at Bedriacum (near Cremona). On the 17th Otho killed himself. Vitellius set off for Rome, where he had been proclaimed emperor. He granted an amnesty to Otho's generals. He entered Rome in June, discharged the praetorian cohorts, and recruited new ones from his legions.

However, Vespasian, whose troops were reducing the last of the Jewish strongholds except Jerusalem, refused to recognize Vitellius as emperor. He himself was proclaimed emperor by the governor of Egypt, Tiberius Alexander, on 1st July; by the legions of Syria on the 3rd; and the army of the Danube, swayed by its general Antonius Primus, approved this choice. Primus marched through Istria and into Italy with seven legions; he captured Cremona at the end of October, chiefly through the disloyalty of Caecina Alienus, the commander of Vitellius's army, and of the fleet at Ravenna. The troops supporting Vespasian occupied Italy as far as the Apennines. In Gaul, where Civilis led a revolt of the Batavians and other German tribes against the Roman garrisons, the troops and officials took sides for the two warring emperors. But during the autumn Valens, who commanded Vitellius's forces on the northern front, failed in an attempt to land troops on the Provençal coast; all the provinces of the West then went over to Vespasian.

Antonius Primus and Mucian, who had brought reinforcements from Syria, marched on Rome in December. As they drew near, Vitellius came to terms (17th December) with Flavius Sabinus, Vespasian's brother, who was still prefect of the city. But the popular elements among the supporters of Vitellius and his party refused to accept the agreement, surrounded Sabinus and his men in the Capitol and massacred them. The Capitol was destroyed by fire on 19th December. Primus entered Rome next day, and Vitellius was killed in his turn.

PART ONE

AUGUSTUS

Chapter One

THE MASK OF THE SOVEREIGN

⟫⟫⟫ I ⟪⟪⟪

THE POLITICAL ACHIEVEMENTS OF AUGUSTUS

'DURING my sixth and seventh consulships, having put an end to all civil strife and being by common consent supreme and universal sovereign, I handed over control of the State to the government of the Senate and the Roman people. For these services the Senate conferred the title of Augustus on me; the entrance to my house was adorned with laurels, and a civic crown was hung on my door. A golden shield was placed in the Curia Julia; the inscription announced that it had been presented to me by the Senate and the Roman people in recognition of my valour and my mercy, justice and piety. From that time forth I had more authority than anyone, but had no more actual power than the other magistrates, my colleagues.'

In these clear and succinct phrases Augustus summed up his political achievements at the end of fifty years' public career. He was responsible for the most far-reaching reforms that the ancient world had known since Alexander, and they were successful only because they had the appearance of a restoration. Caesar, who had adopted Octavian and made him his heir, had realized, like Sulla before him, that the Roman Empire, extending over the whole of the Mediterranean world, could be governed only by a monarch. But the ordinary Roman knew of only one form of monarchy—the *basileia*, which had been set up in the East after the Macedonian conquest, and which depended entirely upon the

might and continued success of some favoured soldier of fortune
supported by a band of friends and mercenaries, and using his subjects
for his own ends. It was thought, with some reason, that such a régime
would be detrimental to the dignity of the Roman people; and so,
although they were well disposed towards Caesar, they did nothing to
prevent his murder by the stupid reactionaries in the Senate. But the
genius of Augustus enabled him to establish a rule as effectual as a
king's, yet without destroying the Romans' feeling of belonging to a
community whose very name—*respublica*—proclaimed it to be the
concern of everybody. This idea of *res publica*, from which emerged
the concept of the State, was never again lost; of all the emperors who
succeeded the founder, not one, however despotic, considered himself
or was considered as anything but the head and leader, and thus the
highest servant, of the Roman Republic.

The success of such a novel and finely balanced solution called for
extremely subtle manœuvring by Augustus during the forty-five years
(31 B.C.–A.D. 14) that he alone wielded power. The one man had to
appear as first citizen (*princeps*) of a republic governed under traditional
law by the Senate, the people and the magistrates; as successor to the
ancient power of the tribunes of the plebs; and as sole head of a permanent army—a new institution, at least in law—whose generals and
men of all ranks came under his supreme command (the proconsular
imperium); and also as high pontiff of religion. But these legal aspects of
his position were not all: as saviour of the homeland, having put an
end to civil strife, restored freedom and subjugated the enemies of
Rome on every frontier, he was officially considered in a very real sense
as the 'Father of Rome', and by being invested with the name Augustus
was likened to the deified founder of the city, Romulus Quirinus.[1] He
was the adoptive son of the god Julius (Caesar), himself descended
from Venus through Aeneas, and he had moreover received from
special protectors—Apollo, Mercury and Diana—a particular favour
that assured him of success in all his undertakings. So in addition to his

[1] The name Augustus had never before been given to a man, although it had
for long had a place in religious terms; it is connected with one of the original
Roman sacerdotal functions, the Augury. According to P. Grimal (*La Civilisation
romaine*, p. 66) it means that the new master has the power to begin everything
auspiciously. Now the chief merit of Romulus was to have founded Rome under
an *augustum augurium*, which assured the favourable destiny of the town; and
according to Suetonius the Senate had hesitated between conferring the title of
Augustus or Romulus (*see* J. Gagé's 'Romulus Augustus' in *Mél de l'Ec. Franç.
de Rome*, 1930, p. 1 et seq.).

legal powers as magistrate (the *potestates*) he was endowed with the divine right (the *auctoritas*), enabling him to do practically anything he pleased. He was a living god to all those whose lives or possessions he had protected or spared, in other words to almost everyone in the Empire.

Some lines of Virgil come to mind:

O Meliboea, a god has provided us with this leisure, for he will always be a god for me; and his altar will often run with the blood of a tender lamb from our folds.[1]

And from Horace's *Odes*:

We thought that thundering Jupiter reigned in the heavens. Our present god will be Augustus, for the extensive Empire he has acquired from the Britons and the mighty Persians.[2]

But this deification was far more complicated than at first seems. Augustus the man was not divine, but the virtue in him was; the old Roman theology contained many subterfuges in order to satisfy both the enthusiasm of the faithful and the scruples of thinking people. It held that each individual had a supernatural self, the genius; so it was not Augustus the man who was worshipped, but his genius, just as every head of a family could have his own genius worshipped by his children, his slaves and his dependants. And when Augustus the man died, the Senate would decree that his genius was to have a place among the gods of the State; while the genius of a humble citizen became a god for his descendants. At no other time, and nowhere else, has a society been governed by such contradictory principles. The 'proteanism' of the Augustan régime was undoubtedly in keeping with the diversity of traditions and customs of the nations within the Roman Empire, and that was probably the reason for its success. But even the most rational historian is unable to see it as a natural and inevitable result of a determined series of events. If Julius Caesar had not been assassinated, if

---

[1] O Meliboe, Deus nobis haec otia fecit
Namque erit ille mihi semper deus; illius aram
Saepe tener nostris ab ouilibus imbuet agnus.
(*Ecl.* 1. 6–8.)

[2] Caelo tonantem credidimus Iouem
Regnare; praesens diuus habebitur
Augustus, adjectis Britannis
Imperio, grauibusque Persis.
(III. 5. 1–10.)

Mark Antony had been victorious, or if Octavian had died from a disease or through a plot, then the Empire might well have become an absolute monarchy in the oriental manner, or even followed the fate of Alexander's Empire and been broken up. At all events, under another leader it would certainly not have taken the form that Augustus gave it; for the system of government inaugurated by him, referred to as the principate, was essentially a reflection of his personality, in its weakness as well as its strength.

⧫⧫⧫ II ⧫⧫⧫

THE CHARACTER OF AUGUSTUS

There were indeed the same contradictions in the character of Augustus as in the 'constitution' that he gave the Empire. In his last years he had a summary of his life's work, now called the Res Gestae, recorded on bronze tablets placed in front of his mausoleum; the wording is known to us from a copy in the temple at Ancyra,[1] and it includes a description of Augustus as he wished to be remembered by his subjects and posterity: noble, serene and lucid, 'master of himself as of the universe'. The writers enrolled by the Emperor's very competent Minister of Information, Maecenas, vied with each other in glorifying the wise and intrepid hero who had put an end to the chaos of civil wars and had restored freedom as well as peace to the world. A very different picture of Augustus was given by Suetonius, who, as state secretary to Hadrian, had access to the imperial archives and was able to delve into secret reports and the private correspondence of Augustus. Writing a hundred years after the latter's death, Suetonius needed to have no more than formal regard for his divine memory, and knew that Hadrian would not be displeased if the glory of his most illustrious predecessor were slightly tarnished.

The chief quality that Suetonius recognized in Augustus was an iron self-command, which served to conceal rather than to overcome his serious weaknesses. The hero appeared as a great *bourgeois*, with all that implies of egoism and hypocrisy. This 'Augustus in his slippers' is a more living and human portrait, and seems closer to the truth, than the other. Yet Suetonius may have been carried away by his addiction

[1] Now Ankara. The inscription was discovered in 1555, and is known as the 'Monumentum Ancyranum'. (Trans. note.)

to gossip and the picturesque, and so missed the qualities that went to make the greatness of his subject—rather like Saint-Simon with Louis XIV. Actually, both the official portrait and that drawn by Suetonius are true and complement each other. If Augustus had been merely the demi-god that he wished to appear, above sensual passions and swayed solely by love of power and the State, his administration would not have had the flexibility which enabled it to be so successful; and his achievements would no doubt have proved as abortive as Alexander's or Caesar's.

Support is given to the written word, moreover, by an examination of works of art relating to Augustus. He had arranged for his physical representation with as much care as for his moral character. Of all his marble or bronze effigies, full face or in profile—nearly one hundred and fifty still exist, in addition to the coins with his head, cameos and earthenware—very few indeed stray from the official criterion that gives the *princeps'* face the ideal proportions of Greek aesthetics, eliminates all traces of suffering and the ravages of age. But a close examination discerns the artificiality in these skilful compositions; their Roman artists had moved away from the realism handed down by the Etruscans. Augustus—as Jean Charbonneaux so rightly says [1]—wore his beauty like a mask. Excavations have revealed the house on the Palatine which was the centre of the private life of Augustus: the house that became the temple of a living god yet retained the modesty of a middle-class dwelling with few comforts. Its comparison with the triumphal arches, temples, altars and other monuments erected at Rome and in the provinces to the glory of the master of the world points a contrast similar to that provided by Suetonius's description of Augustus and the political testament of the Res Gestae.

Augustus was well aware how different his public figure was from his real self, as he revealed just before his death. On the morning of the day he died he examined his face in a mirror, had his hair combed and puffed out his hollow cheeks, then invited his friends into the room; he asked them whimsically if he had 'been a good actor in the comedy of life', and in Greek verse requested them to applaud the player who was about to leave the stage. It is not known what they thought of this smooth exit; perhaps they regarded it as a last instance of the Emperor's cynical humour. This manner of looking upon one's achievements as a kind of game was in keeping with the spirit of the time, which was

[1] *L'Art au Siècle d'Auguste*, Paris, 1948.

sceptical and disillusioned, and contrary to the traditional *gravitas* extolled by the régime; the ancient Roman often made fun of others in private, sometimes of himself, but became serious and pompous again as soon as public affairs were discussed. The attitude of Augustus resulted from the great acumen and shrewdness acquired during the difficult years of his youth, and which saved him from those displays of vainglory that favoured potentates find so difficult not to give way to, and that Caesar himself had not been entirely able to resist. There was no ostentation whatever in the way Augustus organized his life; nor did he have any room for those affectations of familiarity practised by demagogic tyrants. Nevertheless he contrived to place a barrier between himself and others, as impassable as that created by the most ceremonious of courts; and to transform his popular image by myths artfully put about, though rarely given official backing. This work, patiently carried out by entirely original methods, gained for him the supernatural prestige indispensable to every monarch. But it had the inconvenience of isolating him from his friends and relatives more completely than a traditional representation and an openly expressed ideology would have done. His hermetism or duplicity caused his friends and relatives to feel indifferent towards him, and even to revolt. And in the evening of his life the aged Emperor, lonely and weary, must have been cruelly aware of the vanity of a success which deprived him of human affection as much as it did of divine help.

⊱⊱⊱ III ⊰⊰⊰

THE HOUSE ON THE PALATINE

Halfway between the Flavian palace and the temple of Cybele, on the Palatine hill, is a well-preserved house of modest proportions that guides generally refer to as 'Livia's house'. It was discovered and thus named by the Chevalier Pietro Rosa, who was director of the excavations that Napoleon III caused to be undertaken in the Farnese gardens.

In his *Life of Tiberius*, Suetonius says that Livia had lived on the Palatine with her first husband, Claudius Nero, and there gave birth to the future emperor. The frescoes of the house, it has been established, were painted at the beginning of the Christian era. Moreover, Rosa made out the name 'Julia Augusta' on the lead water-pipes; this was the name assumed by Livia after her husband's death. So the identification of the building seemed established. However, archaeologists have learned to be suspicious of clues that appear most revealing. The pipes were examined more closely, and a specialist discovered that the plumbing had been repaired on several occasions and that the name marked on it referred to the empress who was a daughter of Titus. The villa thus lost its original identity. But this was recently re-established, and apparently in a definite manner, by Signor Giuseppe Lugli, a professor at Rome University and a leading authority on the topography of the ancient city.

Quite near the Livia villa are the foundations of a large temple; Professor Lugli has given very convincing reasons for claiming it to be the sanctuary that Augustus built close to his house and on ground belonging to him personally, in honour of his special protector Apollo Actium. Besides, how else can be explained the great respect accorded to 'Livia's house' in the early years of the Christian era, at a time when the emperors were covering the whole hillside with huge edifices? A hundred years after the death of Augustus the modest dwelling of the founder of the Empire was still preserved intact, with his furniture, like a museum. The description given by Suetonius fits in completely with the plan of 'Livia's house' or, as it should properly be called, *Domus Augusta*.

In 44 B.C. Octavian, then Caesar's heir presumptive, bought a villa on the Palatine which had belonged to the orator Hortensius, a rival to Cicero. In spite of the owner's celebrity, it was quite a humble dwelling, without mosaics or marbles, and having a small colonnade of plain Alban stone. The Emperor lived there for forty years, nevertheless, sleeping in the same room summer and winter, although the hard climate affected his already poor health; he meditated in a kind of lofty observatory, which he called his Syracuse or 'little masterpiece'.

After the battle of Actium (31 B.C.) the Senate ordered the purchase of an adjoining building in order to extend the residence of the man who had become the undisputed leader of the state. By another decree —referred to at the beginning of this chapter—his door was decked with laurel and on the lintel was placed the civic crown of oak leaves, the highest military decoration, granted to soldiers who had saved comrades in battle. The house was damaged by fire in 3 B.C. and a public subscription was opened to pay for the repairs; but Augustus would accept no more than a *denarius* from each citizen and a gold coin from the municipalities.

The main building dates from the first half of the last century B.C., which corresponds with the lifetime of Hortensius, who died in 30 B.C. The house consists of a main apartment of five rooms, with additional rooms making a total of twelve. Its plan follows that of the traditional Roman house, centred on the *atrium*, the common- or living-room, which originally contained the hearth and had an opening in the middle of the roof for the smoke to escape and for rain-water to be collected. Visitors today enter the house through this *atrium*, now completely uncovered, and see ahead three rectangular rooms opening from it; they are the *tablinum*, the master's study, and its 'wings'. On the right is another rectangular room, which was no doubt the *triclinium*, the dining-room. All these are now several feet below ground level; but the construction of palaces in the near neighbourhood during the early centuries A.D. had already raised the level, so that today the house has the chill dampness and dreariness of a cellar. It should of course be envisaged as bright and pleasing, though it was always shut in on itself, separated from the street by blank walls.

This desire for withdrawal and occultation, in keeping with Roman tradition though it was, is indicative of a psychic attitude. Augustus could have chosen the plan of the Hellenic palaces which, far from concealing the splendid and voluptuous life of the *basileus*, enabled his subjects to enjoy the sight of his magnificence. The Flavian emperors, though they rejected such ostentation, gave their palace the atmosphere of a public building; citizens could enter the great throne-room and attend the political meetings held by the sovereign. But Augustus's house was representative of a very different conception, one whereby the prince's own life was kept quite separate from his official functions. There was a public part of the building, but it was strictly peripheral, consisting first and foremost of the entrance; the religious and honorific symbols there in evidence gave a sacred character to the doorway—the two laurels set before the doorposts, the crown of oak leaves above the lintel, and the pediment surmounting it all like a temple. This importance given to the front door was in accordance with the most authentic religious tradition of Rome. The prestige of the *janua* was such that the god Janus was invoked at ceremonies before the other gods, before Jupiter even, and his official priest was the monarch himself. The Latin mind, since time immemorial, had attached great importance to rites in connection with change or transition—when the ploughman became a soldier, the family man a magistrate. By merely stepping out of his house Octavian became Augustus again. In order to appear under a more divine aspect still, he had only to enter the temples adjoining his house—either that of Vesta,[1] which was modelled on the shrine in the Forum where her fires were kept burning, and where the Emperor officiated as the grand pontiff, guardian of all sacred doctrine and religious guide of every Roman family; or the temple of Apollo, which was a reminder of the 'epiphany', the miraculous revelation of the cosmic power of the victor at Actium,[2] and which held the secrets of the country's destiny through the Sibylline books kept in the pedestal of the statue. This close connection between sanctuaries and residence calls to mind the similar proximity of chapel and palace of the Christian monarchs. But the temples built by Augustus were intended to enable him to enter into a kind of communion with the people through the practising of rites, more than as a means for private devotions; they were the homes of essentially social cults.

The originality of the course adopted by Augustus was in the fact that the sanctuaries around his house constituted a sacred barrier, fencing him off from humanity; yet without causing him to be likened to the gods, for his house retained its strictly profane character. In such tangible manner did architecture indicate the strange dualism of the Emperor's personality, human yet withdrawn from humanity. Some notion of this can be obtained from the base of a statue preserved at Sorrento; carved on its sides are the deities Latona and Diana with Apollo between them, the Great Mother of the Gods, and Vesta with her priestesses. Augustus does not figure among them; but it was a statue of him that used to stand on the base, thus plainly indicating the subordinate place he gave to the Olympians.

---

[1] Nothing of it remains; it is now thought to have been no more than an altar.

[2] The victory at Actium had been attributed to the intervention of Apollo, who had a temple on the river bank near by and whom Octavian (possibly through the influence of the Pythagoreans) had recently chosen for his protector (see p. 56). Moreover, according to the theological ideas of the time, the day of the battle appeared as the revelation, the 'epiphany', of the supernatural character of Octavian's mission. (See *Apollon romain*, by J. Gagé; and *Trophées romains*, by G. Charles-Picard.)

⋙ IV ⋘

DRESS AND INSIGNIA

The hard-and-fast distinction between public and private life, between the sacred and the profane, influenced the princes of Rome for a long time, in spite of the changes in manners and customs. According to traditional history, which was almost always written by conservative senators, the life of the 'good emperors' remained simple and modest for three centuries, until Diocletian surrounded himself with all the pomp of the Persian kings, in the belief that he was thereby raising the prestige of the crumbling Empire. However, the little weight behind this historic tradition has been ably demonstrated in recent times by a Hungarian scholar, Andreas Alfoldi, through a study of the insignia and dress of the emperors and of the development of ceremonial at court. From his published work we learn that from the time of Augustus the costume and ceremonial varied with the duties and functions.

For normal everyday circumstances, and to go to the Senate in his role of 'President of the Republic', Augustus dressed in the national costume, the toga, which his edicts obliged all the Quirites to wear, in spite of its inconvenience. During 'intermissions' in the civil wars, people had found that the light Greek dress, the pallium, was more pleasant for summer wear; and some daring individuals had even taken to trousers, the dress of the Gauls, finding them practical for energetic exercise and warm in winter. The mass of ordinary people wore a simple tunic throughout the year. Augustus took action against this slovenliness, by setting an example as much as through exhortation. It was meritorious on his part to wear a toga, for the many yards of purple-edged wool lay heavily on his slender body in hot weather, yet gave insufficient protection when the chilly *tramontana* was blowing. But he was anxious to keep up appearances, so only allowed himself some liberty in the choice of rather unusual undergarments. In winter he sometimes wore as many as four woollen tunics over a linen shirt and a jersey,with some kind of puttees wrapped round his legs; and then he put on a thick toga over it all. Such precautions were far from being excessive, for the only heating came from a few braziers. Buildings were better suited to give protection against the heat; as in Mediterranean countries today, people slept in summer under the porch giving on to the *patio*, where fountains played and kept the air cool. Augustus feared the hot sun, and whenever he went out to his *patio* by day he wore a *petasus*, the low-crowned, broad-brimmed hat of the ancient Greeks, such as Hermes wore, and which was not unlike the present-day Spanish sombrero. To uphold tradition, Augustus would not wear any wool that had not been spun and woven at home by his wife and daughter and their female servants. He was opposed to exaggerated modes of dress, and his toga had to be neither too narrow—as had been the fashion among the previous generation—nor too wide, like those worn by dandies of his time. As he thought he was rather short—though his freedman Marathus reported him as being five feet five—he had his shoes made with extra-thick soles. In appearance they were similar to the footwear of the other senators, being purple bootees with an ivory crescent on the toe-cap, and were called *mulleus*—from which comes the word 'mules'. When Augustus returned to his private apartment he took off his toga and shoes, as was customary, but insisted on having outdoor dress at hand.

If Suetonius had not noted such intimate details it would be difficult to imagine them from the statues of Augustus in museums today. Those representing him in the nude can be ignored for the present purpose. Augustus certainly did not pose for any of them. Not through modesty, for like all his contemporaries he felt no embarrassment in bathing with others in Nature's costume. But a convention handed down by the Greeks required that the gods, the heroes or demi-gods and men likened to them, should be represented in the nude—which is why archaeologists speak of 'heroic nudity', an expression that usually surprises and amuses non-specialists. The statues of Augustus naked, or even half naked, are therefore the least realistic of them all; they represent in fact not the human body of the prince but that divine element, the genius or *numen*, that dwelt within him. The bodily appearance has naturally little relation to that of the subject, which was all to the good from an aesthetic point of view; for although Augustus had a well-proportioned body, his chest and stomach were covered with spots and blotches; ingenious flatterers had remarked that they looked like the sign of the Great Bear. When he took a bath he used his skin-scraper so much after the oil—applied instead of the poor-quality soap—had been rubbed over him that scabs began to form. Moreover he had a weak left leg and hip, and used a stick when walking.

Most of the other statues show Augustus wearing a toga or military

uniform. He put on uniform when carrying out duties as army commander or as proconsul; it was no different from that worn by an
imperator in republican times, the most important item of dress being
the *paludamentum*, a long cape dyed purple and attached over one
shoulder, which was the official distinguishing wear of a commander-
in-chief. All titles having been replaced by that of *imperator*, this part
of the uniform had become the distinctive wear of the sovereign, and
the purple eventually symbolized the Empire. Unauthorized use of the
colour was forbidden, to the extent that possession of a cloth dyed
purple was a capital offence. The statue of Augustus discovered at
Primaporta, just outside Rome, shows particularly well the way of
wearing the *paludamentum*. It is attached on the left shoulder and
covers part of his back; but in order not to hide the armour the sculptor
has shown Augustus as having gathered up the rest and drawn it in
tight folds across his stomach and over his left arm.

A plain tunic was usually worn under the *paludamentum*; this was
the dress for travelling, hunting and when in camp. But armour was
put on for fighting. The Greeks had invented two kinds: one consisted
of a metal breastplate and strips of metal or leather to protect the lower
part of the body and the thighs; the other was entirely of leather and
covered the whole trunk, fitting it closely. The latter was preferred by
the Roman emperors for their ceremonial uniform. Several statues of
Augustus show him wearing it, notably the Primaporta statue. The
reliefs carved on it probably represent the metal figures fixed on the
leather uniform, and indicate that the armour was a real work of art
comparable with the highly chased court armour of the late Middle
Ages. The figures in relief on the Primaporta statue symbolized the
ideology of the régime—but we will return to that later. The helmet
and shield, which normally completed the equipment, were rarely
shown on a statue of the Emperor; it was hardly likely, anyway, that
he ever needed them, for he did not engage actively in the fighting, as
Caesar before him had done. When shown with a weapon, that too was
more symbolic than aggressive, being a short Greek sword in a finely
carved sheath.

The Senate had accorded Julius Caesar the right to wear the dress
of a triumphant commander every day. It was a very important privilege, for the *vestis triumphalis* represented the apparel of Jupiter the
Very Good and Great and also the dress of the Etruscan kings who had
first instituted the ceremony of a triumph; it consisted of a purple toga

richly embroidered in gold, a crown of golden laurel, and a long ivory sceptre. The Gemma Augustea shows Tiberius thus attired, while Augustus is wearing Jupiter's mantle, which leaves his chest bare. Augustus had been given the same privilege as his adoptive father, but as he was concerned not to appear a king he put on triumphal costume only on New Year's Day and for great festivals. Statues of him often have a laurel chaplet adorned with medallions, or some other leafy crown, having a religious rather than political significance. But he was always careful not to wear the diadem of the Hellenistic kings; though only a white ribbon, to the Romans it had all the attributes of despotism.

The sceptre aroused less distrust, for in the time of the Republic the magistrates and senators had carried an ivory baton, called the *scipio* (from which was derived the name of one of the most illustrious families of the Roman aristocracy). A distinction was made, however, between this insignia and the long sceptre, which was a divine attribute, a reminder of the assimilation of the victorious commander with Jupiter.

The origin of the ceremonial chair went back to the Etruscans too, being transmitted by the Tarquins to the consuls of the Republic. This curule chair was just a folding camp-stool with a back to it, inlaid with ivory, and was placed on a platform, the tribunal, symbolizing the powers of the magistrate. Augustus had no other throne; and his successors retained it long enough for it to be adopted by the Vandal kings of the early Middle Ages. The 'throne of Dagobert' is still in fact a Roman curule chair.[1]

Another republican emblem, also of Etruscan origin, was the fasces; this was a bundle of elm or birch rods bound round an axe and carried by lictors, and was the emblem of supreme judiciary authority. Augustus had twelve lictors to attend him and walk before him to clear the way.

Augustus is sometimes shown on works of art holding a globe in his extended hand—for instance, on one of the silver cups unearthed at Bosco Reale, at the foot of Vesuvius, and which are now in the Louvre. The globe was meant to represent not just the Earth but the whole Universe, which the Greeks and Romans imagined as a system of

[1] Dagobert was a seventh-century king of the Franks. His chair is in the Cabinet des Médailles (Bibl. Nat.), and is occasionally put on exhibition. (Trans. note.)

concentric spheres. It was a reminder of the supernatural power that the *cosmocrator* was deemed to possess over the whole of nature; and therefore it constantly appeared on monuments and on coins. The globe was often surmounted by a figure of the goddess of Victory, to indicate that the Emperor's victorious powers dominated the world. A statue of this kind was consecrated and placed in the Curia Julia after the victory at Actium, and each senator burnt incense to it before attending meetings—a rite which is sufficiently indicative of the subordination of civil authority to the imperial power, doubly feared for its military support and its supernatural prestige. So much did this statue come to represent the religious and patriotic traditions of the Empire that there was great outcry when, at the end of the fourth century, the Emperor Gratian, urged on by St Ambrose, decided to remove the statue from the Curia. The Byzantine emperors, moreover, retained the globe but changed the figure of Victory for a cross, the symbol of Christ's metaphysical triumph and the talisman of Constantine at the Council of Nicaea.[1] In this form, the orb, it was adopted by all the sovereigns of the Middle Ages; and is still part of the regalia at the coronation of British monarchs.

The insignia of Augustus are thus the origin of the regalia which for many centuries symbolized the divine right of kings. The monarchal character of the principate is made even more evident by the use to which statues of the Emperor were put. For a long time it had been acknowledged that merely to erect a statue of a distinguished person raised him above his mortal condition. The Greeks had allowed stone effigies to be made only of people who had merited such heroic quality by some outstanding exploit, such as a victory at the Games. But this privilege had become degraded, in Greece as well as in Italy, so that eventually all prominent people had their statues in the town square. The statues of Augustus were no different in principle from others; but the idealism of the features, which the *princeps* himself had ordained, was a strong indication that the statues were meant to be more than mere representations. It was not just for aesthetic reasons that Augustus gave instructions for sculptors to modify his features, which

---

[1] According to writers of the early Church, Constantine had a vision in which he saw a cross in the sky just before his battle against Maxentius, which he won. Other writers say it was the Christian monogram ☧ that he saw. But in any case, from the end of the fourth century the cross was believed to have the power of routing the enemies of the Christian Empire, as it did demons. The cross thus became the emblem of victory in the Byzantine Empire.

—by the canon of Polycleitus—were quite regular, but to denote that his individuality was only the temporal form of an eternal and transcendent power. What is even more important is that the images were given a juridical import, and that they became the symbol of the *respublica*. As such they were placed beside the images of the protective gods of the State and of Rome, in forums, basilicas and temples. Medallions bearing the imperial head decorated military standards; and the same profile appeared on all coins, including those issued by the Senate and by municipalities.

Oaths of loyalty were taken on these statues, and their protection extended even to criminals who succeeded in reaching one and clasping it. Eventually any irreverent act towards them was regarded as an insult to the throne, a kind of lese-majesty. From the reign of Tiberius and onwards it became a capital offence to undress in front of an image of the *princeps*, or to go to the lavatory wearing a ring with his head engraved on it, or even having a coin. As one might seem lacking in loyalty by not keeping anything with the Emperor's head on it about the house, the safest procedure was to put such things in the family chapel, beside the household gods.

>>>> V <<<<

CEREMONIAL AND THE COURT

Dress and insignia formed only one aspect of a problem of even more delicate implications, the solution of which was characteristic of the régime founded by Augustus. The problem was that of the ceremonial attached to the Emperor.

The civilizations that had developed before the Roman, in western Asia and around the shores of the eastern Mediterranean, had conceived the relationship between a leader and his people in two quite different ways. In the monarchies of the Near East, although the king was not deified he was considered to be on a higher plane than his subjects. The protocol kept him apart from the world as much as possible; he appeared in public only at solemn ceremonies, and was treated with the deepest respect. It was exceedingly rare for subjects to be admitted into the palace, and if they caught sight of the king they had to prostrate themselves. His private life was kept entirely secret. Between him and the people was a specialized staff whose sole function was to wait upon the master, and its members had no life of their own; many, in fact, were eunuchs.

The position in the Greek city states was just the opposite. The magistrate or, where there was one, the king—at Sparta, for instance, or in the border countries such as Macedonia—led the same kind of life as other citizens. To the Greek way of thinking such equality was essential to the dignity of its civilization; the isolation of the eastern monarchs was regarded as a sign of barbarism. But Alexander, after his conquest of Asia, deemed it necessary to adopt some elements of Persian ceremonial; though not entirely isolating himself—he remained on intimate terms with the Macedonian nobles—he insisted on everyone prostrating themselves before him. This demand raised strong objections from the intellectuals. But after Alexander's death, his successors—the *Diadochi*, the Macedonian generals who fought between themselves for his empire—maintained the protocol that he had elaborated.

Rome, on the other hand, had adopted a compromise solution. The magistrates had maintained the religious prestige of the Etruscan dignitaries and were accorded similar marks of respect; in the Forum the consul presided seated while the assembly of citizens remained standing—whereas in the Greek assemblies the magistrate stood and the people were seated. In each *gens* the head of the household was treated with all deference, not only by relatives but by his 'clients', who came every morning to pay their respects (the *salutatio*) and to receive the presents which were a sign of their dependence upon him. Towards the end of the Republic, so rich had the great men become that they lived in semi-royal state. There were thousands of slaves in their town houses, attending to their every need. Manservants (*cubicularii*) dressed the master in his toga and put on his shoes; it was almost unthinkable for a senator to dress himself, and the wife of one about to be sent into exile asked to be allowed to accompany him to replace the personal servants that were his due, even when in disgrace. No prominent person went out without his slaves; the footmen (*pedisequi*) cleared the way, the *nomenclator* presented to his master the people who wished to speak to him. If he was a magistrate, he was preceded by lictors bearing the fasces. The governors of provinces, especially in the East, readily allowed themselves to be treated as kings, however, and even as gods, and to have temples and statues dedicated to them.

But Roman opinion had not easily accepted the special honours accorded to Julius Caesar, and had in particular disliked his scornful condescension towards the senators and even the people. It had been shocked by Antony's adoption of the Ptolemy court procedure at Alexandria. So Augustus took due note and—having a natural dislike of ostentation in any case—was careful to avoid anything reminiscent of monarchal protocol. He vehemently refused the title of *dominus*, although it was often used as an ordinary form of address when a person could not remember another's name, just as 'sir' used to be. At the theatre he once reprimanded the public for applauding the words 'O Dominum aequum et bonum' and applying them to him. Enthusiastic demonstrations always greeted his return to Rome from foreign parts; he sometimes allowed celebrations by having sacrifices made that converted them into religious ceremonies, but more often than not he arranged matters so that he returned incognito and at night.

He went about the city on foot or carried in a litter; he received his relatives quite simply, and visited them without any ceremony. Once, at an engagement party, he was jostled so much that he gave up attending social receptions.

In spite of this simplicity he was unable to make real friends, and it grieved him. In his youth he had gathered a number of intimates around him; but before long death or the vicissitudes of politics deprived him of them. Several whom he had greatly helped eventually betrayed him: Salvidienus Rufus, a man of humble beginnings, had reached a consulship through the trust Augustus placed in him, but then used his position to stir up trouble; he was brought to trial before the Senate, and committed suicide. Cornelius Gallus, who was also of modest origin, had been appointed prefect of Egypt, a position of the highest importance; but his intrigues obliged Augustus to send him into exile, and the *Patres* compelled him to kill himself. Augustus was distressed by these betrayals of his confidence. The phrase in which Suetonius described his despair has been closely followed by Corneille in his lines:

> O God above, in whom henceforth shall I confide
> The secrets of my heart, the burden of my load?
> Take back the power on me bestowed
> If, given men to rule, I am of friends deprived.

Augustus would not believe that the real cause of this disloyalty was anything other than ambition or inconstancy; but however much he tried to make others forget the unnatural element in his destiny, it was impossible for anyone to remain on friendly terms with a god, even an earthly one. His constant control over himself was a bar to any spontaneity, any genuine familiarity. Even his kindly or charitable acts, such as his visit to a blind senator whom he persuaded not to commit suicide, appeared to be manifestations of a bountiful providence to which one is grateful, but no more. His closest and best collaborator, Agrippa, the actual victor over Sextus Pompey and Antony, suddenly gave up everything and retired to Mitylene. The immediate reason was a clash with young Marcellus, the Emperor's nephew and son-in-law and also his heir-designate; but the real cause went deeper, being the impossibility for anyone to live and work with Augustus on an almost equal footing. Maecenas quite understood this; after the death of Marcellus he cynically told the Emperor that only two choices were open to him: either to have Agrippa assassinated or to compel him to marry Julia and so become the Emperor's son-in-law—in other words, to absorb, as it were, Agrippa's personality into his own.

In contrast to Agrippa, a politician and soldier in the republican tradition, Maecenas was representative of a new order, a product of the monarchal régime: the courtier who was of no importance in himself but wielded power behind the scenes because of his friendship with the *princeps*. This Etruscan of royal blood did not have the true Roman's independent attitude of mind; he did not share the other's scorn of purely intellectual activities, and fully realized the importance of the literary and artistic propaganda under his control. But neither did he have the Roman's sense of honour, nor the distaste for secret intrigue; he turned a blind eye to the liaison of his wife Terentia with Augustus, and he may have even encouraged it in order to have a hold over the Emperor. By this Machiavellism, and freed of all moral scruples, he resembled Livia. However, Augustus was well able to see through his minister, and the wife too, and had no illusions about them. Maecenas, moreover, discreetly withdrew from court during the last fifteen years of his life (23 to 8 B.C.).

There were many other flatterers among the ruling class. The Emperor, who seems to have been touched by the sincere devotion of ordinary people, often showed how weary he was of excessive flatterers and how scornful of eager informers against his enemies. But he was unable to prevent the Senate from becoming servile, in spite of trying to allow it every appearance of freedom of action.

Julius Caesar had shocked the *Patres* by remaining seated before them; his successor did not enter the Senate until all the members were seated, and took his leave of them insisting that they should not move. During the debates he allowed a freedom of expression that was to appear astonishing to people of the next century, who had a servile attitude towards the most liberal princes. One member of the assembly dared to say aloud that he could not understand the Emperor, and another that he was not of the same opinion as the Emperor. At the people's assemblies Augustus took his turn to vote; he made out he was campaigning for his candidates. He could be named as a witness in the courts. All that had no great significance; the Senate would never have rejected a proposition supported by the *princeps*, and when the people's assemblies attempted to take their role seriously a law making them ineffective was quickly voted. But the outward show of freedom still held.

The problem was different where the subject peoples of Rome were concerned. As 'general proconsul' of all the military provinces, Augustus could not be given lesser honours than governors under the Republic. He therefore allowed temples to be dedicated to him, but on condition that he was associated with the goddess Roma. This trend was followed by towns in Italy. But Augustus never encouraged adulation; he dismissed anything that he considered disproportionate, and responded ironically to excess of zeal. When a deputation from Tarragona told him, as though announcing a miracle, that a palm tree had started to grow from the altar that they had dedicated to him, Augustus —although very superstitious, and usually attaching much importance to such wonders—merely replied: 'That shows you often burn incense there!'

Egypt was more a personal domain of the Emperor than a Roman province, and the inhabitants had become used to regarding their foreign overlords as legitimate successors to the Pharaohs. Although Augustus disdained their religion he agreed to assume in theory the functions of king, god and high priest. He was depicted on bas-reliefs of temples restored or built during his reign as wearing the *pagna* and the *pschent* (head-dress of the Pharaohs) and holding the sceptre and the flagellum; and his name in hieroglyphs appeared within the traditional scroll. He did not, however, submit to the consecration ceremony of the Ptolemies.

The solution adopted was a subtle one, entirely empiric, and called for all the versatility of this ingenious and reserved character. The Emperor had chosen the most difficult role with regard to the Romans —that of convincing a carping and touchy people of the transcendence of his personality while continuing to live in broad daylight, of commanding respect without imposing it. He succeeded, with the help of one or two subterfuges. For instance, his glance was believed to have supernatural power; during fighting in the Alps, one look from him was said to have halted a Gaul who was about to push him over a precipice. Augustus held strongly to this advantage; a way of flattering him was to seem dazzled by the light from his eyes, as though by the sun.

Pliny the Younger, it is true, gives a somewhat irreverent explanation of this peculiarity; the Emperor's eyes, he wrote, were placed almost like those of a horse, and he was annoyed if people stared at them. Sculptors naturally tried to reproduce the dazzling quality of his eyes by colouring the pupils. Some traces of polychrome are still evident on the Primaporta statue, and an Italian specialist recently suggested restoring it in order to remove the cold marmoreal expression. The bronze bust from Neuilly-le-Réal still has enamelled eyes, and they do indeed have a kind of fascination. In a country where everyone believed in the evil eye, nothing was better calculated than this for the Emperor to be treated with superstitious veneration, that his agents kept alive in the masses by circulating wondrous tales about the auguries that had announced his birth and foretold his success.

Quite a few of these little stories were collected and written down by Suetonius, who delighted in them. It is odd to find the theme of the Massacre of the Innocents among them. The freedman, Julius Marathus, one of the people used by Augustus for this propaganda, put about the story that a few months before the birth of a son to Octavius an oracle had announced to the senators that a king of the Romans would soon be born; the alarmed assembly decreed that all babies born during the year were to be put to death, but the *Patres* whose wives were pregnant took steps for the decree not to be registered.

While Augustus affected to follow closely the social customs of the times, he was adept at making his visitors feel nervous or confused. In the mornings his house was open to all comers; but along with the 'clients' were seen the most distinguished of the senators, and kings of protectorates or those who had fled their countries, all plainly dressed in the toga, as well as ambassadors from India or the Caucasus, wearing their outlandish garb. The Emperor greeted one and all with a graceful cordiality that enabled him to keep his distance without giving offence, and which left the visitor wondering about the precise meaning of his words. The *urbanitas* of the Romans of those days, like the polished manners of the English, depended on a real technique of social conformity, and was taught in the schools; that of Augustus was closer to the reserved and pessimistic mood of Caesar than to the jovial good nature of Cicero. 'Anyone would think you were giving a farthing to an elephant,' he said one day to a pleb awkwardly holding his petition. During the merry-making of a Saturnalia he ventured to play tricks on his guests; they were invited to take part in a kind of tombola, for which the prizes were sometimes fine cloth, gold and silver, but sometimes sacking, sponges, ladles or wrapped-up pincers with obscure phrases written on the outside.

But on great occasions Augustus organized magnificent ceremonies, taking over those of the Roman religion to begin with, especially the grand processions in which the people, led by the priests, the *flamines* and the vestals, went slowly and solemnly to the temples to appease the gods or to give thanks. The sculptured friezes of the *Ara Pacis*, representing the offering of the sacrifice for the Emperor's return from Gaul and for the peace in the Empire, on 4th July 13 B.C., form a superb pageant of Augustan policy. In the strictly traditional order of the *cortège* there seems nothing that could shock the most conservative of republicans; but this national festival was also that of a family, and a family which was identified with Rome not only at that particular moment but through history, since it was descended from Aeneas—who figured there in the frieze in his sacerdotal function, one might almost say patriarchal, in a biblical sense. It was in fact on this divine family of the *Julii* that rested the pact charging Rome with the mission of organizing the world in accordance with the law of justice and reason.

Such festivals served to link traditional ceremonial with the new ritual which was to develop over the centuries into an imperial liturgy, perfected by the Byzantines and eventually adopted by medieval and modern dynasties. The most significant of these festivals and ceremonies took place in 2 B.C., when the Senate gave the *princeps* the title of 'Father of the Country', which he had often refused. The motion, put by the consul Valerius Messala, began like a prayer, with the 'eulogy' calling for divine benediction on Caesar and his house, and ended with a *salutatio* adapted from the ancient gentilitial protocol, and which later gave form to the feudal homage; and so, from being 'clients' of the *princeps*, the Romans became collectively the children of the new Romulus. The formula pronounced on this occasion only by the consul was later chanted by the whole assembly of senators; this developed into the ritual acclamations of the Senate and the people, which found echo in the coronation and triumphal hymns of the medieval Greek and Latin worlds.

Solemn and stilted religious ceremonies, however, were not enough to satisfy the popular imagination. The Games were a different matter; there was a joyous atmosphere, more likely to bring the populace and its leader nearer together. The Games—whether as chariot-races in the circus or as gladiator fights in the theatre or arena—were originally intended to appease the gods; but they had become huge public entertainments lavishly paid for by rivals for political power, trying by such means to win popularity with the crowds. For Augustus the Games provided the best opportunity to use his gift for stage management; he did so with great skill, drawing most of the popular enthusiasm to himself.

The enormous wealth in his control enabled him to put all his rivals in the shade, and the shows he gave surpassed in splendour and variety anything which had been seen before. While compelling members of the aristocracy to provide displays that almost ruined them, Augustus lost no opportunity to take over from those who defaulted. He noted in great detail the shows that were given in his name or for his heirs: eight gladiatorial fights, in which ten thousand gladiators took part; five athletic contests; twenty-seven ordinary games, consisting of chariot-racing, fighting and dancing; the Mars Games that he founded; the Secular Games of 17 B.C., for which the mystical inspiration was emphasized more strongly than on previous occasions (the significance of this will be examined later); and twenty-six wild-beast shows, at which 3,500 savage and exotic wild animals were killed. Each of these public entertainments was an opportunity for underlining one aspect or another of the Emperor's power. The traditional Games opened with a procession that was both religious and military, in which the statues of the gods were carried; Augustus revived a privilege allowed to Caesar, and had his curule chair placed among them and his Victory among their idols.

Pompey had built the first permanent stone theatre, in the Field of

Mars near the Flaminian Circus. A few years later Julius Caesar, emulating his rival, began the construction of another theatre; it was completed by Augustus, and he named it after his son-in-law, Marcellus, who had met a premature death. Its present-day restored remains, above the Via del Mare, show an imposing semicircle of arcades; they served as model for the architects of the Colosseum. The inauguration of the Theatre of Marcellus, in 11 B.C., was marred by an unfortunate accident; the Emperor's curule chair broke during the performance. Two years earlier a third theatre had been completed by wealthy Cornelius Balbus of Gades (Cadiz), at his own expense.

Augustus enjoyed reading Greek plays, especially the comedies of Aristophanes; and he had tried to write a tragedy about Ajax. He was dissatisfied with his efforts, though, and destroyed what he had written; when his friends asked about it, he replied with a jesting allusion to the suicide of his chief character: 'My Ajax has reached for his sponge.' [1] None of the writers under the patronage of Maecenas, apart from Ovid, tried to add to the existing repertoire. It is particularly surprising that no attempt was made at historical drama like the works of Naevius in the third century B.C., for it would have been an appropriate medium for imperial propaganda.

But Augustus was distrustful of the theatre, and even felt a sort of professional jealousy of it. There was in fact a natural derisive element in the Roman theatre, which had often been critical of the government, and the suspicious mind of Augustus feared—not without good reason —the effect of seditious gibes on public opinion. In his young days he had suffered from satirical jests by singers of lyrics and from lampoons that went the rounds, as he had from the reactions of a fickle public prompt to find some political allusion in the most innocent of phrases. On one occasion a coarse song about the doubtful morals of the priests of Cybele was maliciously applied to him; though another time some flatterers thought to please him by applauding a vague allusion to the *princeps*.

During the disruptive period of the civil wars the prestige of actors had greatly increased. Augustus took steps, under pretence of improving public behaviour, to bring discredit upon the profession again. The police saw that spectators went to seats corresponding to their rank, and that they were respectably dressed. Women had started going to public spectacles; a decree excluded them from attending

[1] The ink on a parchment was rubbed out with a damp sponge.

gladiator fights and athletic games, in which the contestants were naked.
An exception was made for the vestal virgins, but they were given
places far enough back for their modesty not to suffer. A few examples
were made of popular entertainers. Stephanion, the manager of a
troupe who had dared to include in it a lady of high society to play
boys' parts, her hair cut short, was whipped in all three theatres and
then banished. The famous Pylades, who had introduced the mime to
Rome, was also banished, the excuse being that he indignantly pointed
at a spectator who was mocking him, so that the public should boo the
man.

Drama was declining at the same time as the city whose very expression it had been. A new type of spectacle was taking its place, one that
appealed to the base passions of the masses instead of to the intelligence
of the individual. Without any moral scruples, the Emperor pandered
to the lusts of the crowd by offering gladiator fights and the torturing
of condemned criminals amidst exotic scenery, the slaughter of wild
beasts, and lascivious dances and mimes. Massed on the tiers of seats in
the amphitheatre, discontented people forgot about politics, the poor
revelled in the luxury of a spectacle beyond the means of the ruling
class, hatred was stirred up for the enemies of the Empire and a wave of
animal gratitude rose towards the sovereign organizer of all this
magnificence. The Emperor in his box on the podium really seemed a
supreme being, lord of nature, holding the fate of animals and men in
his hands. This metaphysical transposition took so strong a hold on the
public imagination that the Scandinavians came to think of their
Valhalla with a hundred entrances, an idea doubtlessly based on the
Colosseum; and the early Christians, sworn enemies of these devilish
spectacles where so many of them perished, imagined the Last Judgment as an ultimate *munus* at which the place of Caesar was taken by
Jesus and the persecutors suffered the torments of the martyrs.

Augustus was not the originator of these bloody spectacles, for they
could be traced back in a minor form to the funeral sacrifices of the
Etruscan religion and to the triumphal processions of the last century
B.C. with their displays of plunder and tormenting and slaughter of
prisoners. Nor was Augustus responsible for the form they eventually
took when, fifty years after his death, the huge Colosseum was built.
But he was fully aware of their effectiveness as an instrument of power,
as a means of placating public opinion, and he made the utmost use
of them.

The first permanent amphitheatre in Rome was built by the consul Statilius Taurus at the instigation of Augustus, who soon supplemented it at his own expense with a *naumachia*, a large sheet of water for the representation of naval battles. It is to Augustus's credit that he prohibited the *munera sine missione*, those gladiatorial combats from which none might escape alive: no sooner had one of the duellists fallen than another was produced to fight the conqueror, until the entire body of combatants was exterminated. He also had the idea of using the shows to extend the interest he himself had in natural science; the exotic animals that he received as gifts from the potentates of India were exhibited to the crowds—the first live tiger ever seen in Rome, cobras, a python sixteen feet long, a giant tortoise, a rhinoceros, and even a white elephant from Siam.

The people admired these wonders, brought to Rome under enormous difficulties, and thereby received a better idea of the great extent of the Empire and obtained a heightened impression of the Emperor's supernatural power. Augustus was also responsible, however, for increasing the cruelty of the shows by the torture of criminals, which soon became an attraction much in demand. He had the bandit Selouros dropped into a cage of hungry panthers in the Forum, thus introducing this horrible punishment into the penal code; until then it had been applied, only rarely, to traitors.

His excuse—purely relative—was that practically no one was shocked by these spectacles. The most cultured men approved the gladiator fights on the grounds that they preserved the military virtues. Young men of good family sometimes went into the arena, perhaps through a desire to show off such as often comes over idle youngsters in troubled times. Their exhibitions were forbidden by the Senate, but later on Tiberius had to take rigorous action against sons of good family who asked to be struck off the register of their order so that they could become actors or gladiators.

Augustus appears to have used very clever tactics in his dealings with the public, being fully aware of crowd psychology, and working on its weaknesses to his own ends without the slightest scruple. The methods that he invented or adopted to keep the Roman people under his sway have been practised by all sovereigns for at least eighteen centuries since, to arouse in their subjects a religious respect without which a monarchy is indistinguishable from a tyranny. And, in spite of technical progress, there is often a striking similarity between these methods and those employed today by governments—not necessarily totalitarian—to obtain the unanimity of the masses.

The political genius of Augustus is also apparent, and in a very similar way, in the organization of his *entourage*. Without breaking away from the customs of his contemporaries, he gradually and almost secretly surrounded himself with the structure of a political machinery that before long assumed the effective power, and thereby completely sapped the authority of the republican institutions whose apparent restoration had satisfied public opinion.

In the same way as monarchal ceremonial was created out of the ancient aristocratic dignities, the imperial court resulted from the armies of retainers belonging to the millionaire senators in the last years of the Republic.

Augustus, like the other senators, had his *familia* of several thousand retainers. Only a few were domestic servants, attached to the house on the Palatine. The others had their own hierarchy, closely corresponding to the classes of free society. At the top were the specialists and the intellectuals; secretaries, pedagogues, physicians, and especially stewards, or administrators. The latter were people of considerable standing, living in a style in keeping with their great responsibilities; they controlled revenues and estates that in many cases exceeded the patrimony of a rich *bourgeois*, and they could have slaves of their own. The epitaph of one of Tiberius's stewards gives a list of his slaves; it contains a secretary, a cook and several footmen and valets. Privileged slaves such as he were usually given their freedom after a few years, and continued as freedmen to look after the interests of the prince.

The loose definition of the imperial powers naturally favoured the extension of the part played by these semi-official collaborators. The notion of a civil service was unknown to the Roman republic, as to the city states; a magistrate could use the services of a few public slaves, but nothing prevented his employing his own freedmen and slaves to do the work for which he was responsible, under his supervision. The Emperor, in this respect too, could do little else but conform; it was indeed impossible for him to dispense with the help of his retainers to administer the large public funds in his charge. The testament deposited with the Senate gave the statement of accounts together with the names of the slaves or freedmen who held the funds. In the same way it was the prince's retainers who administered his own estates; these immense possessions, spread over all the provinces, were constantly being augmented by gifts and legacies, and constituted what might be called crown lands.

There was a danger in all this, of which Augustus was well aware. The eastern monarchs, whether native or Greek, had made their slaves the ministers and instruments of their despotism, which was a major cause of the rapid decline of their régimes. Augustus's predecessors, Sulla and Caesar, had used their retainers to quell their enemies. Most of these 'specialist' slaves were, moreover, of Eastern origin. They spoke Greek, and were imbued with the despotic traditions of their country; there was therefore a risk that they would break down the nationalism of Italy and destroy the people's sense of human dignity which Augustus wanted to become the hidden strength of his State.

The danger was all the greater because these clever and crafty freedmen soon managed to become rich at the expense of their ex-masters. In order to restrict this development, Augustus applied severe laws to the *liberti*. He also treated his own retainers with a firmness that was sometimes cruel. He had the legs of his secretary Thallus crushed for having revealed the contents of a secret state dispatch in return for five hundred *denarii*; and a freedman much in favour, Polus, was ordered to commit suicide for having bribed some ladies of the aristocracy. The tutor and personal servants of C. Caesar, the Emperor's grandson, were thrown into the Tiber with a weight round their necks because they had feathered their nest while in the East with their master.

Although pitiless where the public interest was concerned, Augustus showed indulgence towards offenders against his person. A slave named Cosimo who insulted him was only put in irons. One day when he was out walking with his steward Diomedes a wild boar charged the two men; Diomedes ran away, knocking over his master instead of protecting him. Augustus merely gibed at the steward for his cowardice. As for the good servants, Augustus treated them with affection and even with honour; they took the place of the friends of his own class that he had not been able to keep.

Augustus needed no great foresight to guess that his successors would not all manage to discipline their subordinates. We know how weak Claudius was with Narcissus and Pallas, and what troubles thereby ensued. Augustus, however, had discovered the remedy for preventing Rome from being dragged down by the intrigues of court favourites. He created important posts, such as administrator of provincial revenues, that were held by knights instead of by members of his own household. These men were salaried officials rather than personal representatives of the *princeps*.

This was perhaps the most important and the more enduring of Augustus's reforms and innovations. The appointment of these procurators laid the foundation of a professional bureaucracy which was to develop into a complex organization a century later; and to become, with the army, the cement which held the Empire together. Augustus can truly be said to have thereby created a new form of administrative government, and one which is still with us today.

⟫⟫⟫ VI ⟪⟪⟪

LEISURE AND RECREATION

His immense responsibilities, the impossibility of sharing them with trusted collaborators and his lack of real friends caused Augustus to live in a state of nervous tension, not unlike Napoleon. Suetonius gave many instances: Augustus suffered from his liver and had the stone, and was glad to lie down after meals; he had a short nap after lunch, without undressing, lying with a hand over his eyes. He worked after dinner, stretched out on a divan, to dictate to his secretary or have his letters read to him. He retired late, and never slept for more than seven hours, often with three or four bouts of wakefulness. When unable to get to sleep again, which frequently happened, he sent for a reader or a story-teller and kept him until daybreak; he never stayed awake without calling someone to his bedside. It was in the morning that he got most rest, so he disliked rising early; when he had business to do in the morning he went and slept near at hand, to have a little extra rest. He caught up on his sleep during his daily travels, too, while being carried in his litter; sometimes he halted his porters for a short time, to rest the better.

He arranged his pleasures, which were simple ones, just as carefully in order to draw the maximum relaxation from them. As a young man he had led a fashionable life and pursued sensual delights in all the extravagant ways available to the rich of his day. But in his late years, according to Suetonius, he renounced such pleasures; not, like Louis XIV, through conversion to a higher ideal—his spiritual development was quite the opposite, as will be seen—but through satiety and by self-discipline.

On the other hand, the intellectual pursuits of his youth, which he had followed as just another means of gaining authority, became a source of pleasure and a relaxation. From his early youth he gave much time to Greek and Latin rhetoric, which was still indispensable to statesmen in spite of the decadence of the political assemblies. He had not Caesar's talent, and because of his weak throat he sometimes had to have his speeches read for him; but he worked hard at his studies, either with his tutors or alone. Later he continued with his education even during a civil war; when he was besieging Modena he used to spend several hours in his tent every evening, reading, writing and declaiming.

He thus achieved an elegant and precise style that contrasted with the bombast and vagueness of speeches by professionals. He was so desirous for his meaning to be quite clear that he always wrote out his speeches, although he was capable of improvising. Fear of letting slip some imprudent remark caused him to make notes of what he wanted to say before giving an interview, and even before conferring with his wife. His knowledge of Greek, however, was never perfect, and he always had his communications to his Eastern peoples translated.

Throughout his adult life he worked from time to time on a massive *Reply to the Cato of Brutus*, and often read extracts to his intimates. He started writing his memoirs too, but never got beyond Book XIII, which dealt with the war in Spain; all that has come down to us is the summary of the Res Gestae. Nothing remains of an *Exhortation to Philosophy* that he wrote, nor of a poem on Sicily, probably didactic and in hexameter, but which was still in existence in the time of Suetonius. That biographer also read a small book of epigrams that Augustus composed while in his bath. As for his tragedy *Ajax*, it never saw the light of day.

He was slightly built, so did not need vigorous exercise. In his youth he had done his military training, both infantry and cavalry, but only because it was necessary to his future as a general. Afterwards he practised only enough athletics to keep himself fit; a ball game, bouncing it against a wall, was his favourite form of exercise. In his late years he went for walks with a little running and jumping. He never had any liking for hunting, but was fond of going fishing; not for the pleasure of catching something, but—Suetonius is positive on the point—for the mental relaxation it gave him.

The poor state of his digestion—finally wrecked by his almost fatal

illness during the Spanish campaign of 27–26 B.C.—caused him to
avoid the pleasures of the table. His favourite feast consisted of coarse
bread, some small fish—anchovies or sardines probably—and buffalo's
cheese rolled in a pig's bladder (called *mozarella* in Naples today), and
finally green figs. It was the kind of meal a labourer was accustomed to
—still is in Italy today—and Augustus may not have taken to it solely
for reasons of health; he liked to make out occasionally that he was
'one of the people', and he was not without that touch of vanity which
is often contained in a show of simplicity. He did in fact vaunt his
frugality even in his letters: 'We had a quick snack of bread and dates';
'While I was returning home in my litter I ate an ounce of bread and a
few Muscat grapes'; 'There isn't a single Jew, my dear Tiberius, who
has kept the Sabbath fast more attentively than I have today; I ate a
couple of mouthfuls in my bath at eight o'clock this evening, before
being rubbed with oil.' Augustus was not a great wine-drinker either;
during the *commissatio*, the ceremonial drinking-match that followed
dinner, he had no more than three cups. In this matter, however, he
allowed himself some latitude in later years; but when he had gone
beyond his evening allowance of six pints—he watered his wine,
though—he made himself vomit before there were any worse consequences. His favourite wine came from Rhaetia (the Swiss Engadine).
Before starting to drink he would have a light meal of bread soup,
some slices of cucumber, and lettuce or a green apple.

These frugal habits did not prevent him giving grand dinners to
carefully selected guests. The customs of the time—which would seem
unmannerly to us today—enabled him to arrive after his guests had
started eating, and to leave without interrupting their meal; he need
not touch any of the food, and such was often the case. Neither was it
considered rude to remain silent or to talk in a low voice with one's
neighbour; it was the host's task to bring everyone into the general
conversation, a matter that Augustus managed very well. Besides,
there were often professional entertainers, jugglers and clowns, to keep
the guests amused. Augustus, though, with his good taste, preferred to
have story-tellers.

He did not share his contemporaries' passion for baths. No thermal
installation has been discovered in or around the house on the Palatine.
Long sessions in a *hamman*, where the Romans spent several hours a
day, were obviously not indicated for a man of Augustus's weak constitution; nor had he the time to spare. He made do with having himself

rubbed with oil and then he scraped away with the strigil, so vigor-
ously that he often took the skin off; or he perspired in front of a big
fire and then had a tepid shower or stretched himself in the sun. His
doctors recommended sea-water baths to calm his nerves, or water
from sulphur springs; but instead of immersing himself the Emperor
sat on a stool in front of a tub and dipped his arms and legs in by
turns.

His one real relaxation, in which he could forget his cares and
worries for a time, he found in games of chance. The Romans of the
first century A.D., though having no real religion, were conscious of
supernatural forces around them and which they called Fortune; to try
their luck by gambling had something mysterious and almost sacred
about it—an attitude that still prevails in southern Italy today. Augustus spent every fête-day at games of chance; his keenness for gambling
is apparent in his letters that Suetonius reproduced:

'My dear Tiberius, I had dinner with the same people again;
Vinicius and old man Sillius joined us. We played dice during dinner,
yesterday and today. Whoever threw a loser or a six put down as many
denarii, and whoever threw the lucky number took the lot.

'We spent the Quinquatrus [1] very happily, playing all day long and
keeping the dice warm. Your brother complained a lot; however, he
didn't lose much in the end, for he won a bit back when it seemed
hopeless. I lost twenty thousand *sesterces* myself, but that's because I
was much too generous, as usual. For if I'd insisted on having the
winnings that I returned to one player and another, or kept what I
gave away, I'd have finished up winning easily fifty thousand. But
I like it better that way—I attain celestial glory by my kindness.'

Such childishness was undoubtedly a sign of old age—the above
letter, and similar ones, were written in his last years—but it fitted in
with a deeply rooted tendency in the man, of which Suetonius gave a
curious example. The elderly prince was sometimes seen playing
marbles in the courtyard with Moorish or Syrian boys, whose pretty
ways and chatter amused him; they had been sent to him by the governors of their provinces. This liking for the company of young lads
could be taken as a sign of that *paederastia* which the morality of the
times regarded as no more than a human weakness. Yet that does not
seem to be the real explanation; for Suetonius, who made no mystery of
Augustus's taste for girls, had nothing to say about his pretty lads, and

[1] Festival in honour of Minerva, on 18th March.

discredited the charges of homosexuality made by his enemies during the civil wars. Rather does it appear that the Emperor was seeking an affection from his young companions that he had been unable to obtain from his own family. Many instances have already been given of his desire for interest in his private troubles. As he felt his life drawing to a close the old autocrat became frightened at being so lonely and at having lost his real self over the years. This turning towards young people was an attempt to retrieve at source the humanity that he had cast aside in order to become a god.

The reaction against an overburdened and artificial life was again demonstrated, and more simply, by a return to nature. The importance given to this theme in the literature of the period is well known; it was suggested, if not a directive, to Virgil and to Horace by the Emperor and Maecenas. This was due in the first place to the economic situation. Augustus had fully realized the danger for Italian agriculture in concentrating on crops for the export market, and had calculated the social consequences of the land being in the hands of a few; he had foreseen the crisis which did in fact begin to affect the country's prosperity after the middle of the century. But there were reasons other than economic, and closer to the individual.

The sculpture and painting of the period treated nature with a realism rarely found in Hellenistic art—one example is the foliage carvings on the *Ara Pacis*. The Roman of Augustus's time had a real love of the country; he escaped from city life whenever he could, leaving the noise and bustle of the Forum for his farm and the peace of the fields. Augustus set the example; when he could take a few days' holiday he went and buried himself in one of his country places, where the only splendour was in the gardens. He had reacted against the extravagant fashion set by Crassus and Pompey, and which had been financially disastrous for Cicero, and refused to turn his country villas into museums filled with priceless paintings and statues brought from Greece. He gave orders for the destruction of the country mansions begun against his wishes by his ambitious grand-daughter. In order to escape unwelcome visitors he often preferred to ask hospitality from Maecenas, or even from a freedman, and spent a few days semi-incognito, going for walks in the woods and fields or fishing in some lake or river.

This feeling for the joys of nature was, however, quite different from the response of the Romantics, with their love of the wild woods

and mountains; it was closer to the pastoral movement of the eighteenth century. The ancient Roman was most at ease in a humanized
landscape, one organized with art and having a refined and easy-going
life of its own; the country folk that figure in it are more often playing
the flute under a tree than digging or weeding. The garden was preferred to the countryside, but it was a garden unlike our own or even
the formal layout of the French. One of Livia's gardens is shown on the
frescoes that have been uncovered in the basement of her Primaporta
villa; behind a low balustrade with shallow recesses are pomegranate
and laurel trees rising above clusters of acanthus and other spiky plants;
a line of cypresses in the background acts as a windbreak; a host of
birds flutter and chirp among the branches. There are no lawns or
flower beds; the climate is against the former, and horticulturists had
not then learned to improve and tend flowers. Only the natural kinds
were known—wild roses, pinks and violets, and bulbs such as irises,
gladioli and lilies; these were used for borders round clumps of
greenery or were grown in a tangled mass in ornamental stands on
low walls.

The main effect was obtained by the use of evergreens, laurel and
myrtle, which were closely planted in front of pine, cypress and plane
trees. Gardeners had learned to train and clip box and fir, and by
introducing wild bushes into the garden managed to obtain two or
three levels of greenery. It is this predominance of greenery on the
Primaporta frescoes that takes the eye; a few splashes of bright colour,
fruits rather than flowers, give very little contrast to the sombre background. But there is water flowing everywhere—gushing from fountains, running in little streams and in cascades contained within marble
and glistening on the mosaic. The Roman garden—one might say the
Mediterranean garden—was a kind of oasis, with a dry, bare soil, but
cut across by numerous channels with running water, beneath dense
trees giving thick shade. People did not seek the sun there, as in our
temperate climate, but escaped from it, under the shade of trees and
close to cool waters, in the company of small animals.

These natural features were considerably modified by architecture.
Suetonius gave a definition of Augustus's gardens in two words that
could have served as the title of Pierre Grimal's book from which the
above information is drawn—*Xysta et Nemora*, Porticos and Shrub-
beries. The mural paintings and actual gardens that have been restored
at Pompeii in the greatest detail present a profusion of pergolas and

c

bowers, grottoes and little temples sheltering statues or mosaics. Living porticos were made by aligning trees and keeping them pruned, and climbing plants dressed pillars in greenery. Statues stood everywhere, often grouped to represent some mythological episode. An idea of such close combination of architecture and sculpture with nature, in a setting where gushing waters make the marble seem alive, can today be obtained at Caserta, near Naples.

It is with some impatience that one awaits the results of the methodical excavations being carried out by the Institute of Architectural History of Rome University, at villas along the Tyrrhenian coast— those 'campanian retreats' that Augustus liked. A fortunate discovery at Sperlonga [1] has already unearthed a magnificent domain that is in the main contemporary with the early emperors; it has grottoes containing statues set between the buildings, and the grottoes are coated with stucco or have a mosaic of glaze or little shells. The relationship of such compositions to the paintings at Pompeii, as well as to the bucolic and mythological poetry, has been rightly emphasized. This art and literature, however, do not just reflect some whimsical taste; they are the expression of a deeply felt need of evasion, which was an essential element of Roman psychology at the time of Augustus. A study of this reveals a hidden aspect of the Emperor's personality, and offers an explanation of the inner struggles and personal tragedy that beset Augustus's final years.

[1] On the coast between Latium and Campania. Excavations have been going on for some years.

Chapter Two

FROM PYTHAGORAS TO ZENO

I⊤ is never easy to enter into the mind of a man of a bygone age; it is even more difficult when he was a past master in the art of dissembling and double practice. However, some chinks have already been noticed in the casing of Augustus's real personality. Let us now try to go further to examine whether this man—who had such great command over himself, who was rightly satisfied with a success that had not only obtained for him the highest position known to man but had also rescued mankind from chaos—whether he did not sometimes ponder over the real value of the power he felt within him.

Corneille's play shows a troubled, uncertain Augustus, on the point of giving up his worldly power when the loneliness of his position suddenly broke upon him; but there is no evidence of any kind to justify such representation. However, one cannot be sure that the poet's intuition does not get closer to the truth than the historian's analysis, especially as Augustus's views on philosophical and religious matters seem at first consideration so complex as to be almost contradictory. In order to assess how far Augustus was capable of judging himself and his mission, and to estimate the extent of the lassitude he sometimes felt, we must endeavour, so to speak, to catch him unawares—to examine his attitude in matters and circumstances where he believed he could relax his watchfulness over himself and others.

In this connection the house on the Palatine is worth further study, not of its plan but of the decorations on its walls.

⫸⫸⫸ I ⫷⫷⫷

THE FRESCOES OF THE PALATINE HOUSE AND THEIR PSYCHOLOGICAL SIGNIFICANCE

There were frescoes in all the rooms, and much of this decoration has survived. The skill of Italian restorers has ensured that they can still be seen on the original site. They are certainly of later date than the building itself, and must have been Augustus's own choice; they thus have great interest, revealing a secret and inner aspect of the many-sided character of the founder of the Empire. Not that they possess any marked originality. The house is a middle-class dwelling, and the frescoes follow the fashion of the period; that is how they can be dated fairly closely. Many mural paintings in the same style have been discovered at Pompeii and Rome; art historians place them in the last phase of what they call the second Pompeian style.

Paintings of that period, however, represent a psychological tendency having little in common with the traditional Roman outlook, which was rigid and disciplined, and which Augustus tried to restore with his code of religious and moral laws. The paintings in fact bear witness not only to freakish taste but also to a desire for escape into a supernatural world, freed of physical bonds as of social obligations.

The primary aim of the decorations in homes during the second and first centuries B.C. was to imitate cheaply the costly marbles and sculptures that adorned the Hellenistic palaces. Pedestals, panelling and cornices were painted on the wall, and pillars which should have stood out from it were painted in *trompe-l'œil*. The innovation of the last phase of the second Pompeian style is the breaking up of the blank wall between the pillars into perspectives that reveal a fantastic world, and which seem to continue behind the wall. Anyone looking at it had the impression of being invited to pass through the wall and enter a world of fantasy, as Alice did through the looking-glass. In the *tablinum* of Augustus's house the wall face therefore appears as a kind of screen, with richly decorated baroque pillars apparently standing in advance of it; this screen is pierced at either end to give a view of tall town houses with loggias and flower-bedecked balconies, and lively crowds going about their business, much as their modern counterparts do in the old quarters of Rome. A lady accompanied by her slave is knocking at the door of a big block of flats, while one of the tenants leans over the balcony to see who is calling on the neighbour.

If it were not for this unexpected scene there would be no warning of the fantasies to follow. In the dining-room to the right of the *atrium* is a most peculiar fresco. An imitation window painted in the middle of a long wall gives a view of a rustic shrine: in the centre of a curved portico surmounted by three hieratic statuettes holding torches is a huge fir tree, and on its branches stands a sort of bronze mass bearing the heads of a stag, an antelope and a wild boar.

It is the domain of some divinity of the hunt—probably Diana. Roman landscape paintings were often sprinkled with small temples, tombs and statues of the gods. Probably one often came across such monuments in the Greek and Italian countryside; the tombs of marabouts that one sees today in North Africa are a survival of the custom. But the constantly recurring sacred element in the scenic paintings may well be indicative of their dreamlike, other-worldly character. In the dream-world the gods rubbed shoulders with mortals. The second-century author of the famous *Key to Dreams* often mentions super-natural apparitions; and the materialistic Epicureans taught that belief in the strange beings of mythology had its origins in nightmares.

Another of the rooms has a frieze painted entirely in yellow; it is an evocation of a journey in the East, perhaps in Egypt, the country Augustus was so proud of having added to the Empire, and which, by reason of its long history, the magnificence of its arts and its peculiar customs, exerted on the Romans an attraction comparable with that of China on Europeans in the eighteenth century.

The house thus gave the impression of being withdrawn from the real world, and to be inviting its occupants into a land of dreams. And this transporting of the mind to another plane is again symbolic of the mythological paintings that have the place of honour in the *tablinum*.

Through the columns of a richly decorated baroque building can be seen an arid, rocky landscape; in the centre, seated at the foot of a column surmounted by the statue of a divinity, is a beautiful young brown-haired girl with a bright complexion and rounded curves; her terrified gaze rests on the bronzed, naked man who is guarding her, armed with a spear and a sword. Behind a boulder and invisible to the guard is the approaching figure of Mercury in his winged headgear and carrying his herald's staff. The damsel is Io, one of Jupiter's many loves; his jealous wife, Juno, had captured her and put Argus, the man with a hundred eyes, to guard her. Jupiter, although lord of heaven, could not face his shrewish wife, and sent his messenger to murder the jailer.

In the fourth century B.C. this somewhat amoral story had inspired a Greek painter named Nicias, who was a companion of Praxiteles; the fresco was based on his work. The choice of such a subject for Augustus's rooms seems in rather doubtful taste. The Emperor, that earthly Jupiter, had in fact the reputation of being only too prone to the failings of his divine patron.

'He never gave up debauchery,' Suetonius wrote of him, 'and it is said that he was too fond of seducing girls, who were procured for him from all quarters by his own wife.'

Considering the risk of scandal, it would seem indiscreet to have given prominence to the theme of Juno's jealousy, for it indicated that Livia was indulgent towards her husband's failings. But art historians provide an answer to that—Nicias had painted two figures only, Io and Argus, without any scenery. The Roman painter, by introducing land-scape, and especially the figure of Mercury, had changed the atmo-sphere and the meaning of the picture. The subject was no longer the terror of the wretched girl held captive by a heartless jailer. Deliver-ance was now at hand, in the person of the winged god, the messenger of divine providence. Considered in this light, all that was shameful and bawdy in the legend was eclipsed by the nobility of the allegory: Io becomes the symbol of humanity held captive in the valley of tears, which Jupiter's herald is about to free from the forces of evil and offer up to love divine.

That may be thought too bold a thesis; yet one has only to consider the range of subjects in the Pompeian paintings of the period. Myths of apotheosis, of metamorphosis or liberation abound—Hercules in the paradise of the Hesperides, Ganymede and Europa carried off by the heavenly beasts, Daphne mercifully changed into a bay tree when pursued by Apollo, Andromeda and Hesione snatched from the jaws of the monster by a gallant hero.

But then we are confronted by another problem. It is certain, and indeed understandable, that Augustus's subjects looked for such a deliverance, that the ordinary people saw the world around them as nothing better than hell, the Emperor's rigid discipline as an unbearable restriction from which they longed to escape, at least in thought. We need only think of the high hopes of seething Israel, whose pride had been so deeply wounded by its loss of independence; or of the Greeks, forced to submit to rapacious and less civilized foreigners. In Italy itself there was not one of the contemporary poets—Virgil, Horace, Propertius—who did not let his fancy roam in a world of peace and justice, such as the paradise of the fourth *Eclogue*, or Clymene and the grotto of the nymphs in the secret underworld.

But how was it that Augustus, in the real world of order, and of Roman order, that complied with the strict morality from the past, with the military discipline of the legions, and the rectitude of praetorian law, how could the restorer of this state of affairs have indulged in such escapism and dreamt of those Utopian shores? If Augustus had believed entirely in his own official doctrine he would not have tolerated paintings of such dangerous fantasies on the wall of his house. To plead thoughtlessness on his part, or a blind following of the fashion, is no answer. For the introduction of fantasy into Roman art—the work perhaps of the Ludius mentioned by Pliny—had, like all artistic innovations, met with opposition from the academic world. One of Caesar's engineer officers, Vitruvius, wrote a treatise on architecture and in Book VII made a critical attack on the contemporary style. Formerly, he wrote, painting was treated rationally, subjects were taken from real life—public buildings, landscapes, themes from the Greek epics; but nowadays, he complained, foolish fashion casts these aside, and chooses to paint the walls with monstrosities rather than actual representations: stems of plants instead of pillars, flowering scrolls sprouting from the roofs instead of pediments.

'What the ancients endeavoured to attain by hard work and application is achieved today by vivid and attractive colours. Fine colours —vermilion, golden yellow, purple, Armenian blue—run riot. Instead of being used artistically, they dazzle the beholder with their brilliance.'

So there was a clash between ancients and moderns, between supporters of a neo-classical figurative style and those of baroque. Augustus, however, was always in favour of classicism, in literature as well as art. According to Suetonius, he wrote in a clear and simple style that was not without elegance. He preferred the Attic manner, and scoffed at people like Tiberius who had a fad for archaisms, and at imitators of oriental orators with their flowery and emotional phrasing. The monuments he built have the same purity of style as his writing. A seeking after balance and clarity governs their symmetrical composition, whether of the friezes on the Emilian basilica and the temple of Apollo Flaminian, carved at the beginning of Augustus's reign, or those on the *Ara Pacis*, of later date; or whether of statues and embossed groupings, or buildings like the Forum centred on the temple of Mars Ultor, or the triumphal monument that still stands on the rock of La Turbie, above Monaco.

This general cold conformism went against the earlier tendency of Roman art, inherited from the Etruscans, which sought to express the whole of teeming life in stone.

Later in Augustus's reign there was a return to classicism in decoration, when the second style was superseded by the third. Large wall surfaces no longer offered an escape into a world of fantasy; long flat-washed panels framed by architectural decorations devoid of relief-work now blocked any wanderings of the imagination, which had to be content with the mythological paintings given the place of honour on each wall. And these frescoes were more than ever concerned with themes of liberation, abduction or metamorphosis. But transitions in the supernatural world henceforth came under the same rules as applied in the real world: only those benefited who had earned the favour of the gods by their birth—a free gift—or at the cost of superhuman exploits in the service of *virtus*.

. . . Few are those, whom just Jupiter loved, or whose ardent virtue raised them to the skies, who, sons of the gods, are able to attain it.[1]

There are the blessed ones, Hercules, Achilles, Jason, Europa; but on the other hand there are Icarus, Bellerophon, Phaeton, who unworthily tried to scale the heights of Olympus and were cast down. The metamorphoses for good, such as Daphne's, contrasted with Actaeon's horrible fate. The similarity of inspiration between this conception of mythology and that found in Horace's works has been rightly stressed. The home of the gods was no longer a refuge open to all who were weary of the world and refused to conform to its rules, but had become the highest reward for the righteous. Olympus was just an eternal Palatine, and Jupiter applied the same laws as Augustus.

⟫⟫ II ⟪⟪

THE PYTHAGORISM OF OCTAVIAN

This evolution reflected the changes in the mind of the *princeps*. In his youth Octavian had come under the influence of one of the great mystical sects which were competing for the control of Roman minds. On the very day of his birth, when the conspiracy of Catiline was in full ferment, the senator Nigidius Figulus had told Octavian's father of the great heights for which the child was predestined. Nigidius Figulus was not only one of the leaders of the conservative party but also the pontiff of the neo-Pythagorean 'church'. He and other distant disciples

---

[1]   . . . Pauci, quos aequus amavit
Juppiter, aut ardens evexit ad aethera virtus,
Dis geniti potuere.   (*Aen.* VI. 128–30.)

of Pythagoras (who had died at Croton in the sixth century B.C.) had developed his teachings as a combination of mysticism and severe self-discipline. This highly intellectual and moral doctrine was directed towards an *élite*. It was in strong contrast to other mystic cults, especially the Bacchant, whose celebrations led to wild and dissolute scenes. Some idea of how wide was this difference can be obtained by a comparison of the frescoes in the Item villa at Pompeii, which portray more or less symbolically the Dionysiac (or Bacchic) initiation rites, with the stucco decorations in a Roman basilica excavated near the Porta Maggiore and which was used by a Pythagorean brotherhood in the first century A.D.

The former depict scenes of an orgy whose sacred character is still apparent, in spite of the sensuality and depravity of the rites. After submitting to the preliminaries, the young woman being initiated is allowed to look upon the unmentionable symbols, of which the chief one is a phallus. Then, stripped of her garments, the initiate is whipped by a winged demon, while a naked Bacchante whirls round in an ecstatic dance. One can realize how dangerous were the influences at work on the men and women taking part in such orgiastic rites. Their immorality had led to a great scandal at the beginning of the second century B.C., which was followed by a bloody persecution. But the cult was revived during the troubled first century, when control was relaxed and morals were looser.

The decorations in the basilica, on the other hand, have much nobility, and draw their inspiration from Greek mythology; indeed, the Pythagoreans, far from taking Plato's view that mythology was to be condemned as immoral and disrespectful to divine majesty, were among the first to give an esoteric interpretation to the trifling and scandalous escapades of the gods and heroes. The apse of the basilica shows Sappho's 'lovers' leap' at Leucadia, an ancient trial by ordeal which the philosophers took as symbolic of the redemption of the soul. The less important subjects decorating the vaulting are all in the prevailing mode. The rivalry between these two cults was carried into politics, in the Rome of Caesar and Cicero. The Bacchants found most followers among the common people, where Greek and Eastern ideas had already spread through the influx of slaves—which had resulted from the captives sent to the markets after each military triumph of the *imperatores*. Support was found, too, in 'advanced' aristocratic circles—Catiline and his friends, for instance—where a lowering of moral standards was

* C

combined with what would today be called 'progressive' ideas. The Pythagoreans, on the other hand, were regarded as conservative; for, in defiance of chronology, they had persuaded public opinion that Numa—traditionally revered by the Romans as the author of their religious system—had been a disciple of Pythagoras.

Bacchism, moreover, had an international character; the cult was powerful in Asia Minor, and had been given an official character in Egypt. So it is not surprising that Mark Antony, having become heir to the Lagid (or Ptolemaic) dynasty through his union with Cleopatra, should have set himself up as a new Dionysus, in imitation of the Ptolemies. He thus drew a great number of Bacchic sects into his service, and their activities in Italy were dangerous for his rival during the war of propaganda, lasting several years, that preceded the armed conflict between the two claimants to Caesar's power. Octavian was therefore inclined towards the Pythagoreans, and in 36 B.C. he took their patron, Apollo, for his protector. This choice has been explained as following the traditions of the Julii family into which he had entered by adoption. But the present writer cannot agree, for Caesar never showed any particular devotion for Apollo. By taking this classical god as his protector, Octavian was already demonstrating his independence of his adoptive father—whom he never renounced, but whose memory he allowed to be smeared by writers in his pay.

The Pythagorean character given to Apollo is evident in the manner he was shown on monuments and coins, sometimes seated and holding his zither, sometimes standing and holding a bow or a lyre. Both forms of representation were taken from the beliefs of the cult; the first showed the victor in the musical contest with Marsyas, the flute-playing satyr with wicked impulses, and the second was the Apollo of Leucadia, standing on the White Rock to succour souls who had just gone through the ordeal of jumping from the cliff.

Octavian may not have been a Pythagorean in the fullest sense, but it is enough for him to have been in sympathy with the cult and come under its influence. Virgil, too, at about that period, felt a similar appeal; the fourth *Eclogue*, that strange message which the Christians held to be a prophecy of the Messiah's coming by the most saintly of the Gentiles, seems to have been inspired by Pythagorean teachers. Apollo, alone of all the gods, is expressly mentioned in it—which obviates any hint of the Dionysiac propaganda of Cleopatra.[1] The

[1] As H. Jeanmaire believed—*Rev. Arch.*, 1924, I. p. 241 et seq.

obvious traces of Pythagorism in the descent-into-hell passage in Book VI of the *Aeneid* prove that the poet remained constant in his opinions until the end of his life.

It was during those critical years, when Octavian became aware of his destiny but not, as then, of its greatness, that he had the walls in his Palatine house painted. The exact date of the frescoes has been much debated. Signor Lugli places it as late as 3 B.C., after the fire that damaged the house. The garlands of foliage and fruit painted on the walls of the 'wings' of the study resemble the sculptured garlands on the *Ara Pacis*, dedicated in 9 B.C. But recent discoveries at Pompeii make a case for putting back the date of the inception of the third style by several years; it was previously considered contemporary with the accession of Tiberius. The Palatine house was given its partly sacred character during the period 31–25 B.C., by the construction of the temples of Apollo and Vesta, and by the ornamentation of the doorway; the interior decorations must have been executed at the same time.

The uncertainty and psychological instability of the young master of the world—Octavian was thirty-two in the year of Actium—appear in early likenesses. A statue in the Capitol Museum has several features adroitly emphasized—the wave in the hair, the knitted brow, the high cheek-bones—which indicate 'the nervousness of a morbid temperament mastered by will-power, the clash of an uneasy spirit with firmness of decision' (J. Charbonneaux). This finely modelled face—strangely like that of Napoleon when First Consul—is marked by remorse for crimes coldly decreed, by the constant menace from enemies often lurking among his circle of intimates, and by amorous desires. That uneasy mind found refuge in a dream-world, in flights of fantasy, and the protection of a pure and serene god.

It was only much later that he found calmness of mind. What distinguishes the revolutionary from the tyrant is that the former sacrificed others and himself in a cause that went beyond him, while the latter's only object was to satisfy his passions. Augustus discovered that people believed in him before he began to believe in himself.

Virgil had already completed the first book of the *Georgics* with his plea for peace, probably the finest and noblest piece of writing inspired by the Roman religion, which was interpreted by Pythagorism:

O Gods of our fathers, and Romulus and
Mother Vesta, who watch over the Tuscan Tiber and the
Roman Palatine, do not hold back this young man
Hastening to help the unbalanced century! For long
Enough we have paid with our blood for the treacheries of
Laomedon of Troy. For long now, the heavenly halls
Envy us Caesar, and complain that he cares only for
Triumphs among men. For everywhere good and bad are
Confused; there are wars throughout the world; so many
Forms of crime, the plough neglected, no respect;
The colonists have been taken away, and the fields lie uncared for.
The curved scythes are reforged into straight blades.[1]
Here it is the Euphrates, there Germania, that stirs up war,
Neighbouring towns, having between themselves broken their
Laws, take up arms; wicked Mars rages throughout the whole world.[2]

ꙮ III ꙮ

THE RETURN TO STOICISM

One wonders what the world would have become if the Emperor
had responded to Virgil's call, and had favoured Pythagorism, as
Acoka had Buddhism. But neither by temperament nor schooling was
Augustus inclined to become a prophet or to propagate a religion. As
was usual in upper-class Roman families, his education had been
entrusted to two Greek tutors; both, Athenodorus and Areios, belonged to the Stoic school. The philosophers of the Porch were

---

[1] This line is a literal translation of an old Eastern saying, of Babylonian origin.

[2] Di patrii, Indigetes, et Romule Vestaque mater
Quae tuscum Tiberim et romana Palatia seruas,
Hunc saltem euerso iuuenem succurrere saeclo
Ne prohibete! Satis iampridem sanguine nostro
Laomedonteae luimus periuria Troiae.
Iampridem nobis caeli te regia, Caesar,
Inuidet, atque hominum queritur curare triumphos.
Quippe ubi fas uersum atque nefas; tot bella per orbem;
Tam multae sceleris facies, non ullus aratro
Dignus honos; squalent abductis arua colonis
Et curuae rigidum falces conflantur in ensem.
Hinc mouet Euphrates, illinc Germania bellum;
Vicinae ruptis inter se legibus urbes
Arma ferunt; saeuit tot Mars impius orbe.

materialistic in the sense that they believed in the great power of the mind and in the identification of divine will with the nature of things; in a world-soul immanent in man. The self-sufficiency of their creed debarred calling on Providence for help; it was opposed to mystical states, although some of the later Stoic teachers, such as Poseidonios, felt attracted by these traditional impulses.

Did Octavian's tutors, who seem each to have been something of an eclectic, let their pupil be tempted by Pythagoreans, or did he escape from their influence for a time? In any case, by the time he consolidated his authority his beliefs were defined. In the year 26 B.C. two significant events occurred. First, the Senate decreed that Augustus should be presented with a golden shield, symbol of the four cardinal virtues of the wise king—*virtus* itself, which was essentially manly courage and valour; mercy, justice and piety towards the gods and the country. Secondly, an order was made banishing Anaxilas of Larissa, a Magian and Pythagorean; this was so much talked about in intellectual circles that St Jerome wrote about it four centuries later. These two acts were as complementary as the halves of a diptych.

By promoting the dedication of the *clipeus virtutis* Augustus was proclaiming in the most solemn manner his adherence to the political creed of the Stoics. For these disciples of Zeno—who were distrustful of democracy, like most of Plato's successors—believed in the human flock being guided by one shepherd, as a delegate of Zeus, provided he was worthy through his virtues and was as much a model to his subjects as he was a leader. And by striking at one of the chief members of the Pythagorean school the Emperor was also proclaiming his break with the last cult that he had tolerated. The Empire born of the victory at Actium was not to be the realm of Apollo, but of Jupiter incarnated in Augustus.

Is this turning-point, so decisive for the future of the world, to be seen as a conversion of Augustus, a sincere adherence on his part to an idealistic philosophy? There can be no doubt that he was passing through a physical and moral crisis during the period 27–26 B.C. Although he had had little effective command of armies, the Emperor decided to take personal control of a campaign which, though of secondary importance politically, proved exceptionally hard and difficult because of the barren mountainous terrain and the courage and tenacity of the enemy. The Cantabri inhabited the mountains of north-west Spain, and had already given proof of their love of liberty and attachment to a strange language, still perpetuated by their Basque descendants today. Three generals had successively won victories over them, but none had been able to break all resistance. Augustus, by his vigorous decision, was meeting the challenge of certain aristocratic generals, such as Licinius Crassus, who would not admit to his monopoly of the victorious power of Rome, which was the essential basis of his political authority.

It was a gruelling campaign; a sweltering heat oppressed the legionaries, increased the numbers of rats and germ-carrying flies, and the only breaks in it were violent thunderstorms that were dreaded even more. One night the litter that Augustus had just left was struck by lightning, and one of his pages was killed. The Emperor took fright; he vowed, there and then, to build a temple to Jupiter the Thunderer, and all that night he clutched a sealskin, which was believed to keep off the lightning. Nevertheless, each time a storm broke he went trembling to shut himself in an enclosed and vaulted room. But much more serious misfortunes came upon him; an infection of the kidneys, that he probably caught from sick soldiers, spread to his digestive system. He was forced to retire to Tarragona and put himself in the care of doctors, who despaired for his life. The usual treatment for such an ailment was to give hot injections, but this brought no improvement. The Greek physician, Antonius Musa, who had the unenviable responsibility for the Emperor's health, then tried a cold-bath treatment; this did wonders, and a cure at a Pyrenean spa completed the recovery. The Senate had a statue of Musa, a well-deserved statue, erected in the temple of Asclepius, the god of medicine.

These trials and sufferings hastened Augustus's intellectual development, understandably enough; but what is surprising is that his confidence in himself, in his own abilities, was thereby strengthened to a point that enabled him to dispense with divine aid. It was exactly the opposite of a conversion in the Christian sense. But Augustus was the very contrary of a Christian. Moreover, other influences were at work to strengthen his determination.

While the Emperor was slowly recovering from his illness, Tarragona had become a world centre for a short time. In the streets its people were astonished to find themselves rubbing shoulders with Parthians sent by King Tiridates and with representatives of Indian potentates, who had a flourishing trade with Egypt. One day an embassy from Mitylene, led by Crinagoras, landed in the town. He was the bearer of a decree that instituted games and sacrifices in honour of Augustus similar to those already celebrated in honour of Zeus; a temple had been dedicated to him, and white calves would be sacrificed there every day. This tribute to him, more solemn than any previously made, probably convinced Augustus of his fitness to give the world the order, peace and prosperity that it needed.

Such a task called for a complete revision of one's character, so the Stoics would have said; a great moral effort to give a truly divine spirit to one's being. Marcus Aurelius, at a later period, endeavoured to do just that. But Augustus was no philosopher. It has been aptly remarked that wisdom did not figure among the virtues that he considered he possessed. And his remark when on his deathbed, quoted by Suetonius (*see* page 19), shows more than anything that he regarded the role of master and saviour of the world in a theatrical sense, like all his other roles; his true personality was not involved, and only when dying did he remove the mask and costume. His one concern was to play the part without faltering, and especially to conceal from the public the change that had taken place; no one must know that the living god had felt any hesitation over the conception of his mission.

A recent discovery in the forum at Arles of a copy of the *clipeus virtutis* reveals the exact date of its dedication, and thereby discloses one of the little deceits that Augustus practised. According to the Res Gestae, the presentation of the shield was made during his seventh consulship, and appears to be a natural consequence of the constitutional arrangement in January 27 B.C. But the inscription on the Arles copy shows that the *clipeus* was not consecrated until 26 B.C. The care taken to conceal the delay, even more than the delay itself, indicates that the symbol corresponded with a new ideology that was being gradually elaborated.

ᗌᗌᗌ IV ᗕᗕᗕ

THE IMPERIAL CULT, A CIVIC RELIGION

A study of monuments and texts reveals the dwindling of Octavian's mysticism, and the setting up of a 'civic' religion with Augustus as the one true god. Apollo had not been immediately affected by the disgrace of the Pythagoreans. Even in 17 B.C., nine years after Anaxilas was banished, the Secular Games (which, this time, officially ushered in the new order) were still placed under the patronage of the twin deities, Apollo and Artemis. Horace dedicated his *Carmen* to them, and it was sung by a chorus of boys and girls belonging to aristocratic families. But a contemporary monument shows that the gods were already being given a subordinate place in the Augustan order of things.

The Primaporta statue commemorated an event that was represented symbolically by the decorations carved in relief on Augustus's armour. In 20 B.C. diplomatic and military pressure had been successfully applied on the Parthian king to return the standards and the prisoners captured after the defeat inflicted on Crassus thirty years previously. Augustus was prouder of this bloodless victory than of any military success; henceforth the recovered standards were given the place of honour on official monuments, instead of the trophies taken at Actium. The Primaporta statue of the Emperor thus shows his breastplate as having, in the middle, the figures of a Parthian handing a standard to a young Roman officer, probably Tiberius. On either side is a woman captive, symbolizing Gaul and Spain, which had been recently pacified. Above, the lord of heaven, Jupiter, spreads his cloak over Dawn's chariot. Below, Earth offers a horn of plenty. Apollo and Diana are there too, one on a griffin and the other on a hind; but they are placed round the sides of the statue, almost under the feet of the two central figures. The Olympians were now only guests of honour, and somewhat in the way, without even a right to front seats.

Their relegation is even more pronounced on the Gemma Augustea, a cameo in sardonyx that was part of the treasure of St Sernin's, in Toulouse, but was eventually acquired for the imperial collection in Vienna. This masterpiece of antique carving represents the victory of Tiberius over the German tribes in 7 B.C. In the upper relief Augustus is seated in all his glory next to the goddess Rome, and surrounded with all the attributes of Jupiter, while Tiberius has left his chariot to kneel in front of him, making the victor's homage which according to the traditional religion was made only to the lord of heaven. The lower relief has soldiers busily erecting a trophy; two others are dragging a man and a woman captive forward by their hair, to chain them at the foot of the trophy. The peculiar dress of these two soldiers has always puzzled commentators, and the two had been generally taken for barbarian auxiliaries of the Roman army. But quite recently they were identified by Ernest Will as Artemis-Diana and Hermes-Mercury. So

Augustus had not only usurped the place of Jupiter, he had relegated the gods to the inglorious position of army supernumeraries! A detail of the carving also gives an indication of the rationalist, and even civic, character of the representation: above Augustus's head hovers the constellation of Capricorn, the sign he was born under. Now in those days astrology was regarded as a scientific theory, a stringent determinism. The glorification of Augustus thus appeared as the natural consequence of the laws governing the world, and no divine favours were needed.

This testimony found in works of art is supported by instances in literature. Horace, in the first books of his *Odes*, published in 23 B.C., did his best to serve and justify the new ideal of Augustus. A natural Epicurean, Horace praised the unshakable sage, *iustum et tenacem propositi virum*, who would stand unafraid if the heavens fell about him (III. iii. 1–10). The fifth Ode begins with the avowal quoted here earlier, in Chapter One, and which could be taken as a comment on the Gemma Augustea: 'We thought that thundering Jupiter reigned in the heavens, but our present god is Augustus.' Horace was probably thinking of the hymn, hardly less cynical, sung by the Athenians of the fourth century B.C. as they installed Demetrius Poliorcetes [1] in the Parthenon as husband of their goddess Athena: 'The other gods are far away or not at all . . . but you are here, and we can see you, not in wood or stone but real.' Horace's third book of *Odes* was also a call to worship the impotent gods, which seems rather illogical; but the ancients felt no scruples about making a distinction between rites and belief. Epicurus himself, an ardent champion of materialism, had his private chapel and his gods, and offered sacrifices. Attachment to tradition and appreciation of the social value of the ceremonies caused people to forget the illogicality of their attitude, which in any case was devoid of hypocrisy.

That attitude provides an explanation of how Augustus could let himself be likened to gods in which he did not believe. As we know only too well today, a materialistic ideology can lead to state-idolatry and leader-worship. The part played in the Roman principate by the cult of the deceased Emperor is more difficult to understand, for it was not just a worship of his memory. Recently published work—that of

[1] One of the Diadochi, the Macedonian generals who fought between themselves for Alexander's empire. Demetrius twice occupied Athens, in 307 and 294 B.C.

Jean Gagé especially—shows that the *Divus Augustus* continued to be the patron of the dynasty. The fortune and the victory of Augustus were guarantees of the successes of his heirs, who instead of being taken for his equals as emperors were regarded more as delegates of the founder of the Empire—in a way similar to the caliphs who succeeded Mahomet.

This is expressed by the Gemma Augustea, where Augustus appears as a deity, hovering in the clouds above Tiberius. It was Tiberius, though, who showed a singular indifference to the outward form of the dynastic cult. On one occasion two Roman knights were denounced to him as having been guilty of lese-majesty. One admitted having invited a mime-actor with vile morals to his house while worshippers of Augustus were meeting there, and having transferred the ownership of his gardens and a statue of Augustus that stood in them. The second man had committed perjury after taking the oath in the name of Augustus. The new Emperor dismissed both men with the disinterested words: '*Deorum injuriae dis curae*'—'Leave it to the gods to avenge offences against them.' Much the same scepticism and disillusion were shown by writers when referring to Augustus's funeral. 'There was not even a single ex-praetor who did not swear he had seen the image of the cremated man ascending to heaven,' wrote Suetonius; while Tacitus made the disdainful remark: 'Finally, when the burial rites were completed, he was voted a temple and a divine cult.' The patricians who solicited the place of imperial *flamen*, to offer the daily sacrifice to Augustus, regarded it only as another social distinction.

These apparent contradictions are more or less cleared up if we consider that Augustus was the embodiment not of a personal divinity but of a decisive moment in historic evolution. The coming of a 'Golden Age' was written in the stars; when the civilized world was at last controlled by a predestined people, the man chosen by destiny to bring order and peace would appear; after his death his successors appointed by him would carry on his work. Such was the reality that could be grasped by enlightened minds. The form of the ritual, the auguries of the mighty work—they were but symbols and signposts for the common herd, who could be beguiled by them as it had been for centuries by the godly images of the Olympians and the ceremonies of their cult.

Chapter Three

THE END OF AUGUSTUS

A POLITICIAN who has gained power early in life rarely benefits by retaining it until a ripe old age, when most of his contemporaries are dead. He usually represents the hopes and aspirations of his own generation, and so hardly avoids disappointing the younger people born during his government. This conflict with the young generation was all the more difficult for Augustus as his only child was among the first to flout his authority. Julia's rebellion was much more than a family matter; the young woman had the support of a considerable body of opinion in her refusal to accept the social discipline that the Emperor was endeavouring to restore. Augustus crushed her, but the movement she had led was later revived, and spread and endangered the whole work of restoration accomplished by the Emperor.

꠹꠹꠹ I ꠸꠸꠸

RESTORING THE MORAL ORDER

The cause and origin of the revolt can be traced to Augustus's intellectual development that we have just examined. It was only his iron command over himself that had enabled him to adapt and discipline his mind and body, which was essential for the great tasks of a man treading 'in the path of history'. He was helped by the asceticism taught by his Stoic tutors; but there were times, as has been mentioned, when the burden of his role felt heavy upon him and he sought relief for a while, often in childish pursuits. But the effort he was making had to be demanded of others too—of all those involved in the great work. The entire Roman people was sternly told to return to the hard disciplined ways of family life, of the soil and of war; especially the aristocracy, who found that their privileges of the easy-going days now had to be earned.

During the period of the civil wars the desire for flight from realities had not only affected the realms of religion and dreams; it had also greatly unsettled the social and moral order. The urge for debauchery that Catiline and his friends, Clodia and her circle, gave way to has provided an easy subject of indignation for moralists. As with the French nobility in the eighteenth century, it was a sign of the revolt of the individual against an outmoded social system, which was no longer worth upholding at the price of renunciation of animal passions.

An interesting aspect of this revolt which has been ignored by traditional historians and by sociologists, is the effort made by women to emancipate themselves. One would like to see a penetrating study made of Clodia, that high-society lady whose immodesty annoyed the social upstart, Cicero, and was a great trial to her lover, Catullus. In the magnificent villa attributed to her by Signor Lugli, the decorations are a striking example of nonconformism, and even more so is the plan of the building; unlike the traditional Roman villa, which was turned inwards on itself to preserve intimacy, modesty and the secrecy of family decisions governed by the strict *pater*, Clodia's villa opened everywhere on to gardens and the Tiber, enabling the idle and the curious to watch Clodia and her noble friends disporting themselves with Bacchantic freedom, but excluding all who did not belong to the 'upper set'—Cicero, for instance, which infuriated him.

Augustus, when a young man, had belonged to such a set during the troubled years of the Triumvirate. Suetonius reproduces the abusive correspondence he exchanged with Antony, and it leaves no doubt as to the complete lack of morals; in the most vulgar terms, Antony flung the names of his mistresses at him—Drusilla, his acknowledged mistress; Tertullia, the wife of Maecenas; Rufilla, Salvia and Titinnia. At a banquet one evening the young Octavian found himself placed next to a young woman whose husband had one of the great names of Rome, Tiberius Claudius Nero. Octavian soon began flirting with her, and the other guests saw the two suddenly get up and disappear into an adjacent bedroom; Suetonius, in telling the story, added the detail that when Livia—for it was she—returned to the dining-room her hair was down and her small ears were quite red! Her husband was among the company, but as he had proposed rewarding Caesar's murderers, had joined Antony's brother in Perusia and then Sextus Pompey in Sicily, he was in no position to show jealousy; a divorce was easily arranged, and Livia gave birth to Claudius's second son, Drusus, at Octavian's house.

The example set by the young triumvir was naturally followed by his *entourage*. Antony accused Octavian's friends of organizing 'strip-tease' sessions, with young women and girls of good family as the actresses. And during a period of famine there was great indignation among the public on learning that Octavian had given a 'mythological' dinner, at which fun had been made of both religion and morals.

However, a change came when the régime was established. Augustus, as mentioned earlier, was never able to control his sexual appetites; but now his laxity was kept secret. The ruler of the world looked very sheepish when, going to meet a curtained litter that he had sent to collect a lady of easy virtue, he saw his old tutor Athenodorus jump out of it. Athenodorus had sent the woman packing and taken her place, and now he started to lecture Augustus on his incontinence. But even if Augustus was not chaste, he meant others to be. Harsh laws were introduced to punish debauchery and homosexuality, while other laws were designed to encourage virtuous families, and privileges were granted to fathers of three or more children. But all that did not lead to a great deal. A fine scandal was caused when Tiberius—who had the hypocrisy of his predecessor—discovered that ladies of the best society were trying to get round police regulations by calmly asking the praetor to register them as prostitutes! Augustus had not realized that the Roman nobility's inclination towards debauchery was not merely a sign of the decadence of a class spent by too easy a life, but also of the need for a more flexible and humane morality. Yet, even had he realized, Augustus would not have found the necessary personal resources to institute a new system of values.

⟫⟫⟫ II ⟪⟪⟪

THE DOMUS AUGUSTA

The already heavy burden that Augustus had laid on the nobility was increased tenfold for his relatives. The monarchal nature of the principate was revealed, as we have seen, by the association of 'the House of Augustus' with the Emperor himself. It was a tradition of the patrician class that each member had greater worth as representative of a perpetual family line than as an individual. The Augustan ideology, by its insistence on the fateful mission of the Julii, emphasized the role of this family which now stood apart from the rest of the nobility and had in fact become a dynasty.

At the beginning of his career Augustus had resorted to that principle in order to establish himself as Caesar's legitimate heir; and had then revived it in order to ensure that his achievements should last. But Augustus's outstanding personality and his role of saviour of humanity, of creator of a new order, placed the members of the *gens Augusta* in a very delicate position. None of them could hope to become equal to the founder; they had to be content with reflecting his supernatural character and consequently subordinating their own personality. They were expected to submit to the discipline that Augustus had imposed upon himself, so there should be no risk of their waywardness affecting the dignity of the divine mission that they were upholding. This obligation was particularly hard on the women. Augustus, faithful to Roman tradition on this point, denied them any political activity and only allowed them the glory of transmitting the divine blood. They enjoyed none of the honorific satisfactions normally accorded to princesses, yet they were subject to the patriarchal morality that Augustus championed.

This complicated role of the *gens Augusta* was reflected in protocol; when the consul Messala proposed that Augustus be given the title of 'Father of the Country', his eulogy associated the family with the Emperor. The sculptured friezes of the *Ara Pacis* form a superb pageant of the imperial family, and in a double aspect: as a model of the *bourgeois* virtues and as the dynasty entrusted with the nation's destiny. The sculptor—thought to have been Greek, but there is no real evidence on the point; he was, in any case, completely Italianized— has understood and rendered the majestic simplicity and *bourgeois* dignity which had become the Emperor's ideal. Behind the *flamines majores*, heirs to the most ancient religious tradition of the Romans, comes Augustus's son-in-law and closest, most loyal collaborator, Agrippa, draped austerely in his toga.[1] His son Lucius, aged seven or eight, is clutching his toga as though afraid of getting left behind; a young woman in the background has a hand on the boy's head—she is

[1] The interpretation of the *Ara Pacis* has been much debated by specialists (the situation as it stands was given by this author in *Rev. des Et. latines*, 38, 1961, pp. 328–36). There is much controversy in particular over the identification of the members of the imperial family. General agreement exists only in the cases of Agrippa, Drusus and Antonia the younger. The identities given here are those favoured by J. Charbonneaux, as seeming the most reasonable.

his mother, the notorious Julia, Augustus's daughter by his first wife. Then comes the Empress Livia, in a long veil and with the dignified air of a matron and priestess. She is followed by a young couple, graceful and at ease; the pretty wife is finding the ceremony rather long and has turned to chat to her husband, while an elderly lady in the background has a finger to her lips in rebuke. She is very likely the Emperor's sister, the unfortunate Octavia; the young wife is Antonia, daughter of Octavia and Mark Antony, married to Drusus, Livia's second son. The young couple's children are there, too: a little boy of three, half lost in his small toga, is holding his mother's hand; another boy, slightly taller, clutches his father's military cloak from behind; in spite of his fine toga and crown of laurels he, too, is getting tired and asks his big sister how much longer it is going on; the young girl is smiling with an amused and protective air, while the uncles behind sign to them to behave.

It all has that mixture of pomp and free-and-easiness which is still such a delightful feature of festivals in Italy today. The sculptor no doubt wished to diminish the solemnity of the occasion, but the effect achieved admirably served the propaganda of the régime. The young female relatives of the Emperor had not to look too much like princesses. They had been brought up in strict seclusion; their day was fully occupied with handiwork in accordance with tradition—such as the spinning and weaving of wool for the family's togas, the Emperor's first and foremost—and with advanced studies that Augustus was kept informed about, so they had little time left for any pleasures. The money they spent on themselves was controlled almost avariciously, and contacts with young men were strictly forbidden. The Emperor sharply rebuked in public a young man of the highest rank, L. Vicinius —for whom he had much regard—because the man had called on Julia without asking permission, having met her on the beach at Baiae.

The consequences of so many precautions were disastrous. Julia shocked all Rome by her misconduct and by openly plotting against her father; and the morals of her daughter Julia were no better. The Emperor's reaction was to banish each in turn and to deprive them of all but the bare necessities. He developed a deep hatred of them; his comment quoted by Suetonius is distressing evidence of it: 'He's a lucky man who remains a bachelor and dies without having had children!' He referred to the two Julias and his grandson, Agrippa, as his 'three abscesses' or 'three cankers'. When an accomplice of one of the Julias, a freedwoman named Phoebe, hanged herself, Augustus coldly declared that he would have preferred having her as his daughter. Such is the reality behind the touching procession shown on the *Ara Pacis*, though it was carved a few years before the great scandal caused by Julia's 'conspiracy'.

⫸⫸ III ⫷⫷

THE CONSPIRACY OF JULIA

Many historians have made a study of this tragic episode, which was as sordid as it was horrible. The eminent writer Jérôme Carcopino clearly shows in a recent book that Augustus's daughter was guilty of far more than shameless profligacy—of a political plot aimed at the assassination of the Emperor, to benefit herself and her lover Julius Antonius, younger son of Mark Antony and Fulvia. But, whatever her excesses, they were surely due, psychologically, to the abnormal and intolerable situation of being the only child of the ruler of the world.

Excuses have been found for her in the separation from her mother Scribonia, who was divorced by Augustus on the very day she gave birth to Julia; in the contrasting effects of a strict upbringing and a liberal education; and in the several marriages imposed on her by her father for political reasons. All these were more than enough to ruin the young woman's morals. But there was another cause, that went much deeper and was, moreover, the basis of all the rest—the misfortune to be the only child of a man who had cut himself off from humanity by setting himself above it.

The inordinate pressure of the Emperor's personality on his daughter had suppressed her own; he had refused to let her have any freedom in her youth, he married her off three times without ever having any regard for her feelings, and—even more serious—prevented her fulfilling her role as a mother. The first two sons she had by Agrippa— Caius in 20 B.C. and Lucius in 17 B.C.—were in fact *bought* by the Emperor, under an ancient juridical procedure, in order to bring them up as his own children. He said to some friends one day that he had two daughters difficult to control and guide—the Republic and Julia. The oppressive affection that 'the Father of the Country' bestowed on Rome was not unlike the affection he thought he was giving his daughter, in the sense that the one and the other were thereby deprived of any free will. Augustus found his justification in the old Roman morality that he aimed at restoring.

It seems almost certain that a marble head recently discovered by Monsieur H. Rolland during the excavations at St Rémy, in Provence, is of Augustus's daughter; this is the only portrait of her known to us.[1] The square face with high cheek-bones and too large a jaw has a rather rustic firmness. The mouth is small and delicate, but the thick nose must have been a 'turned-up' one; the defects are partly redeemed by the long slim neck. But the most striking feature is the insolent way the head is thrown back to look proudly upwards. This gives an impression of defiance, an assertion of stubbornness and haughtiness, all of which correspond with Julia's character.

Her defiance was primarily directed, naturally enough, at the *bourgeois* morality which was the day-to-day and most obvious of her oppressions. Instead of the honeyed hypocrisy of Livia, Julia soon turned to plain audacity. Her disorderly life has been ingeniously explained by Jérôme Carcopino as being a belated consequence of her second widowhood and third marriage, but the present writer is not entirely convinced. The stories of her unfaithfulness to Agrippa were repeated by the younger Pliny, who described the unlucky husband as racked with jealousy, and by Macrobius and other writers. Admittedly the marriage was fertile—three boys and two girls—but Augustus, well-informed as he was, showed as much surprise as pleasure that his grandchildren should resemble their father. The young wife had no hesitation, moreover, in telling the secret to her friends; it was simple enough—to give herself to her lovers only when already pregnant by her husband.

The remark is so typical of her cynical attitude in general that there seems no doubt of its authenticity. Julia did not feel for Agrippa, though, the repulsion that later made her life with Tiberius so intolerable, and hastened her disgrace. It is even possible that she had some affection for the elderly Agrippa, and that she gave him a little of the filial love that had been diverted from her father; it would have been in keeping with the innate fickleness of her character.

She was hoping to injure her father by her deliberate and open flouting of social conventions, and great must have been her rage when

[1] John Buchan in his *Augustus* says there is a bust of her in the Uffizi, and that her head appears with Agrippa's on a gem. (Trans. note.)

her dissolute excesses met only with an Olympian disdain. This
indifference on her father's part was sufficient indication that all love
for her had vanished from his heart; perhaps the Emperor, and in any
case his wife, felt a secret satisfaction that the woman they now considered only as a rival should be lowering herself in the public esteem.
So Julia resolved to attack them in the one way she knew both could be
hurt. The Emperor's sole passion was for his work, for his achievements to last; Livia was doing all she could, urged on by ambition and
motherly love, to ensure the succession for her son, Tiberius. Julia's
idea seems to have been to seduce Tiberius in order to turn him against
his mother and father-in-law.

Jérôme Carcopino has given an excellent account of how Julia's
intrigues first met with little success; and how, following Agrippa's
opportune death, her desired union with Tiberius was forced upon her
by Augustus himself. But Tiberius refused to have any part in his wife's
plans, and the breach between the two widened into a common revul-
sion fostered by hate and scorn. Then came the last act of the tragedy;
Julia, in her despair and folly, launched into a plot that was absurd as
well as criminal. The love affairs she had with leading members of the
Roman aristocracy's younger set—with Julius Antonius, Claudius
Pulcher, Sempronius Gracchus, Cornelius Scipio—were intended,
there can be no doubt, to win over a group of the most ardent opponents of the Emperor, even more than to satisfy her sexual desires. But if
Julia had been in her right mind she would surely have realized that by
doing away with her father she was also destroying the one political
value she possessed. With the Republic restored, the parricide would
have found the indignation of her family's clients and the suspicions of
the sincere republicans directed solely against herself. And one can be
sure that her lovers would not have hesitated to cast all the odium on
her, once her usefulness had ended, and made her the scapegoat for
public opinion. But Julia was not really an ambitious woman; for her
politics were merely a means of gratifying her hatred against nature for
having clouded her intellect after destroying her finer sentiments.

None but a madbrain and a wanton could have conceived the demonstration that led to the discovery of the plot. Certainly no organizer of
a *coup d'état* would approve of her assembling her raffish set in the
Forum at night, in the very centre of Rome, where the police—however rudimentary a body—could hardly avoid them, and there giving
an orgy that has never been surpassed in wild dissolution: yet was

perfectly harmless to the authority of the State. There was, admittedly, a religious significance to this witches' revel. As Monsieur Carcopino has shown, it was placed under the patronage of the satyr Marsyas, whose statue was set up in front of the Rostra and symbolized—for a reason still unknown—the liberty of the Roman Republic. This satyr was a companion of Dionysus-Bacchus and so an enemy of Apollo, who eventually flayed him alive.

Bacchism, though, had been a subversive element in Rome since the second century B.C., and was directed against political institutions and the social order as well as against morality. Julia and her friends must have organized the kind of seditious gathering banned by the Senate and the Emperor, and it was undoubtedly a full-blooded and copious Bacchanalia. This was probably the reason for Augustus expressly denying his daughter any wine during her exile on the island of Pandataria. However, if these details make the demonstration seem less peculiar, they do not make it appear any the more sensible. The 'conspiracy of Julia' was far more like a wild party of the raffish younger set than a revolutionary *putsch*. Augustus realized this, and had only Julius Antonius executed, while the other accomplices of his daughter were banished. Julia herself was kept in exile for the rest of her life, first on Pandataria and then in Rhegium; those sixteen miserable years were alleviated only by the presence of her mother, the hapless Scribonia, who would seem to have survived her repudiation by Augustus only to succour Julia in her disgrace.

⫸⫸⫸ IV ⫷⫷⫷

EXTENSIONS OF THE CRISIS

When ordering those stringent and inevitable measures, Augustus should have realized that he was not free from blame himself, and should at least have tried to avoid similar errors with regard to his grandchildren. It was too late, though, to make any changes in the education of the three eldest, Caius, the younger Julia and Lucius, who were respectively eighteen, sixteen and fifteen, and so were practically adults for the times. The elderly Emperor turned with all the affection he was capable of to Caius and Lucius. They had been taken away from their mother at a very early age, as already explained, and Augustus himself had taught them to read; they always dined with him, and rode by his side or just ahead when accompanying him on his travels.

Unfortunately it was as oppressive to be the object of Augustus's affection as of his severity. He was fond of his grandsons not for themselves but as reflections of himself. According to Suetonius, he made them imitate his own handwriting; and sculptors gave them a resemblance to the Emperor that was more or less imaginary. They were forced into public prominence and given responsibilities too soon, and their arrogance was increased by the flatterers surrounding them. The new title of 'princes of youth' designated them as leaders of the rising generation, of that active section from which the military leaders emerged and which was the social equivalent of the equestrian order.

They were supposed to be as gifted as their grandfather, especially the elder of the two, who was made a senator and pontiff at thirteen, consul at seventeen and vice-emperor of the whole of the East at eighteen; Caius certainly stood in need of the early maturity and exceptional capabilities which had enabled Octavian, when as young, to win over Caesar's legions and to foil the intrigues of crafty senators. Portraits of the two heirs presumptive were set up by municipalities and constituted bodies all over the country. Their features, at every stage in their brief lives, are probably the best known to us of all the personalities of antiquity. Caius, even in the year of his birth, was shown as Love riding on a dolphin, near the statue of his grandfather that was discovered at Primaporta. On the Gemma Augustea, which commemorated the victories of Tiberius in Pannonia in 7 B.C., Caius is shown wearing a breastplate, between the Emperor and Tiberius; here is clearly seen the latent conflict over the succession, which was solved the following year by Tiberius going into voluntary exile on Rhodes, not without some bitterness, and where he remained for seven years. There is a bust in the Vatican of Lucius as a young child, and another in Athens of him when eleven or twelve.

Their mother's disgrace did not appear to upset the young brothers very much; they had probably already broken with her, as Jérôme Carcopino suggests, because of the clash of ambitions. In 2 B.C. Caius was sent on a roving commission to the eastern provinces; this was a difficult assignment, for the removal of Tiberius had encouraged the enemies of Rome in Armenia and among the Parthians to stir up trouble. A little later Lucius was sent on a mission to Spain. Augustus may have intended the young Caesars to specialize each in a different half of the Empire; if so, his plans were brought to nothing by successive disasters, in which the elderly and superstitious Emperor saw the avenging hand of a Nemesis whom he had never ceased to fear. Lucius fell ill in Marseilles and died there in 2 A.D. Caius, who had obliged the Armenians to accept Ariobarzanes of Media as their king, was caught in an ambush and badly wounded. His arrogance, which had caused people to fear he would become a tyrant, soon slipped away from him; he sank into a state of neurasthenia, and announced his retirement from public life. A marble bust of him made then shows him sad and bitter, indifferent to his easily acquired honours, brooding over his approaching end; his death occurred on 21st February A.D. 4.

There was great consternation throughout the Empire at the deaths of the two brothers. Evidence of it still exists: in France, there is the Maison Carrée at Nîmes,[1] possibly the most harmonious of Roman temples; on the Aegean island of Thasos, the French school at Athens recently excavated the *hieron* of Lucius, with a statue modelled in the best tradition of Praxiteles; a fine inscription at Pisa gives the order of the funeral procession held by the colony. Acerra, like Nîmes, dedicated a temple; Athens, Corinth, Epidaurus, the Aegean Islands and towns in Asia Minor all dedicated statues.

Neither the death of Marcellus nor that of Agrippa had been marked by such widespread mourning. This cannot be explained by loyalty and adulation alone; the two brothers, in spite of their vanity and arrogance, had won a popularity comparable to that of Augustus after the victory at Actium. In many instances this was undoubtedly aided by people's fear and dislike of Livia and Tiberius; at Nîmes, the statues of the latter had been overturned. But the principal reason was that the 'princes of youth' represented the hopes of a whole new generation, the men who had grown up during Augustus's reign and were getting tired of the old man's rule.

There can be no other explanation for the fresh attempts to overthrow Augustus, following the deaths of the two princes. In A.D. 4 Cornelius Cinna led the reactionary senators in a conspiracy, since

---

[1] Built about 20 B.C. by Agrippa. On the death of the two 'princes of youth' the magistrates of the colony dedicated it to their memory. The two successive dedications are known from marks made on the architrave and the frieze by supports to the bronze lettering. The second inscription was made out by J.-F. Séguier in 1758, the earlier one only in 1919, by Émile Espérandieu. See Jean-Charles Balty's *Études sur la Maison Carrée*, Brussels, 1960.

made famous by the tragedies of Seneca and Corneille. Not for twenty-five years had there been such a plot against the imperial power. Faced with this peril, Augustus recovered the abilities of his youth; when the conspiracy was revealed, he pardoned Cinna and made an ally of him, even giving him the consulship for the year 5. The agitation had spread well beyond the Senate; the people's assemblies, which for more than thirty years had been meekly registering the laws proposed by Augustus and electing his candidates, were now becoming assertive and vocal. Cinna showed the sincerity of his new loyalty by passing a law that practically confined decisions to a preparatory commission whose members were carefully selected.

The recently discovered inscription at Magliano [1] which has given us this hitherto unknown text also reveals that these members, senators and prominent knights, were deemed to be expressing the posthumous wishes of Caius and Lucius. The reason behind the reconciliation of Augustus and Cinna is thus made clear. The Emperor had convinced the bungling conspirator that he risked turning the rebellious movement against his own class. The Magliano tablet also confirms that the popular agitation was linked with the deaths of the two princes, since it was necessary to make out that the suppression of the people's civic rights was an order of the young Caesars from beyond the grave.

Order at home had hardly been restored than the provinces and the barbarian tribes began to revolt. In 6 A.D. all Illyria and Pannonia rose in open insurrection, and a large army had to be deployed against them instead of marching on the Marcomanni, whose leader, Marbod, had formed a powerful independent kingdom in Bohemia. The Cherusci in Westphalia seized the opportunity to recover their freedom, and the consequence was the disastrous loss of three whole Roman legions, a tenth of the Roman army; commanded by Quintilius Varus, the legate of Germania and a relative of Augustus, they were surrounded and massacred somewhere in the Teutoburger Wald by Arminius, the son of the Cheruscan chief. The despair of Augustus on learning of the calamity is well known; of how he wandered about his house crying: 'Varus, Varus, give me back my legions!' It was a great contrast to the calm manner in which he had received the news of the deaths of his grandsons:

[1] A bronze tablet discovered in 1948 at Magliano, in Tuscany, gives the text of the posthumous honours accorded to Germanicus, which followed those bestowed on Caius and Lucius. Cf. A. Piganiol, *Hist. de Rome*, p. 549.

His last years have a similarity to those of Louis XIV: the aged monarch left lonely by the deaths of his near ones, and threatened with the collapse of all he had striven for, having sacrificed his own happiness and his family's too. The anguish that finally distorted the mask of the *Imperator* was occasionally conveyed by sculptors, notably on the small bust from Neuilly-le-Réal.

The deaths of the princes left only one man whom Augustus could call upon. Tiberius, recalled from Rhodes on the death of Caius, had once again proved his great worth as a general and a statesman. He subdued Pannonia, and, though unable to reconquer Germania east of the Rhine, he stabilized the Empire's frontiers on that river. Livia could rightly insist on the value of her son, who was alone capable of preventing the collapse of the régime. Although there was a son of Julia and Agrippa still living—Agrippa Postumus, a tall man of great bodily strength—he was half an idiot and a degenerate; *ingenium sordidum et ferox*, Suetonius said of him. However, Augustus adopted him at the same time as Tiberius, in A.D. 4. But three years later the Emperor banished him to Sorrento; then, as his madness increased, to the little island of Pianosa, just off Elba, where he was kept under military surveillance. The young man had undoubtedly inherited weaknesses due to his mother's loose living. His sister, the younger Julia, who married L. Aemilius Paulus (a descendant of the conqueror of Macedonia), had the morals of her mother; all the ancient authorities are agreed on her sexual depravity. Only one of her lovers, Silanus, has been mentioned; but her scandalous behaviour was understandably concealed as much as possible from the public. Livia must have influenced Augustus to remove this rival to her son in the succession; when Julia was banished in A.D. 8 she was pregnant. The birth of a great-grandson to the Emperor, and one bearing the name of an illustrious republican family, would certainly have weakened Tiberius's claim to the succession. The poor baby was in fact declared illegitimate and condemned to be left to starve to death, by virtue of the inhuman authority that the ancient Roman law vested in the *pater familias*. Livia, who subsequently showed hypocritical concern for the exiled mother, and gave her a small allowance, naturally tried to have her responsibility in this State crime glossed over. But Julia was not the only one to be punished; Ovid seems to have been implicated in her downfall, for the same year he was sent to practise his wit on the Scythians.

The real cause of Ovid's exile to the bleak shores of the Black Sea remains obscure, as it probably was for the poet himself. But Livia and her faction were undoubtedly instrumental. Ovid was one of the last exponents of the spirited licentiousness that Augustus was penalizing with increasing severity as he grew older. There are good reasons for believing that Ovid was connected with one of the Bacchic sects suspected as much of political conspiracy as secret excesses. Their gatherings no longer constituted a threat to the State, and Ovid himself certainly lacked the character to lead a conspiracy, but Augustus had a regrettable tendency to vent his spleen with erring members of his family on their followers and supernumeraries; Ovid's exile was a result of this, as was the putting to death of Caius's tutor and servants.

The aged Emperor's hatred of Julia's family did not, however, extend to his remaining grand-daughter, Agrippina; he appreciated her intelligence, and had married her to Tiberius's nephew, Germanicus. The Emperor had always shown a preference for his younger stepson, Drusus, who had been born in his house after Livia's scandalous divorce, and of whom he may have been—so people had whispered— the real father. But Drusus had not escaped the fate that seemed to await those Augustus loved; soon after his triumphant campaign against the German tribes, in which he advanced as far as the Elbe, he had a curse laid on him by a Druidess—or so it was said—and died from an illness some days later. Augustus then turned his affection to Drusus's son, Germanicus, and obliged Tiberius to adopt him as heir, to the detriment of Tiberius's own son, Drusus junior. The marriage of Germanicus and Agrippina was most fertile; they had four sons and three daughters, in whose veins ran the blood of Augustus, Mark Antony and Agrippa. This happy family was popular with the people; Agrippina shared all the dangers of her husband's campaigns, and the children were born in military camps. The soldiers used to play with the boys and dress them up in uniforms; the youngest, Caius, was called Caligula—the name he later made so notorious—by the soldiers of the Rhine legions, from his wearing small *caligae*, or soldiers' boots.

The Egyptians, who hoped to see the principate become an hereditary monarchy, for their traditional subservience would ensure them a leading role, were full of enthusiasm for Germanicus and his family. It was probably the leaders of these ultra-monarchists who, in A.D. 23 or thereabouts, had a cameo made to aid their propaganda. This famous cameo, which is now in the Cabinet des Médailles of the Bibliothèque Nationale in Paris, has even more figures carved on it than the Gemma Augustea in Vienna. Tiberius is shown in the centre, adorned with the attributes of Jupiter, like Augustus on the Vienna cameo; but Livia, not Roma, has the place next to him. And the 'living Jupiter' has been given a heavenly patron absent from the Gemma Augustea—brooding in the clouds is Augustus, supported by a figure in Eastern costume who probably represents Aeneas, the mythical ancestor of the Julii. He is greeting Germanicus, who had died in Syria. The latter's family throng around the imperial pair, pressing them to acknowledge their legitimate claims; the widow Agrippina is there, with her eldest son Nero, and Drusus tertius, and little Caligula, who is clutching his mother's skirts but already wearing a breastplate. The Vienna cameo hints discreetly at the rival claims of Tiberius and the 'princes of youth' to the succession, but the Paris cameo shows plainly the many claims that Tiberius had to contend with, and which finally wore him down, allowed Sejanus to gain his confidence, and resulted in the banishment and then the murder of Agrippina and her eldest sons.

The primary cause of those horrible tragedies lay with Augustus. His gravest fault was to have unconsciously sacrificed his family, through overriding ambition but also through egoism and hardness of heart, to what he believed to be his mission in life. Admittedly his responsibility is attenuated by the part played by Livia, *gravis reipublicae mater, gravis domui Caesarum noverca.*

Towards the end of his life Augustus relaxed a little and was less hesitant to show his need of real friendship. He even turned to Tiberius, as his letters reproduced by Suetonius prove, not realizing that he had alienated his stepson by his distrust and rebuffs. Livia remained until the end a relentless schemer, cold and prudent, incapable of any warm-hearted act. It must be said on her behalf that her life with Augustus was a long and difficult balancing act. She had won him in the first place by her physical attractions, but these had waned; she could not rely on family ties, as their only child had been still-born, nor on reasons of state, for Augustus distrusted his wife as he did everyone else, perhaps more so, and had refused to give her an official status. There was not even the minimum of intimacy between them that is possible to any royal couple, however hedged around by protocol; Augustus spent all his spare time, all his moments of relaxation, away from his wife. It was only during his last years that Livia came to have any part in his daily life, when the lonely old man was seeking a little affection from the few people still close to him. His last words to her

D

on his deathbed, 'Farewell, Livia, be mindful of our wedded life', could be taken as ironic if the authority of Livia during the final years of his reign did not attest to the influence she had ultimately gained over him. Her official status, which had been for so long refused to her, was conferred by Augustus's testament. By an oddity of ancient Roman law, because of the accepted principle of agnation a wife was not considered a member of her husband's family, although she came under his *manus*; so that Livia did not in fact belong to the *Domus Augusta*, which had achieved all the prestige of a dynasty. In order to bring her into it, the dying Augustus had to—adopt his widow, whose name was changed from Livia to Julia!

The testament gave her the title of *Augusta*, and thereby associated her with that mysterious *auctoritas* which was the source of all the Emperor's extra-constitutional authority. This was an important stage in the transformation of the principate into a monarchy; previously the co-regents had all been men or youngsters, legally able to assume magisterial office. For the first time, against all established custom and laws—but in common with Eastern royal practice—a woman was closely associated with the ruler. And this unheard-of innovation had been brought about not by a decree of the Senate but simply by a testament. Augustus thus destroyed the fiction he had preserved until the end, and treated the State as a private possession.

Livia at once became the object of flatterers and petitioners. Ovid, who was still in exile at Tomis on the Black Sea, appealed to his wife— living in Rome and an old friend of Livia—to intercede for him with the Empress:

> Yet with your mouth praising Caesar's spouse
> Who stands out by her virtue, so that by her chastity
> Ancient bygone days are not supreme over our centuries.
> Who, by having the beauty of Venus, the character
> Of Juno, is alone judged worthy of the heavenly couch.[1]

Artists in all parts of the Empire did in fact adorn statues of Livia with the attributes of Venus, Juno or Ceres. Roman traders who

---

[1] 'Caesaris at coniux ore praecanda tuo
Quae praestat uirtute sua, ne prisca uetustas
Laude puricitae saecula nostra praemat.
Quae Veneris formam, mores Iunonis habendo
Sola est caelesti digna reperta toro.'
(*Epistolae ex Ponto*, III. 1. 114–18.)

travelled across Asia to the Chinese silk markets took presents to the Indo-Scythian rajahs of Afghanistan of medallions bearing a portrait of a rejuvenated Augusta wearing the crown and veil of a goddess. The Senate prepared new decrees to confer on her the title of 'Mother of the Country', to have the words 'son of Julia' added to the Imperial protocol, and to set up an altar commemorating her adoption by Augustus.

But Tiberius knew his mother. . . . 'Tiberius kept saying that a limit must be put to honours bestowed on women . . .; and in particular, being riddled with jealousy, and fearing the effect on his own prerogatives, he would not allow her to have a lictor, forbad the altar and all proposals of that kind. But he requested the proconsular *imperium* for Germanicus Caesar.'[1]

When Livia died, her son was opposed to her apotheosis. Not until the accession of the easy-going Claudius did Augusta join her husband in the Mausoleum, the official pantheon.

⋙ V ⋘

THE ULTIMATE PEACE OF MIND

In the end it was a fruitless effort that Augustus had made to break the sacred circle he had drawn around himself and to enjoy a little human friendship in the evening of his life. He had perhaps managed to give himself some illusions as to the feelings of his wife and his stepson, but he certainly had none about the noble senators who were under his sway.

'In the third place in his testament (after Tiberius and Livia, and the family of Germanicus) came the great names of Rome, most of whom he detested, merely mentioned for show and for his greater glory in posterity.'[2]

This was yet another, and final, instance of his urge to assert himself with disdain, to make even his favours a means of humiliating people, which we have seen as a constant feature of his character.

However, as though to compensate him for the 'ingratitude' of the chief beneficiaries from the régime, the ordinary plain people showed

---

[1] Tacitus, *Annales*, I. 14.
[2] ibid. I. 8.

how much they worshipped him. Shortly before his death Augustus was on his way his villa at Sorrento when he saw the crew of a ship from Alexandria coming ashore; they were dressed in white, were wearing floral wreaths and carrying censers, and they sang a hymn in his honour: 'Through him we live, through him we sail the seas, through him we enjoy freedom and riches.'

Augustus was so entertained by this demonstration that he distributed forty gold coins among his companions, for them to buy goods from Alexandria. And the incident greatly helped in creating a relaxed and cheerful atmosphere during the last days of his life. It was early August; the towns and villages of Campania were holding popular festivals, and people on holiday from Rome joined in. The Emperor happily presided at gymnastic contests and ordained disguises to be worn; he improvised some Greek verse, and asked his astrologer Thrasylles to guess the author. 'Whoever he is, they're excellent,' he prudently replied.

The Empire was in a happy condition; for the first time in history peace reigned from the Atlantic to the Euphrates, from the North Sea to the Sahara. Men could use their energy in producing, and in improving their conditions, and the taxes they had to pay in exchange for their tranquillity took only a small part of the fruits of their labour.

The naïve hymn sung by the Egyptian sailors expressed the gratitude of a hundred million souls. What, then, did the recriminations of a few thousand privileged persons matter? Especially as the middle classes, who were gradually gaining control of the trade and economy of the Mediterranean, also held the military power because the army was recruited from their ranks. Augustus had not worked for the benefit of the aristocracy from which he sprang, but for a new and growing middle class; and it was a class that, before long, would be composed of Romans, Italians and provincials alike.

The strength of the principate was in its understanding with that class. The deification of the Emperor—which, as we have seen, had no mystical or metaphysical importance—had let him slip from the control of the ruling class. It established a communion between the Emperor and the majority of his subjects, and thereby created a gap between him and his personal circle, who regarded him only as *primus inter pares*. The family tragedies that darkened Augustus's life, and his inability to keep friends of his own class, were therefore consequences of his successful achievements in the social sphere.

This explains the striking analogy between the isolation of the founder of the Roman Empire and that of other great sovereigns—all destroyers of an old ruling class, and indirectly responsible for the creation of a new social order—Louis XI and Louis XIV in France, Ivan the Terrible and Peter the Great in Russia.

Augustus suffered from these conflicts for most of his life; only at the end of his days did he recover some serenity and peace of mind, when the true purpose of his efforts was mercifully revealed to him— that it was not to restore a cruel and rapacious Republic, but to create a world community, a commonwealth, in which Mediterranean man was to find the happiness and peace, for quite three hundred years, that his condition allowed.

PART TWO

NERO

Chapter Four

THE DREAM-WORLD OF NERO

⟫⟫⟫ I ⟪⟪⟪

THE PROBLEM

WHEN the friends of Domitius Ahenobarbus went to congratulate him on the birth of his son on 15th December A.D. 37 his response to their compliments was that 'nothing but evil and misfortune for the State could be born from the union of himself and Agrippina'. This sinister phrase was probably fabricated, but was worthy of a great lord aware of his hereditary defects; in any case it laid an early curse upon the last Roman emperor of the Augustan dynasty. Throughout the ages, even when Classics were little studied, he has been the best known of the Caesars. In his case it is difficult to distinguish history from legend; his renown is not that of an illustrious ruler but of a criminal of the deepest dye. Christians, who hold him responsible for the persecutions, are not alone in attributing to him a devilish malevolence. According to tradition, which modern scholarship has been unable to shake, he was a monster in the original meaning of the word: an abnormal being created by the gods to warn mankind of grave disorders in the affairs of the world. However naïve that idea, there is no doubt that Agrippina's son remains the only ruler of his kind, not merely in the history of Rome but probably of the world.

What makes him unique is not his undoubted moral and physical defects, but rather the extraordinary ideal which he set himself and strove all his life to attain, breaking down more and more pitilessly every obstacle to its realization. Nero was assuredly the only monarch to consider himself as primarily an artist. Many others, Hadrian, for instance, have been outstanding connoisseurs, sometimes even creative artists and capable of solving technical problems. But Nero wanted to be a professional artist, and that was more important to him than being Emperor. Indeed he did not hesitate to jeopardize his political prestige by acting in the theatre. When the 'moment of truth' arrived it was not his crimes that he deplored but the shabby situation he found himself in, and he chiefly bemoaned the premature loss to the world of his talents. There has surely never been any other sovereign who could have taken for his maxim, instead of 'Politics first' or 'I serve God', that of 'Aesthetics first'. Marcus Aurelius, Julian, were more philosophers than Caesars; Elagabalus sacrificed the Empire to the ideas he had of his priesthood. But their attitudes, like those of many pious sovereigns—Acoka, Saint Louis and others—were in accordance with the accepted values of their times. With the exception of Elagabalus, their subordination of the State to a higher ideal in no way undermined their authority. Nero, though, ran counter to the largest and most powerful party among his subjects, and lost the purple and his life in the struggle. His ideas were not strictly his alone, but were shared by a very limited group, foreign to the Roman tradition; and they very likely exceeded even the wishes of those few. That called for a certain kind of courage on his part which should not be underestimated, even if it is considered absurd.

This attitude has not been fully understood. The historial works of the ancients that have come down to us (all those favourable to Nero were eliminated) regard his artistic activities as an expression of his vanity, his intemperance and immorality; by condemning them out of hand, the historians made no attempt to estimate their worth. A few modern writers have reacted against that attitude. 'Although he was a sot,' says, for instance, André Piganiol, 'he was not without taste in theatrical and literary matters, and this had some small influence on the art of his time.' Yet this side of Nero's behaviour does not appear ever to have been properly examined. It remains to be seen—and this is obviously the most difficult—whether his artistic activities were due to a genuine talent or whether they were merely the result of feelings and urges such as are often found in the scions of great families on the decline, and which make dilettantes of them but not real artists.

We must therefore attempt to analyse Nero's personality—a task which has often been undertaken and always been found of absorbing interest. Although Tacitus and Suetonius both drew as black a picture as possible of the last of the Claudians, they have at least left a 'dossier' on him that, in the aggregate, is a careful and penetrating compilation. There are many astonishing things in it, but none is completely unbelievable, and that cannot be explained with the help of modern psychology or by reference to his social background, which advances in archaeology and epigraphy have made clearer.

⟫⟫⟫ II ⟪⟪⟪

THE NATURE OF HIS ARTISTIC YEARNINGS

Nero's father was a degenerate scion of the *gens Domitia*, who had produced several clever generals renowned for their harshness. He had inherited from them a sadistic brutality and a lust that even the court of Tiberius was amazed at, and he was covetous to the point of being dishonest. It was said he once ran over and crushed a child with his chariot, on purpose, on the Appian Way; and that he was guilty of incest with his sister. The best service he ever did for his son was to die of dropsy, when Nero was three.

The boy then came completely under the influence of his mother. Agrippina was the youngest daughter of Germanicus and Agrippina the Elder, whose mother had been Augustus's daughter, Julia. The disorderly life that Julia had led, the imbecility of Agrippa Postumus and the mad streak in Caligula are sufficient evidence of the blemishes in that branch of the imperial family. Agrippina the Younger fortunately took after her mother most of all, and her great ambitions were served by a cool and clear intellect. That her morals were non-existent is hardly surprising; when a child she had seen her mother beaten up by a centurion with such violence that one eye was permanently blinded; and then her mother died of voluntary starvation; her two eldest brothers had suffered a like fate, by order of Tiberius. The death of the latter and the accession of her brother had only improved the situation in appearance. Agrippina was obliged to be a partner to the indecencies of the demented Emperor, and was later sent into exile leaving Nero, still a child, in the care of a barber and a dancer. When Claudius succeeded Caligula, her most dangerous enemy became the notorious Messalina. Finally, after much intrigue, Agrippina had realized the

*D

desire inherited from her mother, and became the wife of an emperor; but her ambitions were not satisfied with an indirect and precarious power, at the mercy of an old man's whims. By getting rid of her husband, and securing the succession for her son, her intention was to reign alone, after the manner of the Eastern queens.

There is no point in emphasizing the unwholesome and turbid side of the relations between Agrippina and her son; Tacitus and Suetonius, especially, have given enough information about that unpleasant subject to satisfy the most probing of psycho-analysts. Even allowing for exaggerations, there can be no doubt that Nero was sexually attracted towards his mother, and she encouraged him probably in order to dominate him the more. At the same time he wanted to shake off her hold—a contradiction only in appearance—which he managed as soon as he dared, by having her murdered. This complex obviously explains why he never succeeded in leading a normal sex life. All that need be said on the point—Suetonius gave all necessary details—is that he never found one single kind of sensual gratification to satisfy him. Until the end of his life he indulged variously in normal sexual relations with his successive wives and his numerous mistresses; in active homosexuality, notably with the hermaphrodite Sporus; in passive homosexuality, in bestiality, sadism and probably masochism. The pathological character of these dissolute practices is beyond doubt.

In addition to psychological causes there were physical, probably endocrine, disabilities that contributed. Although he was ill on only three occasions during his life—in spite of a most unhealthy way of living—he had thick jowls and neck, a fat stomach that wobbled on his thin legs, and there were ugly blotches on his skin. Suetonius's description of him is confirmed by the portraits that escaped the destructions due to the *Damnatio memoriae*. His features seem regular, in spite of the bloated face; there is still a hint of bewilderment in the small, deep-set eyes, although the pigment that once made them look alive has vanished. It is a weak face, especially when compared with the masterfulness of Augustus's or the sternness of Tiberius's, and gives an impression of a shifty and uneasy character.

Nero was fearful and untruthful throughout his short life. This autocrat who wielded absolute power, through the disciplined administrative and military organizations built up by Augustus, went continually in fear—of his mother to begin with, then of his tutors, the Senate, the people and the army, spectators at the theatre, judges at competi-tions, slaves and women. He was incapable of standing up to firmness, and hated himself for his weakness; so his decisions, when he managed to make them, were hasty and often followed by counter-orders. When the dominating hand of others became unbearable he found only one way of freeing himself: by assassination, and by means used by the weak—poison or infernal machines. Contrary to accepted belief, Nero never killed for pleasure, but through fear. As will be shown later, he was fundamentally gentle and indulgent; not only at the beginning of his reign, when he refused to sign death sentences, but in the midst of terrible crises, when he stopped proceedings against Lucan's mother, and gave orders for Seneca's wife to be spared. His ideal was to see the abolition of the death penalty, of the massacres in the arenas, and even of war. But when in the grip of fear he struck out like an animal trapped in its lair. Britannicus, Agrippina, Octavia, all those who had the blood of Augustus in their veins, were killed off one after the other until none remained to claim any part in the special 'grace' that the founder of the Empire had passed on to his descendants. The Christians were killed with horrible tortures as expiatory victims so that the Romans should cease suspecting the Emperor of having set fire to the city. Then came the turn of his tutors, his friends, and even his wife, of whom he was fond, for Nero was unable to feel affection for anyone without having a sense of inferiority and fear; so that he showed a great fondness for almost every one of his victims right until their last moments—and it would be a mistake to regard that purely as hypocrisy.

Nero thus offers the most notorious example of a tyrant's lunacy, such as Plato had described four centuries earlier in his *Republic*. Yet his psychosis, unlike that of the early dictators, did not originate in fears of an opposition. The failure of Piso's conspiracy proves how difficult it was, in the middle of the first century, to stage a revolt; and the uprising in 68 succeeded only because of the Emperor's lack of energy. There were three factors contributing to Nero's mental dis-orders: his physical and moral defects, which finally reduced him to apathy; the domination of a corrupt mother; and, finally, what might be called 'a harem complex', of which history gives many examples—Cambyses, the son of Cyrus the Great, and Constant II, the son of Constantine, several of the Byzantine *basileis* and—in quite recent times—the Sultan Abdul Hamid and the last Chinese emperors. In Nero's case Claudius was primarily responsible for having allowed women, freedmen and eunuchs to gain the upper hand. Moreover, there were powerful economic and social influences that tended to transform the Empire into an oriental despotism. Many historians have seen that as sufficient explanation of the Neronian crisis. But Nero was never merely a disciple of the great kings of Persia; though it is true that Eastern influences at the imperial court were stronger in Nero's time than at any period until the accession of Constantine. The revolution in 68 was, among other things, a reaction of the West that restored the balance between the various nations of the Empire for the following two centuries and more.

Nero tried all means of escaping from his *entourage*, whom he feared and hated. In his young days he slipped away at night to visit the drinking-booths and places of ill-fame in the teeming, low-class districts. Dressed as a ruffian, and with a few companions, he beat up respectable men returning home late, and was quite prepared to receive some hard knocks in return. Throughout his life he picked his close companions from the common horde, preferring them to the great ones of the earth. One of his mistresses, Actea, was a freedwoman; she was the first woman to give him enough confidence in himself to enable him to resist his mother.

'Vatinius', wrote Tacitus, 'was one of the most detestable monsters of that court. Brought up in a cobbler's shop, his deformed body and vulgar jokes got him accepted as a butt, to begin with; then, by denouncing all the decent people, he came to have so much power that he surpassed the most malicious in influence, wealth and destructive strength.'

Honours and riches were showered upon a money-lender of menial origins, whose grotesque name, Cercopithecus Paneros ('Monkey-with-a-tail, Full-of-love'), had probably amused the Emperor. But Nero was scared of the common people, too; like many of the ruling class, he was haunted by fear of a social revolution and the spectre of Spartacus. In spite of the people's protests and the reserve of many senators, he had the whole four hundred slaves of the prefect Pedanius Secundus done to death for not having tried to prevent the assassination of their master.

In later years he sought escape by change of scenery, by travel. The East exercised its influence upon him; and although he eventually decided against going to Egypt, his voyage to Greece was the most important decision of his final years. In the last great crisis he thought of becoming prefect of Egypt, then of fleeing to Parthia.

This desire for evasion is the basis of Nero's artistic yearnings. If he had possessed a truly creative spirit he would have discovered, probably after some fumblings, which of the arts was most suitable to his talents, and would have gone on to produce a body of work. But all his life he hesitated, dallying with poetry, sculpture, and painting, taking an interest in architecture, and finally putting his efforts into music and the theatre. Such eclecticism, with an eventual preference for the interpretative arts, indicated his awareness of an inability to create; and it was this feeling that led him to humiliate and punish himself, that caused him to tremble as he awaited the public's verdict. It is particularly interesting to note that his artistic efforts were not an assertion of his personality but a concealment of it; and that his master-piece, the Golden House, was intended first and foremost as a refuge, a hiding-place, a self-created paradise, like a child letting his imagination roam in his play so that he can exercise an authority not possible in real life. There should be no surprise in finding that the hero of Nero's poem on the Trojan War was the dissolute, effeminate and cowardly Paris, whom Homer treated with scorn. In the athletic contest forming a main incident in this epic, Helen's lover had a brilliant victory over the virtuous and brave Hector.

At every period the arts have offered a means of escape to individuals restricted by the social order and unable to express themselves other-wise, but never more so than in ancient Rome. During the Republic the only impartial search after beauty had come from 'liberal' circles, who were damped and discouraged by the general conservatism. Augustus had endeavoured to put a disciplined art at the service of the new order he was instituting. It is a marvel that such dictatorial inter-vention in the field of arts should have been understood by Virgil and the sculptor of the *Ara Pacis*. But with the passing of those two geniuses neo-classicism rapidly deteriorated, became conventional and lifeless. One has only to consider the sculptured reliefs of the 'Altar of Augustan Piety', dedicated by Claudius, which was closely based upon the *Ara Pacis*. The obligation to follow the lines of the great work obviously weighed heavily upon the sculptors.

'These reliefs', writes Cagiano de Azevedo, 'try to amalgamate affected aulic expressions with an elegant neo-atticism, which here degenerates into mannerism, there gives an impression of fatigue and weariness, or betrays an expressive immediacy that is rough and ready or of rustic simplicity.'

The Augustan discipline had become a restriction, broken whenever the artist had an opportunity to use his talents freely; so that the most interesting of the reliefs are the minor scenes showing a bull being dragged to the altar by the *victimarius* and its slaughter by the priests.[1]

A similar urge to recover creative liberty can be discerned in the Pompeian frescoes of the last phase of the third style. That school is dealt with at some length in the first part of this book; the artists, it will be remembered, abandoned vast perspectives that gave the viewer the impression of being about to penetrate a dream-world and concentrated on a central scene, taken from Greek mythology, which was confined within large areas of flat-wash. The architectural design surrounding this central picture was purely ornamental, and was treated with a mannerism that has always marked the transition from classicism to baroque. The slim pillars of the edifice sheltering the picture 'float above their base rather than rest on it, and the decorations above seem unreal by contrast with the monochrome panels' (K. Schefold). The panels have borders of delicate arabesques intertwined with fantastic creatures and stylized foliage. So rationalism had triumphed only to reveal its incapacity to satisfy the spiritual needs of imperial society.

Nevertheless the almost servile dependence of artists upon the aristocracy, itself controlled by the central authority, would have stifled all escapism if the Emperor had deemed it necessary to maintain the Augustan tradition; under Claudius there had already been a return to classicism, undoubtedly due to imperial directives. But the accession of a prince who was himself inclined to rebel against the established order suddenly broke down all barriers; rationalism gave way to subjective art, 'drawing on the magic of dreams, the mysterious and the extraordinary, sensually confusing mind and matter' (J. Bayet). Nero's part in this reversal of artistic values—which may be considered ridiculous, but which inspired some of the most original of Roman art— should not be underestimated because of the non-creative nature of his talent or the limitations of that talent. The sudden reversal has often been rightly compared with those precipitating the baroque and the romantic movements. And Nero was a romantic, if only because of his vices—the physical and moral defects that weakened his will-power and his intelligence also heightened his sensitiveness. His guilt-complex and fear of failure—that he never managed to overcome—made him

[1] In my opinion they are imitations of models made by the sculptor of the *Ara Pacis* in his old age. (G. C.-P.)

moody and uneasy; his vanity and immoderation prevented him from distinguishing the limits of possibility and the boundaries between reality and unreality. This confused and troubled aspect of his character, admirably captured by Tacitus and perceived to some extent by writers at all periods, explains why dramatists have always been much more attracted by Nero than by Tiberius, Caligula or Domitian. So it could be said that Nero's overriding ambition to achieve immortality through the arts was eventually satisfied, though as a subject instead of a practitioner.

ᗞᗞᗞ III ᕗᕗᕗ

NERO'S ARTISTIC WORKS: POETRY AND MUSIC

Psychological analysis enables some estimation to be made of the inadequate, and contradictory, judgments we have of Nero's poetical works. The accusation made by Tacitus, that the Emperor was not the real author of the verses ascribed to him, is obviously a calumny and can be dismissed. Suetonius, with an archivist's scruples, was more objective in the matter:

'I have handled tablets and notebooks that had very well-known verses written in his own hand; it is quite evident they were neither transcribed nor dictated by another person but were the spontaneous work of a thinking and creative man; there were thus many erasures, insertions and additions.'

So Nero wrote fluently, but did not think this absolved him from going back over his work. The last thing he can be accused of, in any of his artistic efforts, is a lack of professional conscientiousness.

Some fragments of his poems have come down to us, the most interesting being some verses quoted by Persius—one of Nero's worst literary enemies—as an example of an 'effeminate and Hellenistic' style:

They fill the curved horns with airs of the Mimallones, and a ravishing Bassaride having torn off the head of a fine young bull, and a Maenas holding a lynx with strands of ivy, give the Evoe! Echo obediently replies.[1]

---

[1] Torua Mimalloneis implerunt cornua bombis
Et raptum uitulo caput ablatura superbo
Bassaris et lyncem Maenas flexura corymbis
Euhion ingeminat, reparabilis adsonat echo.

(*Satires*, I. 99–102.)

Reading these four hexameters aloud in the original, one cannot help being struck by their musical quality. The hunting-horns of the Bacchantic women can be heard sounding in the first line; the last is harmonious with its subject; and to sustain the song the composer has —contrary to general usage—made alternate lines rhyme. The accumulation of Greek words, which was criticized by Persius, introduces much the same feeling of confusion and mystery as does the use of proper nouns and exotic expressions in Victor Hugo's *Legend of the Centuries*. One should not forget that Nero's poetry was intended to be sung and accompanied on the lyre, so should be compared to lyrics.

'It is permissible to think that Nero's preference was for something picturesque and colourful, with frequent sonorous effects, or with sensational and pathetic parts. Many a young poet begins in like manner: with sound and fury, horror and pathos' (P. Charlesworth).

Nero's romanticism appeared not only in his own work but also in his choice of pieces forming his repertoire. His favourite ones came from the most tragic and shocking of Greek myths, or were prompted by the mysteries of orgiastic cults: the massacre of Niobe's children, Canace pregnant by her brother, Orestes the parricide, Oedipus tearing out his eyes, the wrath of Hercules, Attis castrating himself in a sacred frenzy. These roles, which appealed to Nero's troubled and diseased mind, happened to suit his voice; according to Quintilian, it was a sort of deep muffled bass (*fusca*, cavernous). However, Nero also liked to contrast these moving items with a few refined, finical pieces, such as the description of a dove's feathers ruffled by the wind, that Seneca quoted with approval, or of the course of the Tigris, that closely resembled the geographical passages in Lucan's *Pharsalia*.

It would be a very narrow basis for judgment if we could rely only on these sparse elements of what was a considerable body of work— the literary part of which still found readers and admirers after Nero's death, when their critical sense was in no wise influenced by adulation. In a recent study of Nero, Attilio Levi advances a most odd and original opinion on this subject—that the Emperor, far from associating himself with the 'romantic' movement, was attached to the classical tradition which was still supported by a kind of Roman Ronsard called Calpurnius Siculus! But if Signor Levi had extended his study beyond the realm of literature he might well have revised his opinion.

⧓⧓⧓ IV ⧓⧓⧓

THE GOLDEN HOUSE

Fortunately a considerable part of Nero's creations in the field of architecture and interior decoration still exists. The grandiose remains of his most famous and most discredited undertaking can be visited; this was the Golden House, a huge and fantastic palace that he considered his masterpiece, and which expressed his whole idea of art as well as what he conceived a sovereign's life ought to be.

Augustus's successors were not as modest as he in housing themselves. Tiberius, although economical and little inclined to ostentation, had bought most of the northern upper slope of the Palatine—where Augustus's house already stood—and there built the first imperial 'palace' worthy of the name. Unfortunately its ruins are today almost completely buried under the Farnese gardens, which were laid out in the fifteenth century; only the extent of the building—390 by 490 feet —has been determined. One of its façades overlooked the Forum. Little is known of the interior, which in any case underwent many changes; emperors used the *Domus Tiberiana* as a residence until the fourth century, and during that period restoration was carried out on several occasions following fires.

Caligula, too, wanted a palace, and had his built opposite Tiberius's, at the northern end of the hillside. The mad Emperor transformed the venerable temples of Castor and Vesta into vestibules to his palace, so that his subjects should be more convinced of his divine nature. And he built a wooden bridge across the open space to give him direct access to the great temple of Jupiter on the Capitoline and to enable him to talk as an equal with the lord of Olympia. Practically nothing remains of these constructions, except a small room for an *impluvium* that forms part of the Byzantine church of Santa Maria Antiqua.

Many archaeologists attribute another small building to Caligula, at the southern end, on the *Palatium* properly called; now covered by the basilica of the Flavian palace, it is still elegantly decorated with frescoes belonging to the last phase of the second style, and wholly inspired by Egypt and the mysteries of Isis. The friezes have *uraei* forming a framework to lotus blossom and implements of the cult. Between the fanciful architecture can be seen the hieratic silhouettes of a Pharaoh and a priestess. These frescoes have been reproduced in a book, and its editor, Giulio Emmanuele Rizzo, supports the view that this *aula* was built by Caligula, contending that the Emperor favoured Egyptian religion through hatred of Augustus and Tiberius, who had both banished it. And the eminent Belgian writer on Roman religion, Franz Cumont, has an attractive and bold theory that this hidden chapel was the *Hermaeum* where Claudius secreted himself while his nephew was being assassinated, and where he was discovered by the Praetorians who, to his great surprise, elected him to the purple. But, unfortunately, it hardly seems possible that the second style, which came to an end at Pompeii in the last years of Augustus's reign, could have continued in Rome for another generation. The question remains one of the many enigmas giving rise to sharp discussions between specialists.

Claudius, too, built on the Palatine; but his buildings were destroyed in the great fire of 64, and their remains vanished when the Flavian palace was constructed.

Nero, on his accession, therefore came into possession of a great many buildings of his predecessors, most of them being vast but probably not very pleasant. In spite of these additional constructions, the Palatine was still far from belonging entirely to the Caesars; there were a number of private villas on the hill, as well as many temples, and thousands of tall houses let by rooms or floors. So the emperors suffered as their subjects did from a closely packed and overcrowded city, and from all the disgusting inconveniences such as Juvenal described in one of his satires. The *Domus Tiberiana* in particular appears to have been a great barracks of a building, receiving little light and air from its interior courtyards and having no 'green spaces'; Tiberius never went to live in it, preferring his villa on Capri. However, the dynasty had gradually acquired a number of parks and gardens on the Esquiline, where many wealthy senators had built villas. Maecenas had planted his gardens there, on the site of an old burial-ground that had been filled in, and at his death he left them to Augustus, together with all his possessions. Other inheritances, and confiscations, had brought in the neighbouring gardens of Lamia, Maius, and of Lollia Paulina and Statilius Taurus, victims of Claudius and Agrippina. So that when Nero came to power the imperial domain was contained in two large areas, separated by the Forum in the valley between the two hills; there were the great buildings on the Palatine, and the villas standing in their own parks on the Esquiline.

Nero's grand design was to make a whole of these two groups. There were several stretches of rough ground between them; for instance, where the Colosseum now stands was a swampy depression. And, too, the Carinae district in the folds of the Esquiline was a mass of narrow, winding, evil-smelling streets crammed with houses that swarmed with people. But these obstacles did not deter Nero from starting on the *Domus Transitoria*, right at the beginning of his reign; as its name implied, this was intended—as Tacitus pointed out—to link the Palatine and the Esquiline. It was therefore a vast construction, with breaks in it where existing streets passed through. Some of its remains have been rediscovered, notably a group beneath the great dining-room of the *Domus Flavia*, on the Palatine. Nero's architects had there built on foundations at two different levels, joined by marble staircases, because of the hollow between the two summits of the hill, the Germal and Mount Palatine itself. On the lower level was a pavilion standing on columns and pilasters of polychrome marble; water flowed down the retaining wall, between green and red marble columns with bronze capitals. The rooms, or kiosks, outside and around the pavilion, which were also kept cool by playing fountains, have a flooring of coloured marble and a vaulted ceiling decorated with frescoes illustrating episodes from Homer.

This gracious summer-house, erroneously called 'Livia's Baths' in the past, probably gave on to a flowered terrace, or perhaps a bathing-hall with a gymnasium beyond. Another building believed to have been part of the *Domus Transitoria* was a large round room with a cupola and a mosaic paving, which Hadrian destroyed when making the foundations for his huge temple that he dedicated to Venus and Rome, in the Velia district. Vestiges of Nero's palace have been found all round the Colosseum; so that one can form an approximate idea of what his vast and grandiose construction was like. It seems to have been not so much a palace, though, as a succession of open pavilions with fountains playing everywhere, and linked together by long colonnades. Nero had already shown his preference for the Greek architectural plan, introduced into Italy by Clodia and her licentious circle, which—contrary to the enclosed plan of the Roman—left houses open to the sun and air, without thought for privacy, and so was a deliberate defiance of the modesty of Roman matrons and the *Patres*.

On 19th July 63 fire broke out in the shops where stocks of merchandise were stored, around the Circus Maximus. The blaze spread to the

Palatine and swept through the new buildings of the *Domus Transitoria* towards the Esquiline, where it was finally halted; but only after six days, and even then another outbreak occurred, fortunately much less disastrous. Nero was at Antium when the fire started. He returned to Rome without haste, and set up his quarters in Maecenas's gardens —a reasonable thing to do, for that was the area where attempts were being made to halt the fire.

People always look for a scapegoat when such disasters occur, and usually accuse the authorities or the government. The idea soon gained ground among the public that Nero had ordered the fire to be started, for the thrill of it and to clear the way for his town-planning. But there is little to support this accusation; Suetonius accepted the arguments in its favour, Tacitus merely stated them without giving an opinion. It was reported that Nero's slaves had been seen with tow and firebrands; but none was caught setting fire to the shops. Suetonius wrote that the accusation originated among the consuls; they were Nero's worst enemies, which makes it suspect. The other argument he gave is even weaker—that the artillery was ordered to knock down the remains of the stone buildings after the fire; this was obviously a sensible precaution against accidents from damaged walls suddenly collapsing. However, there are psychological arguments against Nero, which will be examined later; and altogether the question remains far from clear.

All writers are agreed on the praiseworthy efforts of the Emperor, after the terrible fire, to achieve a more open layout of the Roman streets and to prevent a repetition of the disaster. His edicts included the widening of streets and squares, an increase in the number of waterpoints, building in stone brought to Rome at State expense instead of with inflammable materials; the State also undertook to pay for the building of elevated terraces, designed by Nero himself, in front of houses and apartment blocks, to give firemen more freedom of movement. And emergency aid was given to victims of the disaster.

It was Nero's errors and blunders, though, which roused opinion against him, not only among the ruling class, which was already hostile and had started hatching the plot that Piso led, but also among the common people. As usual, these blunders were due to his determination to put aesthetics before politics. One of these errors, venial in itself but which caused him much harm, was the famous poetic declamation given from a tower in Maecenas's gardens, in which Nero compared the recent disaster to the burning of Troy. The incident was so typical of

Nero's character that there seems no reason to doubt it. But the chief fault of the Emperor was to continue with his building projects, on the sites cleared after the fire, with a magnificence and on a scale that were an insult to the misfortunes of the people.

The *Domus Transitoria* had been badly damaged, so instead of repairing it Nero decided to replace it with a group of buildings which would cover the whole area from the Palatine to the Esquiline, without leaving any space for streets or public buildings. The palace itself eventually occupied the centre of this area, which was about two thousand yards in length and over a thousand at its widest part. This huge building set on the slopes of Mount Oppius, one of the two summits of the Esquiline, was a square exactly facing the four points of the compass; what remains of it today still covers an area of about one hundred by three hundred yards. In front of where the Arch of Titus now stands a portico a thousand feet long was built as a kind of vestibule, divided into three parts by the Via Sacra and the Via Nova. The foundations and a few architectural remains are still visible, between the House of the Vestals, the Arch of Titus and the basilica of Constantine. Behind this portico was erected a statue a hundred feet high, the work of a sculptor in bronze, Xenodoros, which represented Nero as the Sun and wearing a star-shaped crown with points twenty feet long. Strangely enough, this colossus was respected after the death of its model. Vespasian did no more than change the face for a conventional image of the divine planet, and Hadrian had the statue moved when he built the temple of Venus and Rome. In fact it came to be treated with superstitious awe, and the priests and people placed flowers round it on 8th January every year, regarding it as a guarantee of Rome's eternity. So it remained standing until the Goths captured the city. Its name, however, still remained, and was given in the Middle Ages to the nearby Flavian amphitheatre, the Colosseum.

But the parks and grounds were the most amazing part of the domain of the Golden House. The swamp at the bottom of the valley, where the Colosseum was later built, was deepened to make a lake, and the installations of a mock port were built around it. Clumps of bushes were planted on the slopes of the Caelian hills, to give the impression of a young forest; over towards the Carinae, on the site of the present Via Annibaldi and Via Colosseo, artificial meadows were created for herds of cattle and wild animals. Vineyards and orchards were planted on the slopes of the Oppius and the Cispius. This vast sylvan creation may recall the pastoral follies of Marie-Antoinette at Versailles, but there is certainly no other instance in European history of a sovereign claiming for his exclusive use such an enormous area in the very heart of an overcrowded and expanding metropolis. The Golden House and its grounds formed a barrier to any extension of the city to the south-east. Moreover, the cost of the work was enormous, and added to the already crushing expenses of reconstruction. The tax-collectors were obliged to invent new means of bringing in money and to increase the pressure, not only with regard to the rich—whom Nero simply put to death in order to annex their fortunes—but to the small tax-payers, both Italian and provincial, and to guilds, temples and munici-palities. Public discontent began to express itself more openly, in the form of pamphlets and songs; one of the latter, alluding to the idea of the Romans emigrating to Veii after the Gauls had captured the Urbs in the fourth century B.C., suggested they should now move to that ancient Etruscan town twelve miles away—unless, the song went on, the Golden House did not end up by stretching as far as that.

The emperors who succeeded Nero were obliged to take this public feeling into account; Otho was the only one to continue with the building scheme, and he poured vast sums of money into it during the few months of his reign. Vespasian and Titus made use of the buildings that had been completed, but gave up most of the grounds. Vespasian had Nero's lake filled in and started to build the Colosseum there; Titus erected a thermal establishment on the Esquiline. Later Trajan had the palace itself buried, and built another thermal establishment, larger than any already in existence, on top of it. However, this work of destruction in fact preserved the buildings it was meant to hide for ever. The kernel of the Golden House, filled with earth and rubble to its doors and windows, survived the centuries in a protective solitude, like a tomb or a buried city; so that today its architecture is intact, and its stucco decorations and its frescoes too.

To go down and visit these ruins today, from the public gardens on the Oppius, is like passing through a succession of gloomy, damp cellars. Trajan's builders had blocked in the façade in order to erect the walls of a great apse against it. This entirely changed the aspect of Nero's building, which originally had large doorways and windows opening on to a terrace; moreover, the interior courtyards and the skylights were covered with rubble, adding to the general gloom. It is to be hoped that renewed excavations will one day restore light and airiness to the building, in keeping with its painted and sculptured decorations that are full of fantasy, exuberance and the joy of life.

The building is strung out along the foot of the Oppius, and was protected against landslides from the steep slope above by a long gallery, the crypto-portico, along the north side. The one façade faced south, and is almost cut in half by a large trapezoidal courtyard, opening outwards. Instead of leading to the heart of the palace, as one might expect, it gives access to only one room—a sumptuous room at one time, for here was the gilded vaulting that so enthralled Raphael. The wings on either side of this false entrance are completely independent, and each is built to a different plan. The west wing is a rectangle with a court and peristyle in the middle; a vestibule connects the courtyard with the façade, and on either side of this vestibule is an apartment consisting of a bedroom, a dressing-room, a chapel and a kind of waiting-room. The two apartments are quite similar to each other; they were probably intended for Nero and Poppaea. The east wing has five rooms radiating out from a semi-octagonal hall with a cupola; these are believed to have been reception-rooms.

❧❧❧ V ❦❦❦

THE CONCEPTION OF THE PALACE. THE PROBLEM OF EASTERN INFLUENCES AND MYSTICISM

The plan of the whole building seems original and somewhat illogical. It is not easy to see why the architects should have built right up to the hillside, cutting into it and erecting the rear of the building against the rubble, when they had so vast a space at their disposal. The rooms at the back were deliberately sacrificed; this is especially evident in the east wing, where all the rooms built back from the octagonal hall were almost completely deprived of light and air from the moment of construction. In the west wing the rooms of the two apartments stretch parallel with the façade, on a level with the portico, and each room has a door opening on to it. In fact the palace is really an immense pergola; everything is subordinated to this façade.

But then it is puzzling to note that the whole extent of the façade was not immediately visible to a visitor entering the domain by the magnificent portico on the Velia, nor even while following the line of

gardens prolonging the Via Sacra. The palace was in fact built parallel
to this axis, instead of perpendicular, so that the prospect was of the
lake and the porticoes stretching into the distance. There should have
been another building to set this off, on the opposite side of the lake,
where Agrippina had started to build a temple in honour of her husband, Claudius—whom she had helped on his way to join the Olympians. Nero had this sanctuary almost completely destroyed—having
no great regard for the memory of his 'adoptive father', as one can
imagine—in order to erect in its place a *nymphaion*, a large grotto with
statues of nymphs, as being more in accordance with the design of his
park. But Vespasian redeemed this sacrilege by seeing that the unfortunate Claudius had his temple.

The Golden House was in fact conceived as an adjunct to the park,
and therein lies the answer to the riddle of its peculiar plan. Pierre
Grimal has explained its connection with the Hellenistic tradition,
which had inspired the open plan of Clodia's villa. There can indeed be
no doubt that the Golden House was based upon the princely residences of the Greco-Asian potentates; the west wing closely follows
the plan of the Prytaneum at Palatiza, built by Antigonus Gonatas
when King of Macedonia in the third century B.C. The *Diadochi* were
influenced in the building of their palaces by the 'paradises' of the
Persian rulers. This explains the overriding importance of the park, the
little pavilions or kiosks arranged about the parkland and the colonnades extending beyond the façade. Such architectural disposition, of
Babylonian or Iranian origin, spread to the Far East as well as to the
West; the 'forbidden cities' of the Chinese emperors were one result,
and their relationship with the Golden House was not fortuitous; while
the Turkish sultans carried on the tradition in the seraglios of Con-
stantinople.

These archaeological comparisons would seem to support an
estimation of Nero based upon the social trends of the imperial court,
which under Caligula and Claudius had come to resemble an oriental
harem. All the precautions taken by Augustus to prevent the ministers
obtaining political power had been ruined as much by social changes as
by the ineptitude of his successors. The aristocratic Senate, by refusing
to collaborate sincerely with the régime, had obliged the emperors to
fall back on the only intermediaries whose devotion was not suspect.
Ambitious mistresses and princesses had built up, through their followers and *entourage*, a power that was entirely contrary to Roman

tradition. The smooth-running state services created by Augustus had the effect of placing finances and administration in the hands of the freedmen who became procurators.

Claudius had been governed by his 'Prime Minister', the freedman Narcissus, who was for long closely associated with Messalina; and then Agrippina had ruled through the 'Minister for Finance', Pallas. These *Graeculi* were not deterred by the scorn and disdain of the senators, for they had the backing of their kindred, all the merchants of Eastern origin who had gained control of the sea trade and the industries of Italy, and who worked in close liaison with relatives trading in Syria and Egypt. This switch of power to the East, that Cleopatra had been unable to bring about by force, was apparently accomplished quite peacefully by the pressure of economics and intellectual influences. The Emperor was still a Roman by blood, but the introduction of certain customs and modes of life—which had so quickly exasperated the rugged Macedonian generals who inherited Alexander's empire—was soon to make him worthy of succeeding the Pharaohs and the Persian kings. Eunuchs made their appearance; Claudius even appointed one to superintend the generals who were conquering southern Britain, and decorated him with the *hasta pura* which was reserved for senior officers. So Nero was following an established trend by replacing the Roman *domus* of his predecessors with a harem where he could lead a secret and voluptuous life amid his slaves, his favourites and his mistresses.

A Danish scholar, P. L'Orange, has put forward an archaeological theory in support of the foregoing argument. The Golden House contained a room—the exact site has not been discovered—which was roofed by a dome that revolved with the firmament. Now it is known that the throne-room of the Sassanid kings of Persia, who reigned from the third to the seventh century, was covered by a moving cupola on which were painted the heavenly bodies. L'Orange says the significance of this can be found in Mazdan theology, whereby the Shah was the earthly delegate of the Lord of the Heavens, Ahoura Mazda; and so Nero's revolving dome was probably copied from the Persians. Pliny the Elder wrote that Nero was initiated into 'the banquets of the Magi' by King Tiridates, brother of the King of the Parthians, who in 66 A.D. came to make homage to Nero and to accept the crown of Armenia from his hands. Franz Cumont has concluded from this text that Nero had become a worshipper of Mithras. This would explain Nero's

conduct during the last years of his reign; beguiled by Persian theo-
cracy, he endeavoured to transform the Augustan principate into a
monarchy by divine right, and to introduce the ceremonial of Eastern
courts to Rome. Mithras was closely associated with Helios, the sun-
god; and there can be no doubt that Nero wanted to be a sun-king.
Many instances of this assimilation appeared in the literature and art
of the period. At the beginning of the reign Seneca, in his wicked satire
on the apotheosis of Claudius, compared the new Emperor with the
sun. The theme was later taken up by Seneca's nephew, Lucan, who
introduced some rather heavy-handed astrological references:

> Nevertheless, Rome owes much to civil war,
> For all acts were done for thee. Thou, with thy
> Mission fulfilled, will later reach the stars; and the
> Heavenly halls will greet thee with the rejoicing
> Zenith: whether thou hold the sceptre or in Phoebe's
> Flaming chariot ride round the earth, this change of
> Sun encircling it with a shining light will in no way
> Frighten it. Before thee all will bow; and nature will
> Relinquish to thee the right to be whatever god thou
> Wishes, and to rule the world from wherever thou wilt.[1]

The Golden House is the palace of the Sun; it merits the name, for
the yellow metal had the planet's colour and brilliance, the cupolas
gave an imitation of the heavens, and the rooms disposed in a semicircle
recalled the passage of the sun. Beams of light came through circular
openings in the roof and brightened the gilded stucco. At the entrance
stood the great statue with a star-pointed crown, copied from the
Colossus of Rhodes, which was a statue of the sun-god Helios. About
the year 65 a wealthy *bourgeois* aped the Emperor by having his *casa
d'Apolline* at Pompeii decorated with themes taken from the Golden
House. One of the murals shows three deities within the usual architectural framework of the fourth style. The centre of the wall is occupied

---

[1] Multum Roma tamen debet ciuilibus armis,
　　Quod tibi res acta est. Te, cum statione peracta
　　Astra petes serus, praelati regia caeli
　　Excipiet gaudente polo: seu sceptra tenere
　　Seu te flammigeros Phoebi conscendere currus,
　　Telluremque nihil mutato sole timentem
　　Igne vago lustrare iuuet: tibi numine ab omni
　　Cedetur: iurisque tui natura relinquet
　　Quis deus esse uelis, ubi regnum ponere mundi.
　　　　　　　　　　　　　　　　(*Pharsalia*, I. 44–54.)

by an elegant baldaquin on pillars, reminiscent of the kiosk in the *Domus Transitoria*; it covers a throne with a rounded base on which Apollo is seated in a pose full of grace and dignity. On either side of him is a half-draped goddess under a square canopy; Apollo, leaning on a sceptre, is holding out his left hand to one, while looking at the other with annoyance. Both Richard Harbig and Karl Schefold have recognized the former as Venus and the one in disgrace as Hesperus, the evening star. The astronomers of ancient times had believed a personal rivalry existed between these two, which had not then reached complete identification as two aspects of one planet.

Eastern influences are discernible in the decorations to this strange allegory. The three deities have each been given a halo, which was an invention of Syrian art to indicate the brightness of the astral gods, and was soon to be applied to human monarchs. Apollo is seated under a baldaquin that has side extensions to cover the dignitaries, such as was used by the Great Kings of the Orient. These emblems of theocratic sovereignty here made their first appearance in Western art; they were often found in the iconography of the late Empire, and then in Christian art.

Nero copied Apollo in lesser ways; he played the zither, and drove chariots, especially one drawn by ten white horses that was supposed to be exactly like Phoebe's.

Finally the ceremonies in connection with the homage that Tiridates made to Nero were placed under the sign of the Sun. The procedures instituted by Augustus were considerably modified for this occasion, although the political circumstances were reminiscent of those surrounding the return of the Roman standards by the Parthians in 20 B.C. For many years Romans and Parthians had been fighting bitterly for the possession of Armenia, but without definite result for either side; a compromise was inevitable, and it was decided that Tiridates, the brother of the Parthian king, would reign over the contested country but would go to Rome to accept his crown from the hands of Nero. The ceremonies were spread over two days; on the first, the King knelt before the Emperor, who was seated in his curule chair, on the Rostra, amid a great parade of troops.

In spite of its unusual splendour, this part of the ceremony conformed in essentials to Roman usages, by the choice of place and the military display; on the silver bowl from Bosco Reale, Augustus is shown receiving homage in almost similar conditions. But there was nothing traditional about the ceremony the following day, which took place in Pompey's theatre in the Field of Mars. The whole vast stone edifice was given a covering of gilt in twenty-four hours; above the tiers of seats was stretched an awning showing a constellation, with the Sun's chariot in the centre—and the Sun had Nero's face. The ceremony was in keeping with this wondrous atmosphere. Tiridates, prostrate, recited a prayer, the words of which were noted by Dio Cassius:

'I, O Master, descendant of Arsaces, brother of the kings Vologaeses and Pacorus, am thy slave; and I have come to thee who art my god to worship thee as Mithras, and I shall become whatever it may please thee to decide, for thou art my Destiny and my Fortune.'

The wording, as Franz Cumont has explained, was inspired by the currently accepted theology at the Persian court. Bas-reliefs recovered from temples of Mithras show the ancient god crowning the Sun with similar procedure to Nero crowning Tiridates. The latter was, moreover, a king-priest, being a member of the ancient Persian priestly caste, similar to a Magi. His visit to Rome has been suggested, in more than one bold exegesis, as inspiring the story of the Three Wise Men in the Scriptures.

Such are the facts that convinced Franz Cumont of Nero's conversion to Mithraism, and led P. L'Orange to give his interpretation of the Golden House. However, their views have been challenged by other scholars, A. Boethius and P. Charlesworth among them, for those views imply that Nero was a mystic. But Suetonius denied him any real religious feeling:

'He despised every religion, whatever it was, with the exception of the cult of the Syrian goddess. And he even came to disdain her, to the point of making water against her statue. Another superstition had taken hold of him, the only one he retained. An unknown plebeian had given him a statuette of a little girl that would save him from snares and dangers; this was just before the conspiracy [of Piso] was discovered, and he began to honour the statuette as though of a great deity, making sacrifices to it three times a day; he wanted people to believe that its warnings enabled him to know the future. A few months before his downfall he also took to reading the signs in the entrails, but without ever obtaining divine approval.'

The text is impartial, and is in keeping with Nero's psychological make-up; his aesthetic appreciations were given too much importance in his sense of values to leave room for piety. As in the case of Augustus, superstition went with this scepticism, and had drawn him to the cult of the Syrian goddess, the most vulgar and savage of the Eastern deities introduced into Rome. Neither was there any contradiction between Nero's irreligion and his 'Apollonism', for the Delphic god was simply a symbol of his ideals and not an object of worship. Any connection between Nero's cosmic representations and Mithraism is only apparent, for Seneca's *Apocolocyntosis* and Lucan's *Pharsalia* show that Nero's assimilation with the Sun had been imagined by that circle of writers some ten years before Tiridates came to Rome; it owed its origin to the philosopher Posidonios of Apamea and the astrological speculations in which he had engaged the Stoics in the second century B.C. The ritual of Tiridates's homage in no way implied that the Emperor had become converted to his vassal's religion; the ceremonial and its surroundings all resulted from the aesthetics of the Golden House and not at all from Mithraic rites. It was Tiridates who had decided to make homage in the form of a Mazdan prayer, possibly as a means of attenuating his humiliation. Similarly, having been obliged to take part in a *venatio* in the arena, he had succeeded in giving it the form of a Persian sacred hunt. But Nero refrained from any condescension towards the practices of one whom he considered a conquered barbarian; his response that Dio Cassius quoted was charged with haughty menace. As for the 'initiation' mentioned by Pliny, it was explained by Suetonius simply as recourse to Magian necromancy in an attempt to appease the ghost of Agrippina that was haunting his nights. The experience was not satisfactory, anyway, as towards the end of his reign Nero returned to the more orthodox practices of the Haruspices, the interpreters of a victim's entrails.

Persian influence hardly seems to have been any stronger in the political sphere. The Persian monarchy, from its very beginnings in the sixth century B.C., had followed the example of the Mesopotamian dynasties and isolated the sovereign from his subjects in order to increase his mysterious prestige. A strict protocol, which surprised Herodotus and left its traces in the Book of Esther, precluded high court officials and even the royal wives from meeting the king except by prior arrangement. Nothing could be more contrary to Nero's conduct, for he was continually seeking contact with the crowds, and was not averse to kneeling before them. Far from trying to establish a monarchy by divine right, Nero was so conscious of the democratic origins of the principate that in the moment of supreme crisis he

thought of going to the Forum, and from the Rostra asking the sovereign people to re-elect him or at least to pardon him for his errors and
send him into honourable retirement. So it is hardly likely that he
wished his Golden House to have an audience hall on the Eastern
model, to impress his subjects with his superhuman majesty. His
revolving dome covered a dining-room, and there was nothing stilted
about the banquets given by Nero. The comparison with the Sassanid
throne-room made by L'Orange has been rightly challenged by A.
Boethius, for the descriptions of it date from the seventh century A.D.,
and such a complicated mechanism was hardly likely to have been in
use six hundred years earlier, by the previous ruling dynasty. It may
well be—as P. Charlesworth has suggested—that, instead, Tiridates
copied Nero's revolving dome; and, as we shall see, the history of
technical progress makes this quite feasible.

⤷⤷⤷ VI ⤶⤶⤶

NERO'S POSITIVISM AND MODERNISM

Nero was far too conscious of representing the most advanced
civilization there had ever been to wish to copy or learn from barbarians. This sense of progress is one of the strangest aspects of his
psychology and links him in a curious way with modern times. The
Golden House might well have contained one element or another
reproduced from earlier palaces, but as a whole it was an entirely new
conception, far in advance of its greatest prototypes. Its construction
marked the beginning of that Golden Age so long foretold by the
prophets. But, unlike those mystics who expected the earthly paradise
to be brought about by divine intervention, Nero meant to create it
himself, relying on his own genius, the inexhaustible economic
resources at his disposal, the skill of his engineers and craftsmen, and
the talents of his artists.

This is not the place to discuss Nero's economic policy. Tacitus and
Suetonius rightly regarded his inordinate spending as a chief cause of
his downfall. It should not be forgotten, however, that he enforced
some very wise measures, notably in matters of commerce; for instance, by making North Africa instead of Egypt the main source of
Rome's food supplies, Nero greatly reduced the cost and risks of sea

transport; and he also helped shipping with his great building schemes. But Nero's mistake was in thinking that the Empire's resources were boundless, and in continuing to pour them into his programme of sterile magnificence.

Like many statesmen with exaggerated ideas of grandeur, Nero was no financier; but on the other hand his interest in technical development was in advance of his time. Many modern historians maintain that a cause of Roman decadence was the failure to create new sources of production and to plough back profits against times of economic recession. But Julius Caesar had realized the need of harnessing natural forces; this is evident from the writings of his engineer officer, Vitruvius, and also from his own works. But Augustus and his successors, as in many other matters, did not follow the dictator's lead. It was Nero who revived Caesar's projects. The magistrates of the Republic had provided Italy and the provinces with an excellent network of roads, but had not realized the importance of inland waterways. Caesar, probably getting the idea from Egypt, had planned to cut two canals, one through the Pontine Marshes to link the Tiber with the coast of Campania, and the other across the Isthmus of Corinth. There was an obvious economic advantage in both these schemes. By the former, the ships supplying Rome would avoid the dangerous coast of southern Latium; and the inconvenience of the port of Ostia, which could only be used in summer, would be overcome. By the latter, ships would no longer have to face the storms round Cape Matapan, which every year took a heavy toll of human life and wealth. Nero sent for the plans which had been lying in the archives for more than a century, and ordered them to be put into effect with the new techniques available— an order which naturally caused him to be taxed with megalomania by Tacitus and Suetonius. But once again politics had prevented these grandiose schemes being carried out; in A.D. 68, as in 44 B.C., the Roman conservatives could boast that they had caused a 'sound financial policy' to prevail over the needs to improve communications.

It was in Alexandria that Caesar had realized the importance of artificial waterways; and there, too, he had found the most advanced institutes of scientific research in the world. He took back with him to Rome the mathematicians who formulated the calendar still in use today. The members of these Alexandrian institutes had for a long time been well on the way to practical discoveries which, if pursued then, would have led to the practical use of steam and compressed air at that early stage in history. One of the most remarkable of these scientists, a barber named Ctesibios, had invented a pressure pump in the third century B.C., in the reign of Ptolemy III. The long accounts that Vitruvius gave of his discoveries prove that the dictator had been particularly struck by them, and had probably introduced them into Italy. Unfortunately little is known of the 'Polytechnic' in Alexandria, and the date of Ctesibios's most important successor, Heron, is uncertain. He invented several scientific toys, among them a miniature machine that worked by steam. Many scholars have blamed the Roman conquest for the break in scientific progress in Alexandria. But two texts by Suetonius, which seem to have been disregarded on this point, show that scientific engineers were still pursuing their researches in Nero's time, and that the Emperor encouraged them as much as had Caesar. In fact Suetonius also wrote that in the middle of the Vindex revolt Nero 'wasted' the whole of one day in demonstrating to some of the highest State dignitaries the workings of a new hydraulic organ that he had just received, and in taking it to pieces. The hydraulic organ was one of Ctesibios's inventions; its principle is the same as that of the pressure pump. Nero was doubly interested in it; as a musician (he was said to have vowed to play it at the theatre if the revolt was quelled), and as a mechanic, since he was capable of taking to pieces this very complicated machine. It is no doubt regrettable that a principle in physics which could have harnessed hydraulic forces to useful purposes should have been put to purely aesthetic use. Still, according to Suetonius, Nero's engineers were capable of building a mechanism of perpetual movement. The famous revolving dome of the Golden House, which has been considered almost entirely from a symbolic and religious point of view, was evidently turned by a powerful source of energy, since a considerable mass, probably of metal, had to be moved; and it was regulated like a clock, since its rotation synchronized with the movement of the stars. Unfortunately no historian thought it necessary to explain the principle on which it worked; but as the absolute regularity of its movement excludes the possibility of its having been worked by man or animal power, one may reasonably assume that the axis of the hemisphere was joined by cogs to a water-wheel driven by a carefully regulated flow of water. Thus it seems to have been a combination of a water-mill and a clepsydra. Now the water-mill was first described by Vitruvius, and appears to have been invented in Asia Minor in the first century B.C.; while the clepsydra, which was already in existence in the sixth century B.C. in a primitive form, had been greatly improved by the Alexandrians, who perfected water-clocks with various ingenious accessories.[1] These indications throw some light on the problem of the revolving dome, which in Nero's time represented the epitome of technical progress. It was the result of years of scientific study by the Alexandrian school founded by Ctesibios. Since the time of Caesar, Greco-Egyptian engineers had been attracted to Italy; and Nero, more than anyone, encouraged their immigration. For the Roman Government could not allow men capable of constructing powerful military weapons to enter the service of Parthia, the traditional enemy of the Empire. The Iranian kingdom therefore found itself at a disadvantage in the matter of technical knowledge. Tiridates noted this during his visit to Rome, and cunningly took advantage of Nero's thoughtless generosity by obtaining a loan of 'artisans of all kinds'. This piece of information supplied by Dio Cassius destroys, as P. Charlesworth points out, L'Orange's theory of the Persian origin of the revolving dome. The English scholar also suggests that the Roman engineers lent by Nero might have constructed the first model of the 'cosmic throne-room', while the Arsacid dynasty was still ruling in Parthia. If so, this would be an odd instance of rivalry between East and West in the search for progress!

There was a close co-operation between Alexandrian 'mechanics' and Roman architects in the constructing of the Golden House, as in carrying out other ideas of Nero. Technicians of eastern origin were undoubtedly the more numerous in the team gathered together by the Emperor, but it was led by two Italians, Severus and Celer, who had the chief responsibility. Tacitus called them *magistri et machinatores*— master-workmen and engineers; and they were in fact architectural engineers in the tradition of Vitruvius. 'They were clever and bold enough', Tacitus added, 'to use technical means to overcome Nature itself, and they made light of the requirements of the prince.' It may have been their team that designed the boat intended for getting rid of Agrippina—the cabin roof automatically descended as the hull let in water—though Tacitus attributed that infernal machine to a naval officer named Anicetus.

There were many similar, but less diabolical, contraptions in the

---

[1] Vitruvius described water-clocks fitted with automatic floats which 'struck the hour' by tossing pebbles or eggs into the air or by emitting warning whistles. See *Daily Life in Ancient Rome*, by Jérôme Carcopino, p. 147. (Trans. note.)

E

Golden House, e.g. roofs that let showers of flowers and perfume descend on the guests. The buildings became a vast research workshop where plans just off the drawing-board were put to the test. The present excavated remains, mere skeleton of the great monument though they are, still bear witness to its original innovations. In the east wing, the central plan based on the octagonal domed room has no known earlier form; in fact it included some of the very latest architectural novelties of its time. The roofing of the octagonal room is the oldest known example of a cupola allowing light to enter through the top; this necessitated the solving of problems of stress and strain, especially as the dome is supported by eight quite slender pillars with wide apertures between them. The light enters not only through the summit but also through a kind of crown or circular rim contrived between the extrados of the dome and the wall. This was a result of quite two hundred years of research and experiment by Roman architectural engineers with a material unknown to the Greeks—rubble mixed with cement—and with a form of architecture—the vaulted roof—also unknown to Hellenic art. By dispensing with dressed masonry the Romans were able to erect a cupola over a larger surface than previously and to leave apertures in the roofing; and it was still solidly built, without the risk of decay in wooden beams. The technical revolution thus achieved is comparable to the transition from Romanesque to Gothic, and more particularly to the invention of reinforced concrete. The methods used for the first time to build the cupola of the Golden House were later employed on a greater scale by Hadrian for the dome of the Pantheon, which in turn served as model for Renaissance churches.

One can imagine the joy of those brilliant architect-engineers, able to carry out the boldest experiments without feeling restricted by any financial or material consideration. It is almost possible to follow the progress of their experiments. The east wing, markedly different from the other, is of later date; it was still uncompleted when the insurrection of 68 interrupted the work. The desire to apply the latest discoveries was so strong that the details were not fully worked out before being put into effect. Professor Lugli has aptly drawn attention to the inconsequence of fitting the octagonal hall and its adjacent rooms into the rest of the wing; as the frontage was straight and the other rooms rectangular, there were inevitably triangular spaces, completely walled in, where the octagonal part met the rest. The rooms that received no light from the cupola were left gloomy, as well as being difficult of access. It does seem that this wing was originally planned like the other, but the inclusion of the octagonal room threw the conception completely out of line. The attempts of Severus and Celer were in fact leading to a new style entirely opposed to classicism; angles and curves were being introduced, against all the traditional principles of regularity and symmetry.

There was undoubtedly a relationship between the later parts of the Golden House and the pavilion of the *Domus Transitoria*. The room with a cupola was developed from the latter, which also had other small buildings radiating out from it. The fountains in the corner recesses of each of the rooms built around the octagonal room are a sure indication of this derivation, for which there were two ideological reasons. First, a desire to introduce into the centre of the buildings those principles of architecture that corresponded to a grand and voluptuous conception of life, and which had previously been allowed only on the outskirts of the palace. Secondly, the 'celestial' system of letting light in through the cupola so that it was distributed over the rooms evoked Nero's desire to be assimilated with the Sun.

⟫⟫⟫ VII ⟪⟪⟪

ARTISTIC SENSIBILITY AND ROMANTICISM

This positivism, this interest in material progress, is a rather unexpected aspect of Nero's character, and presents a great contrast with the routine tendencies and subservience to authority that stifled scientific inquiry in the minds of the outstanding men of the period—Seneca and the elder Pliny, for instance. One wonders if Nero escaped because he had been such an intractable pupil; for it was the philosophic teaching which had turned men's minds from materialistic research, and Plato bears a heavy responsibility in this respect. It is to Nero's credit, then, that he was mentally curious, though his mind worked more by intuition than by rational processes. He was aware of this, and only really felt at ease in an aesthetic surrounding; so it is from that viewpoint that we must consider the value of his contribution.

The principle of 'art for art's sake' was applied to the Golden House with so much enthusiasm and refinement, and so little objectivity, that the decorations extended to the minor rooms, where the almost complete absence of light prevented anyone enjoying the decorations; such is the case with the great crypto-portico between the back of the buildings and the hillside. The most richly ornamented ceiling was the vaulted one covering the room behind the trapezoidal courtyard. When this was discovered by Renaissance artists they named it the Golden Vault; and one of them, Francesco d'Olanda, had the happy idea of making a very detailed reproduction of it. His water-colour still exists and is the only record we have of this masterpiece, which has been completely destroyed through four centuries of vandalism and of being exposed to the weather. The name given to it was due to the gilt stucco that went round the square sides of the ceiling and also divided it into sections containing paintings or reliefs.

In the centre of the vaulted ceiling was a fresco of Jupiter among the clouds with one of his loves, a work executed in a style that has been compared to Tiepolo's; in each of the corners of the ceiling was a smal medallion representing the abductions of Europa and Helle, and the Nereids riding on sea-monsters. The remainder of the ceiling was divided into small squares or rectangles, each containing a scene from Greek mythology. The gilded border used to be heightened with enamel to imitate precious stones; pinks and blues were thrown into prominence by a dark-red background, traces of which can still be seen.

The centre-piece, following a convention already employed in the basilica of the Porta Maggiore, represented the heavenly spheres where the ruler of the world reigned, but was subordinated to Love—in other words, according to Plato's exposition, to the attraction of eternal beauty. The secondary, smaller representations symbolized the efforts of creatures to attain that paradise. So here the Neronian ideology was expressed by the plastic arts. The methods employed were not new, and probably went back to the Ptolemies. But the concordance between the disposition of the pictures and the structure of the vaulting, and especially the vivid polychrome, was completely in line with Nero's liking for ingenious techniques and magnificent display.

During the Renaissance, and again in the eighteenth century, artists made copies of other ceilings in the Golden House. Some of the paintings there can still be distinguished, notably a Victory on a light background with flower-work and winged beasts around; a 'chapel' in the east wing, which perhaps contained the famous Laocoon group, still has its coffered stucco ceiling.

Parts of the murals still remain, but give little idea of the great compositions that once covered the entire walls; fortunately, here again it is possible to refer to reproductions made in the eighteenth century. The lower part of the wall was simply painted to represent a marble panelling, but above this was shown a stage with people on it, and stretching back in perspective were complicated structures with tiers of arches set on slender pillars, and with projections separated by windows or doors opening on to courtyards or porticos. Most of the people shown on the stage are standing near these openings, so as to establish a link between the real world of the onlooker and the fantasy world extending beyond the stage.

Many pages would be needed to give a complete description of all this wealth of detail and rich decoration. Elaborate treatment was given even to details that were too small and high up to be seen properly. It was impossible, for instance, to make out the subjects in the small mythological paintings on the vaulted ceiling. The painters had aimed at a gradual transition from substance to living matter, from real to fantasy. Slim columns rise from clumps of greenery, and their shafts become distorted into climbing tendrils; animal and human figures peep out from the ornamentation or support the corbels. The same figures from mythology people the tri-dimensional area above the stage, and appear in some of the pictures and reliefs. These secondary scenes were painted in a style owing much less to tradition, a kind of impressionistic work by which colour and light blurred the outlines and yet gave a slightly unreal radiance to the subject.

This decoration had obviously been inspired similarly to the architecture of the palace. The Golden House was the centre of a universe undivided by any barriers, of a wonderful universe in which only the dictates of art mattered. So there were open fronts, with 'kiosks' spreading light and the sparkle of water. The actual architecture and that shown on the frescoes had an exact resemblance, and resulted from theatres and gardens which were closely connected in the minds of the ancients and were entirely governed by ideals of beauty. The Golden House had nothing whatever in common with the old patrician *domus*, and surpassed the Greek and oriental palaces in its perfection. It was a paradise of its own, where nothing was allowed to come between the dream-world and reality.

Nero thus attained an ideal that Roman artists had been striving for since the previous century. Architecturally his Golden House derived

from the Clodia villa; the murals are in the fourth style, and show by
their basic inspiration that they owe much to the second. Nero's artists
'reopened' the long stretches of flat-wash of the third style, and reintro-
duced the perspective of a dream-world. The connection is so obvious
that a specialist in ancient Roman painting, Ludwig Curtius, believes
that the fourth style may have been a continuation of the second,
without any time-lag, and that the third style was merely a deviation,
contemporary with the beginning of the fourth. But this theory is
not compatible with the dating of the Pompeian villas; and, moreover, is belied by the fact that several innovations of the third style are
continued in the fourth—for instance the little columns and many
decorative figures taken from Egyptian art.

The re-emergence of the evasion theme, the escape into a dream-
world, is explained by the history of ideas. At the end of the Republic
this theme had expressed the non-conformism of 'libertine' circles, and
its disappearance was a logical consequence of Augustus's revival of
traditional values. But those 'progressive' elements continued, in spite
of the apparent austerity of the first two emperors; and with the
accession of Nero an end was put to the neo-classicism imposed by
Augustus, thus liberating the most original trend in Roman art. Artists
who had been suspect until then, because of the little convention they
showed, found themselves supplanting the academics by favour of the
Emperor.

One of these revolutionary painters is known to us, thanks to Pliny
the Elder. His name was Fabullus, and he executed much of the decoration in the Golden House besides being responsible for the whole; the
palace became the prison of his art, commented Pliny. It is surprising
at first to read that all his production was in the four years 64–8, for
according to other details about him given by Pliny he seems to have
been already middle-aged. But until Nero's accession Fabullus very
likely lived and worked in obscurity, as the French Impressionists did
until the end of the nineteenth century. One has only to visit the
museum at Naples, to look at the many boring repetitions of mythological themes copied from the same Greek original, and then pass on to
a landscape seen by the bluish light of the moon (oddly akin to Far
Eastern paintings), or to this or that romantic villa boldly painted, or that
masterpiece of ancient Roman art, the flower-gatherer from Stabia—and
one realizes that there were as many different styles of painting in the
first fifty years of that era as in the second half of the nineteenth century.

The most interesting of these paintings from the Campanian towns overwhelmed by the Vesuvius eruption in 79, and the one that even writers little convinced of any Roman originality admit to be free of traditionalism, shows the Wooden Horse entering Troy. It is night, and the only light thrown on the scene—apart from the feeble moon—comes from burning torches held aloft by a group of women in long white robes, in the centre of the painting. The horse is a sinister and gaunt figure looming through a breach in the walls, with men bending and straining to drag it forward. On the left of the scene is a 'sacred landscape' wrapped in gloom that could be regarded as a mere convention were it not for a large statue of Athena in armour standing on a rock, and a mysterious figure, very likely some divinity, in the air above; both are pointing in the same direction, the way the horse is headed. To emphasize the dramatic meaning of these personifications of the fate awaiting Troy, the painter has placed the dejected silhouette of Cassandra at the extreme end of the two scenes. The artist's use of chiaroscuro enabled him to eliminate detail, and he obtained his dramatic effects by concentration on two lines of movement: the vertical sweep of the horse and the torch-bearers is repeated by three onlookers in the lower right-hand corner, while the oblique movement of the striving men is taken up, as it were, by the main branch of a pine tree and carried across to the divinities conducting the fatal operation. The only figures kept aloof from the main composition are three 'foremen', and their disorganized, almost grotesque, attitudes symbolize the unawareness of human beings that it is not they who order their lives but supernatural forces. In the whole of antiquity there is no other painter, and probably no other artist of any kind, who has succeeded so well in conveying, by the bold use of novel techniques, this Sophoclean conception of an inflexible destiny. The concern of this great painter was akin to that of Seneca and his school, who believed in both an immutable determinism and the goodness of a God, and had run up against the apparent injustices of the world which they had tried to explain—in almost the same way as Christianity did later—by recourse to a divine prescience that brings about a temporary evil in order to create a future good. Seneca's mind was so taken up by this problem of undeserved suffering that it appeared in his tragedies as well as his philosophical essays. There is, then, nothing surprising—especially when, like Karl Schefold, one remembers the close relationship at this period between literature and the plastic arts—in a talented painter expressing through his particular medium this fundamental theological problem.

However, in giving this deeper significance to his picture, the unknown painter had been moved to modify the traditional setting of the episode. This was a bold innovation, for painters at that time felt themselves obliged to keep to the accepted representation when treating a classical subject. Virgil, in the *Aeneid*, had the wooden horse being taken into Troy at the end of the day; this was reasonable, as the Trojans had to be given time to get to sleep before the Greeks emerged. And, far from being gloomy, the introduction of the wooden horse was an incident of light relief between two horrible episodes, the killing of Laocoon and the sack of Troy. Reference to the 'Iliac tablets' used to illustrate scholastic studies shows that Virgil had kept to the traditional story commonly followed by the figurative arts. But in the Pompeian fresco the incident takes place at night and in an atmosphere of foreboding. The artist was undoubtedly influenced by the Alexandrian school. One has only to compare this work with a series of paintings of the nocturnal ceremonies of the Isis cult; there is the same mystic effect of vague figures emerging from the night, and the same contrast is obtained by the frenzied attitude of sacred dancers and the rigidity of priests in their long white robes. The initiation description by Apuleius shows, moreover, that a theatrical staging helped to create the right atmosphere of troubled agitation. There were twisted trees in the Alexandrian paintings, too, and rocks with statues of divinities standing among them. However, it is not suggested that the Pompeian fresco was a copy of an Egyptian painting. Its effects were exactly the same as those obtained by contemporary poetry; by Lucan, for instance, when describing the human sacrifices of the Gauls in the dark Druid forests or the horrible necromancy practised by Thessalian sorcerers. And the techniques employed artistically by the painters and poets of the Lagid court were adopted in the fresco as in *Pharsalia* to express a philosophical idea of a high order.

We thus avoid two errors that often arise when 'Neronian romanticism' is discussed: it is either seen as but a servile reflection of Hellenic art; or, on the contrary, taken to be a reaction that was specifically Roman, owing nothing to Greek tradition and influence (a mistake into which Attilio Levi has fallen). Both attitudes are due to a too simple view of Hellenistic art, which contains both a romantic and a classical current, and of the new movement that began to spread in the middle of the first century A.D.; this owed its inspiration to Latin-speaking westerners who had absorbed Greek culture and who were completely outside the national trends—contrary to what certain modern Italian historians would have us believe.

It is almost incredible that any scholar should have denied Nero any part in this artistic development, and presented him as a reactionary. His influence as sponsor becomes apparent merely by comparing the decorations in his Golden House with those in the contemporary Pompeian villas, the luxurious mansions of the Vettii and the statues of the Dioscuri that were restored soon after the earthquake which partly destroyed Pompeii in 63. The artists there, as might have been expected, adopted the new ideas and techniques without entirely understanding them or succeeding in reproducing their carefree elegance. On the Pompeian murals, the spaces between the scenes of fantasy are painted red, the famous Pompeian red. In the Golden House, Fabullus had preferred white as being more luminous and imparting airiness to the 'flying' figures in the centre position. This is given over, at Pompeii, to large mythological groups which are not only in the classical tradition but are more faithful to Greek models than frescoes of the same subjects painted in the third style. The artists of that period had given greater importance to the landscape border, thereby toning down the central figures. These heroes of mythology recovered their prominence in the fourth style, and the border was thus reduced to a simple decorative element. Very few of the frescoes in the Golden House had mytho-logical scenes; the human body only appeared in a few small groups of Bacchants or priests, etched in impressionistically, or figured among the complicated architectural designs. It was probably Fabullus who had the bold idea of placing the gods and the heroes of tradition among those structures, thus reducing them to the role of actors.

His name alone—Fabullus, or Amulius, according to one account—proves he was Roman and not Greek. Pliny wrote that he maintained Latin dignity to the point of working in a toga, even when spending long hours on a scaffolding. His graveness and severity, emphasized by Pliny, made an odd contrast with the fantasy in his work. It is most interesting that an Italian artist should have had such an important part in the aesthetic development sponsored by Nero; for in the time of Augustus another Italian, Ludius, had given a fresh impetus to land-scape painting. In the face of such commonly accepted facts it is diffi-cult to understand how many modern archaeologists can affirm that

* E

Greek-speaking Easterners practically monopolized the arts everywhere in the Roman Empire. It would seem, on the contrary, that Westerners, who were not so tied down by tradition, represented the vital force in painting and literature; whereas the Hellenes were content to reproduce the masterpieces of the past. This is true, so far as the first century A.D. is concerned, not only of painting—which became the guiding art, something it had never been in Greece—but of architecture and even of sculpture, in which the only interesting works belong to the strictly Roman fields of political and historical bas-reliefs and of portraiture.

Nero certainly called upon Greek painters as well, such as the Dorotheos mentioned by Pliny. He, too, experimented with new methods and techniques, but followed a different line from Fabullus. He painted a portrait of Nero on linen—now in a gallery of the Horti Mariani, on the Esquiline—that is more than forty yards high. This example of the 'contemporary folly'—a phrase of Pliny's—could therefore vie with the bronze Colossus, the work of another Easterner, Xenodoros. It is worth noting that Dorotheos had painted an Aphrodite Anadyomene for the temple of Venus Genitrix in the Forum Julium; some scenes of nude young women frolicking by the sea, which were copied by eighteenth-century artists from frescoes in the Golden House, may have derived from Dorotheos's painting; as may have done a group of mosaics showing the goddess of love being crowned at a sea festival. These representations of mythological gambols were probably inspired by the nautical diversions of the 'Neronian society'. The virtuosity of Dorotheos in painting on linen makes it likely that he was of Egyptian origin, for the technique—which mummifiers had passed on to immigrant Greeks—was revived in the second half of the first century, and some vivid and individual work was produced. Dorotheos's influence can readily be seen in the major mythological paintings of the fourth Pompeian style, which appear to owe nothing to Fabullus; some of the large figures, obviously inspired by statuary art, give an idea of the 'colossal' style of Dorotheos. A striving after luminous effects and colourings—which make one think of Rubens—show that, while keeping to traditional subjects, this school was not afraid of applying new techniques and treatment.

This 'Easternizing' school broke away quite openly from the 'Atticisant' neo-classicism which had triumphed under Augustus, and it looked towards the schools in Asia Minor—urged on by Nero, who showed the same romantic taste for pathos and tragedy in the plastic arts as he did in poetry and music. The famous Laocoon group in the Vatican Museum—the most celebrated example of passionate 'rhetoric' captured in stone by the Rhodian sculptors—was discovered in one of the rooms of the Golden House, or perhaps in the Baths of Trajan, having been removed there when the palace was buried. There were practical reasons, too, for the spread of this Eastern-style sculpture: a very active school of sculptors was at work at Aphrodisias, in Caria, a district of Asia Minor with a coastline on the Aegean.

After Nero's death in 68 there was a natural reaction against the tendencies that had found favour during his reign. Nevertheless impressionist painting continued to hold its own under the Flavians; and, as can be seen from bas-reliefs, there were efforts to express movement in three dimensions and a taste for the fantastic which were obviously a continuance of the tendency during the previous reign. But the general trend was a return to classicism, and this hardened under Trajan, and more especially under Hadrian.

Yet this reaction, which was in keeping with the accession of a *bourgeois* ruler little inclined to fantasies, did not completely stifle the innovations of the 'Neronian school'; there was a revival of impressionism towards the end of the second century, as well as a return to the pathetic in the arts. The value of Nero's patronage of the arts was strikingly and unexpectedly revealed fifteen hundred years after his death, when the digging of foundations brought to light, by sheer chance, what were then believed to be the grottoes of the Baths of Titus. Renaissance painters went and stared in amazement at the frescoes, which still retained the original brightness of their polychrome, and hurried to make copies of them. Raphael was inspired by the art of Fabullus, rescued after centuries of seclusion; the figures of fantasy among the columns and the foliage reappeared on the loggias of the Vatican, and were given the name of *grotteschi*. Many other painters, Giovanni d'Udine, Caravaggio, Domenichino, went down below ground to study the work of Fabullus, and scratched their names on the walls of the room with the gilded vaulting. The resurrection of Neronian art thus contributed to divert the Renaissance from classicism, and prepared the way for the emergence of baroque. This partly explains the connection of the art of the *Secento* with that of imperial Rome, and enables art historians to speak of antique baroque in no vague manner.

The Neronian academy numbered not only architects, painters and sculptors, but musicians too. The most celebrated was the zither-player, Terpnos; Nero had him come to the palace, and used to spend whole evenings listening to him.

The literature of the period shows there was a reaction against academics, too; in short, the aesthetic revival went wide and deep, and was a deliberate, reasoned movement. Seneca was prominent in the attempts to break away from the artificialities of classical eloquence and to recover the spontaneity of the language; and his ex-pupil, although turning against him to the point of hating him to death, did not escape his influence. Seneca's tastes for 'obscure finesse, bombast, padding and highly coloured phrases' were in similar strain to the impressionism of Fabullus, with his vivid and rather glaring poly-chrome and weird, 'grotesque' figures. Seneca was also interested in the effects of passion; but whereas Nero abandoned himself to passion in the search after ecstasies, the moralist in Seneca led him to study it in order to curb its effects. This explains the concordances, to which Karl Schefold calls attention, between the themes of Seneca's tragedies and the mythological repertory of the fourth Pompeian style; the writer and the painter both chose the most pathetic examples of the potency of love and its excesses.

Nero's relations with Seneca's nephew Lucan throw a curious light on the circle of aesthetes who formed the imperial court. Lucan was the son of the least brilliant of the three Annaeus brothers, Mela, who had a modest career as a jurist, and of Atilia, the daughter of a renowned orator. While still a youth, Lucan had shown a talent that his tutors thought marvellous. Nero accepted him into his circle of intimates, made him a senator and a quaestor, and appointed him to the college of augurs. The young man's ambitions were on a par with these honours; he wanted to renew epic poetry in a bolder manner than Virgil by following in the tradition of Ennius, which meant drawing on contemporary history and not the old legends for his subject. The one he chose was daring—the civil war between Caesar and Pompey, which had been the origin of the imperial régime. And in Lucan's social background, which was conservative and stoic, no secret had been made of sympathy with Caesar's worst enemy, Cato. Fortu-nately, ever since Virgil, it was generally agreed that the principate had restored national unity. So by introducing the Stoic theme of divine prescience, Lucan was able to present the war as a necessary prelude to the golden age of Nero, and to link its 'republican' sentiments with flattery of the Emperor—which was, however, so overdone that some scholars take it for irony. Actually this prodigy was incoherent and regrettably lacking in dignity, which is hardly a mark of talent.

This became obvious when he fell into disgrace; Nero refused to allow him to read his poetry at the literary meetings which were almost the only means of making one's work known. According to Tacitus, this edict was due to jealousy. But Nero could well have had enough of the poet's excessive vanity. In any case Lucan reacted in the way writers often do when they feel victimized by a government—he went over to the opposition. He continued his *Pharsalia* in secret, decrying Julius Caesar and praising republican liberty, and he joined in the conspiracy of Piso. When denounced and arrested he was promised impunity if he revealed the names of some of the plotters; he began by naming his mother, who was innocent and whom Nero did not proceed against, and then denounced many others. However, he was still forced to open his veins:

'As his blood drained away, as he felt his hands and feet going cold, while his heart was still warm and his mind lucid, he remembered a poem he had written in which he described a wounded soldier dying in much the same way; and he recited these verses; they were his last words.'

It would be difficult to be more of a man of letters to the last!

When Lucan had spoken to Nero and his circle of renewing epic poetry, one of the most prominent and favoured members of the coterie had been highly critical:

'And then take this huge subject of the civil war; whoever tries his hand at it without abounding in literary knowledge will collapse under the weight. For it is not just a matter of putting events into verse (historians do that much better) but of maintaining a flow of inspiration, through tortuous detours, divine interventions, fabulous and brilliant complications, in order to produce a prophetic rapture rather than a story based on a religious respect for the records.'

Petronius put this opinion into the mouth of a ridiculous poet whom he called Eumolpus, and followed it with three hundred epic verses that were an obvious parody of the first book of the *Pharsalia*. Lucan was just the kind of writer to aggravate the *arbiter elegantiae*, the 'director' of the palace entertainments, who was as far removed as possible from the enthusiasm for romanticism. Petronius, of all the Latin writers, is undoubtedly the one who would feel most at ease in the modern world. The *genre* he created brings him close to us—his *Satyricon* was very different from the wonderful or erotic tales of the Greeks, and on a different level from the psychological and moralizing essays of Theophrastus and Menippus. Petronius's originality was in his unbridled realism, and especially in his choice of characters, who were not so much Encolpus or Eumolpus, or even Trimalchionis, but were representatives of a class, the new 'working class' of Rome and southern Italy, a mixture of the uprooted people from all over the Mediterranean that can be compared in a way to the present-day population of New York. By writing in different styles and in a rambling manner, Petronius brought out the varied characteristics of this swarming mass; each character has a life of his own, and speaks in a particular manner, so that the *Satyricon* is a mine of information upon contemporary Latin slang, far removed from the noble language of the educated classes. These plebeians uprooted from their ancestral environment, and descended for the most part from slaves, had lost all sense of tradition, particularly—superstitions and mysticisms excepted—religious and moral sentiments. Nevertheless they had considerable material power, controlling the economic means to the making of quick fortunes. The *Satyricon* was therefore connected with a definite moment in history, the brief period between the collapse of the Roman nobility—still all-powerful under Augustus—and the economic revival of the provinces. In the last quarter of the first century that revival was to place the economic and political power in the hands of an emergent middle class descended from conquered peoples but firmly settled in new territory and attached to its principles. Everything that was outrageous and excessive in the Neronian episode is largely explained by the instability then existing in the lower strata of society. The *Satyricon* is a document of the first order on the social background to Nero's activities; though it would be ridiculous to see the work as a political pamphlet in which the Emperor and his circle are ridiculed through the persons of Trimalchio and his friends—as many humanists have tried to do, from the Renaissance to the nineteenth century.

This accounts for Petronius having been so little understood; his *Satyricon* could hardly be other than unintelligible to humanists of the seventeenth to nineteenth centuries, living in an aristocratic or *bourgeois* society and knowing only the superficial fringe of the ancient Roman world. The age-long misconstruction of Petronius's work was due in the first instance to Tacitus; the admirable portrait he drew in Book XVI of his *Annales* omitted the creative genius of Petronius, of whom he thought enough, though, to compare his suicide with that of Seneca. Ronald Syme, in his study of Tacitus, explains this apparent negligence by an attitude of dignity—history, being a noble study, did not have to take account of a comic romance like the *Satyricon*. Obviously no one considered (not until the nineteenth century) the importance of the lower classes in historical studies, and probably Petronius himself had not realized the sociological significance of his work, which was written with his usual elegant indifference. Nevertheless one should remember that Nero took an interest in low-class life, for reasons that were more or less pure, and had succeeded in establishing a certain measure of popularity among the masses, especially in the last few years of his reign when the conspiracy of Piso had definitely separated him from the aristocracy.

Chapter Five

THE NERONIAN REVOLUTION

❧❧❧ I ❧❧❧

AIMS AND METHODS

IF NERO's activities had been restricted to gathering around him the most outstanding artists and writers of his time, he would have received the praise that history gives to Augustus, Lorenzo the Magnificent and Louis XIV. Classical scholars would probably criticize him for encouraging a break with tradition (Boileau's idea, expressed in an epigram directed against Perrault, was that Nero's greatest crime was his lack of respect for the ancients), while periods such as ours, which strain after novelty, would find it a matter for praise, But Clio is a tidy old lady and does not gladly suffer extremists. In our times she excuses even bloody revolutionaries provided they had good motives and sacrificed one section of mankind for the benefit of the rest. Now Nero was a revolutionary, but with no serious motive; he endeavoured to reform the world for which he was responsible, not to make it a better place but to make it more beautiful from his personal point of view. He was not content with organizing his own life aesthetically, with a complete disregard for the sacrosanct principles of Roman morality, but tried to impose the same mode of existence on his subjects by destroying generally accepted ideals and replacing them with those of his own choosing. He even went to the extent of thinking he could make nature itself conform to his ideas. Art, as André Malraux has said, is the creation of a world removed from the real one. But Nero made the mistake of trying to fit the real to his dream-world, by using and abusing the power he had and overestimating its strength.

The Golden House played a major role in this extraordinary endeavour. It cannot be regarded as a private residence, nor as a sanctuary for a sacred sovereign, nor even as a motiveless work of art; it was a real 'instrument of government', permitting the master of the world to lead a life whose perfection would inspire such awe in people that they would meekly submit to his power, and in following his example would achieve an earthly paradise, that 'Golden Age' which every Roman emperor had promised to inaugurate. It never occurred to Nero that he was in any way neglecting his duties or wasting public money, for he considered that he was creating the means of human salvation. This peculiar sense of altruism lay behind the Emperor's words, on the day of dedication, which astounded Suetonius by their modesty: 'At last I am beginning to be housed as a man should be.' The humility of this satisfaction is a reminder that Nero's strange philosophy was always humanistic; having achieved within himself the ideal man, he was able to act as guide and example to common mortals, and rescue them from their wretchedness. There was indeed in that strange period a feeling for the dignity of the individual, and a solidarity between men, even in places where one would least expect it. Trimalchionis was thus led to say to his wife when he pulled her out of the river: 'Hominem inter homines feci.' And Juvenal's feminist later proclaimed: 'Homo sum.'

In order to carry out his task the Emperor needed assistants, and— like a good Roman—well-organized assistants. So he created a graded society of which he was naturally the head. As its aim was to impose a 'dictatorship of art' on the world, it was led by the artists and men of taste in the palace coterie. Thus the 'Neronian Academy' became in a sense a party, a sort of church or militia, whose work was not in the field of politics, religion or war, but in the realm of aesthetics. The organization acted chiefly through public festivals; these served to bring the members together, to arouse the public's admiration by their splendour, and to break down moral opposition to the new ideal by publicly flouting the old values. Several of the orgies held have been mentioned by historians. The biggest and best known, thanks to Tacitus, was the banquet given to the Emperor by Tigellinus, just before the great fire, on the lake made by Agrippa in the Field of Mars. The banqueting hall was built on a great raft pulled by ivory-and-gold decorated ships. The rowers had been recruited from the city's perverts, and were arranged in an ingenious order according to their special talents. Brothels had been built on the banks and were filled with young women belonging to the best Roman families, while nude professional dancers had to be content with posing like statues. The evening began with suggestive ballets, followed by a grand illumination of the surrounding scene.

Water-fêtes of a similar kind had been given by Caligula in the past, on the famous pontoons of Lake Nemi (which were discovered under water and recovered during Mussolini's rule, but were destroyed during the war). The Ptolemies had been the first to build floating palaces in which to hold banquets, having got the idea from the Pharaohs; it had most probably originated as an entertainment given by the harem, for the Pharaohs had delighted in watching lightly clad concubines or dancers performing on the artificial lakes in their gardens. These displays had contained a religious element, as in Syria water-festivals were held in honour of the Great Goddess, queen of the seas and of love, in which nude slaves attached to her temple took part. And at a festival of the old Roman religion, the Floralia, in honour of the goddess of flowers, it had been customary for the women dancers to strip naked. However, public morality at the time of Nero disapproved of such practices, and he was quite aware of the scandal he was causing by flaunting these spectacles in the very centre of Rome. It was not that he did not care; he was acting with deliberate provocation, in defiance of the modesty and the moral standards of most of his subjects. Nero was not really debauched, but immoral and essentially hostile to any ethical code.

'Several people told me', wrote Suetonius, 'that he was quite convinced that no human being was chaste or pure, in any part of the body, and that most people hid their vice, concealing it cunningly; and that was why he excused all their other faults to anyone who admitted to a depravity.'

Tigellinus's banquet can be considered as the inaugural ceremony of a sect whose members were carefully graded according to their vices, and who had the practice of sexual perversions in common. The initiation in fact consisted of the erotic act, performed in the most spectacular circumstances. This is the explanation of Nero's 'marriage' to Pythagoras:

'He himself, having besmirched himself in every possible way, normal and abnormal, and being unwilling for anyone to outdo him in depravity, a few days later (after Tigellinus's banquet) married Pythagoras, one of the members of the contaminated band (i.e. one of those at the orgy), with all the ritual of a real wedding. The Emperor put on a bride's wedding veil; everyone saw the auspices, the dowry, the marriage-bed, the nuptial torches; indeed, everything which night hides with its shade, even when a woman is concerned, was enacted before the onlookers.'

⟫⟫⟫ II ⟪⟪⟪

AMORALITY AND REVOLUTIONARY TRADITION

However monstrous these practices appear, they are not incomprehensible if considered from the psychological and the historical point of view. Nero's aversion to morality is explained by his upbringing; from his earliest age he could have had no illusions about the behaviour of his family and all those around him. Seneca's lessons served only to strengthen his scepticism; his tutor certainly taught austere principles, but did not practise what he preached. During the reign of Claudius he had openly been the lover of Agrippina's youngest sister, and he was known to associate with business men of doubtful reputation who exploited the provincials to such an extent that revolts broke out; moreover, he was a treacherous and intriguing politician. His lack of moral fibre, which was more serious than Cicero's, did not prevent him from being strongly attracted by virtue, the highest form of 'public morality'. Whether Nero really understood his tutor's thought or not, he certainly came under his influence and felt a mixture of fear and respect for him. But this feeling of dependence aroused resentment in a weak character like Nero, which he finally indulged by condemning Seneca to death—an action probably justified from a political point of view.

The awareness of a vocation that was thwarted by his *entourage* and by convention must also have convinced Nero, as has happened with many artists in all ages, of the incompatibility of art and ethics. As he refused to isolate art from life, he found himself on the path of a militant immorality, an immorality which was influenced by Bacchism. Nero was certainly no more a worshipper of Dionysus than of any other god. But his impassioned romanticism had much in common with the cult, whose liturgy attracted him because of the arts that it had nourished—the theatre mainly, but also poetry and painting. Now, in Rome even more than in Greece, Bacchism had been a suspect and persecuted cult, and had adopted a revolutionary attitude, morally and politically, from the very first. In 186 B.C. a senatorial decree had banned its rites, as much for their sexual *flagitia* as for the murders and political conspiracies for which the members were held responsible. Even when allowances have been made for what popular imagination and the malevolence of conservative society added to the depravities of the cult, it is obvious from monuments due to the participants themselves that in some gatherings the initiate had to submit to certain sexual practices which were probably presented as a means of union with the goddess.

A notorious 'affair' which Nero must have known about, as it helped to clear the way for his accession, proves that these 'naturalistic orgies' had spread to court circles in spite of the interdict of Augustus. The debauchery during which Messalina 'married' her lover Silius, in defiance of her husband the Emperor Claudius, was in fact a Bacchanalia; the Empress played the part of Ariadne, while Silius represented Dionysus. Although Messalina was a mortal enemy of Agrippina, Nero appears to have modelled his conduct on this rival, for his 'wedding' with Pythagoras was based on her scandalous behaviour. However demented Messalina may have been she could hardly have thought her husband would overlook her bigamous action; and if she had seriously considered assassinating Claudius, as Tacitus indicated, she would have taken some precautions against his getting rid of her first. But the centurion ordered by Narcissus to kill her was able to carry out his mission without any difficulty. The whole matter becomes a little more understandable when one remembers the kind of 'parallel' life that many of the Roman nobility led, those excursions into a dream-world of unreality. This does not make Messalina's actions any less abominable, either from the point of view of modern ethics or of the traditional ideology of Augustus that Claudius was trying to maintain. Messalina was repeating Julia's rebellious action by the most outrageous conduct against public modesty and decency, upon which the political as well as the moral order of the Empire was based. Narcissus must have made Claudius understand that, to have obtained from him the sentence of death which was quickly put into effect.

It was this undermining of the very principles of society which gave a sacrilegious and revolutionary aspect to immoral practices. When the Senate had first banned the Bacchanalian gatherings it had considered the State equally threatened by their debaucheries and their opportunities for political conspiracy. The connection between revolutionary action and the orgiastic rites of Bacchus was so strongly established that Catiline, the leader of a subversive political and social party, considered it only natural to give the meetings of its members the character of an orgy, and to surround the taking of oaths with rites similar to those at the initiations into mystic cults; while Julia, and then Messalina, whose chief desires were to cast off the yoke of *bourgeois* morality, found themselves obliged—almost against their own inclinations—to engage their depraved followers in seditious action, followers who were as ill prepared as themselves for the harsh realities of politics.

It would be a mistake to explain away this revolutionary attitude of Bacchism in Italy by theological reasons or by a sort of 'incompatibility of mood' between the prophets of the cult and the pontiffs of the *respublica*. Roman order was vested in the patriarchal family, the *gens*, a social unit introduced into Italy by the Indo-European conquerors. Now Dionysus is believed to have been originally a pre-Hellenic god, belonging therefore to the races conquered by the Aryans; and instead of his cult being incorporated into the latter's religion it was always practised among secret societies which recruited their members without distinction of lineage.

The *Bacchae* of Euripides shows that in Greece, from the fifth century B.C. at least, the orgiastic cults attempted to undermine the authority of the *genos*, the Greek equivalent of the *gens*, by wrenching women away from domesticity and by suppressing the magistrates who tried to oppose them. In earliest times in Italy the cult of a god whose name spoke of liberty—Liber—had spread among the non-Aryan peoples, especially the Etruscans. Bacchus became the symbol of seething, discontented forces which were for a long time kept in check by patriarchal discipline and strict moral codes. The destructive power of those forces, which Augustus tried in vain to restrain, has been referred to here on several occasions. It was the cause of scandal in the highest social circles throughout the first century A.D.—women of good family asking to be registered as prostitutes or, like Messalina, entering brothels incognito; young men going into the arena to fight in defiance of official regulations; highly respected notabilities going on the stage to act—some of them Nero's most active opponents: Thrasea, a leading Stoic philosopher, and Piso, who headed the conspiracy of 67. Nero, who himself felt oppressed by the old morality and its conventions, found a large section of public opinion was ripe to approve and support him. But his difficulty was not so much to crush the old order as to create a new one afterwards; and in that Bacchism could be of help to him. After the Macedonian conquest, which had destroyed patriarchal authority, some of Alexander's successors had found in the celebration of Bacchic festivals a means of establishing a spiritual communion between the immigrant Greeks and the conquered native population. The Ptolemy dynasty in particular had made good use of this means in Egypt.

A Dionysiac idea of royalty took shape at Alexandria, its most perfect expression being the 'inimitable life' of Antony and Cleopatra, and it was the opposite of the Stoic concept of power as adopted by the Antigonid dynasty in Macedonia. Both concepts demanded of the sovereign that he should prove himself worthy of his power by his 'virtues'; but the 'Dionysiac virtues' were more like attainments, in a modern sense, depending on 'magnificence' and implying benevolence, generosity, encouragement of the arts and their practice: Cleopatra's father Ptolemy XI was known as Auletes the Flute-player, and her mother as Tryphaena the Magnificent. The Ptolemies exercised their power more by persuasion than force; the myth of Dionysus conquering the East, which had grown up around his name in Alexandria during the third century B.C., told of the god disarming his enemies by magical powers or driving them mad—a notion probably derived from witchcraft, and still found among some primitive tribes. The Ptolemies, however, had developed these barbarous tactics by applying 'psychological action': the second king, Philadelphus, who reigned in the third century B.C., increased the empire founded by his father less by warlike means than by judicious use of his great wealth and by giving splendid festivals, beginning with his coronation procession—which had both a Dionysiac and a military character. This 'Apollo with fair, curly hair, surrounded by the Muses', writes Bouché-Leclercq, 'soon became convinced that he had to choose between brute force and intelligence, between vice and virtue; that he had to be a just ruler to his people, and an enlightened protector to the scholars and scientists of his court' (*Histoire des Lagides*, 1, p. 95–6). The portrait could apply word for word to Nero. The system of government was the antithesis of the Roman; yet Cleopatra had proved its worth by almost succeeding in conquering the world without recourse to military power, solely through the attractions of the refined civilization that this woman, who was somewhat lacking in physical charms, had represented.

Nero thus appears as heir to the social revolutionary movement in Italy and to the traditions of the Ptolemies. From the former he assumed the militant immorality which aimed at the disruption of the social system founded on the old patriarchal family; while from the latter he obtained the concept of a monarchy based on the attraction of the sovereign's life of splendour. Nero's prodigality which emptied the state coffers filled by Pallas, and for which the Emperor was blamed by Suetonius, was not the heedlessness of a spoilt child with too much power, but a conscious process of government.

'He did not believe that riches and money were meant for anything but to be spent lavishly,' wrote Suetonius. 'He considered that people who counted their money were mean and sordid, and that those who wasted it and ruined themselves were dashing and truly superb. So he put no limit on his munificence and his spending. He gave Tiridates—it seems incredible—eight hundred thousand *sesterces* a day, and had more than a hundred million counted out for him when he left. . . . Never did he wear the same clothes twice. He played dice for four hundred thousand *sesterces* a throw. He went fishing with a gilt net and ropes woven in purple and scarlet. It was said that he never travelled with fewer than a thousand vehicles in his train, that his muleteers were dressed in fine cloth, and his charioteers and messengers were covered with bracelets and decorations.'

This policy of prestige drew subjects eager for a better life into the Emperor's service, and discouraged foreign monarchs from attacking such a rich Empire. But Nero was ignoring the fact that pomp and ostentation are only worth while politically when reflecting the prosperity of a productive economy, as had been the case with the Ptolemies in Egypt at the beginning of the third century B.C. Italy, however, was entering on a grave economic crisis, and the Emperor's prodigality was soon to lead to the first inflation in the Empire's history; the high cost of living and the heavy increase in taxation were played upon by the opposition to great effect, in Italy and in the provinces.

⋙ III ⋘

THE APOLLINISM OF NERO

Unfortunately for Nero he refused to see the danger, although he was warned in the reports from his procurators. It seemed impossible to him that men could be so stupid as not to realize what a wonderful future he was preparing for them: freed from the old restrictions, from wars and poverty, under him they would lead a life of paradise, such as his predecessors had only promised them or let them catch a glimpse of. Whilst taking the basic elements of his doctrine from Bacchism, Nero meant to surpass all the Greek rulers who had adopted the cult— it was to be a new Apollo, not Bacchus, who would found the 'Golden Age'. At first thought it seems extraordinary that Nero should have taken for his patron this stern god of the Pythagoreans, the eclectic Stoics and of Augustus just when he was setting an example of a way of life directly opposed to asceticism. But our surprise arises from a narrow and rigid conception of the Greco-Roman deities. Although they had undergone a kind of naturalization, each was regarded not so much as a personality as a combination of virtues and powers (*numina*) which could be called upon—provided the correct approach were made. It mattered not at all that these offerings—which were controlled by groups of specialists—included practices which seem contrary to one another; for instance, the goddess Demeter required her worshippers to be quite chaste yet at times expected them to perform sexual acts, symbolically at least. Only philosophers found fault with this illogicality. And Nero was no philosopher, any more than the great majority of his subjects. Tacitus mentioned how the Emperor cited Apollo to Seneca, to justify his desire to sing in the theatre:

'Songs are sacred to him; he appears as a musician, not only in the Greek cities but in Roman temples; he is a great and knowledgeable power [*numen praecipuum et praescium*].'

Those last words gave an exact idea of what Apollo was to Nero— the personification of power, of 'virtue' that showed itself through song, music and poetry, sometimes through intellectual or intuitive spheres.

It was very convenient for Nero that the founder of his dynasty had at one time relied upon some of the characteristics of Apollo, for he could refer to that example—but without being obliged to call upon the same aspects of the classical god's *numen*, nor to follow the same procedures. The Apollo of Augustus had been a Pythagorean and political god, very similar to the one at Delphi; there the cult had retained a strict and ordered character which corresponded with the moral conceptions of Augustus. The Pythia, the priestess, made her prophecies without any hysteria; before entering the shrine she prepared herself by purifications that had no ill effects on her physical and intellectual integrity. But it was very different in sanctuaries elsewhere; the Sibyl priestesses went into a frenzy or fit, and the sacred message from the god dribbled out incoherently. This delirium would seem to have been induced by some form of intoxication, and was given an erotic meaning; which would explain some at least of Apollo's mythical adventures.

That irrational and passionate Apollo was much like Dionysus, with whom he was often associated by the cult, and who was given an almost similar appearance by artists. Now Bacchus was generally considered to inspire poets and artists; Plato, in his *Ion*, had expressed a theory about artistic creation which had a wide influence in Roman times. 'Poets do not work to a technique,' he wrote, 'but compose under the effect of a divine force, similar to that sending the Corybantes and the Maenades into a delirium.' This suited the romantics in Nero's circle; Lucan's description of the Delphic oracle was influenced by it, and his Pythia was falsely represented as a delirious Sibyl, running madly through the temple, shrieking and foaming at the mouth, yet unable to get rid of what was burning her inside and which finally killed her. Nero and his friends decided in favour of the impassioned and affectionate Apollo and disregarded the other; they could best work in a state of suspended thought, a condition encouraged by drink and erotic practices. The 'surrealist' paintings and the fanciful passages of the *Pharsalia* were probably produced during such 'spasms of enthusiasm'. The originality of the Neronian doctrine, however, was contained in the idea that inspiration did not bring exemption from the use of techniques. Nero even appears to have felt the need of a hard discipline, which replaced the morality he had rejected. Suetonius wrote that he subjected himself to training sessions over a period of years. To develop his breathing muscles, he spent hours on his back with a heavy lead weight on his chest; he had enemas given him, took emetics, and followed a strict diet from which fruit was excluded. When taking part in singing competitions he was careful to observe all the rules; according to Suetonius he never dared to spit, and he wiped the perspiration from his brow with his arm. He once dropped his sceptre while acting a tragedy, and hurried to pick it up for fear of being eliminated from the competition because of this mistake; and he was reassured only when another competitor told him that the public, in its enthusiasm, had not noticed the incident.

It was undoubtedly this feeling that he needed to make an effort and to have some difficulty to overcome that caused Nero ultimately to

prefer Apollo to Dionysus—though there were political and astrological reasons as well. After all, worshippers of the god of wine
obtained satisfaction easily; there was no need to strive and struggle.
Nero's ideal was on a higher plane; for him immorality, love-making
and drunkenness were but preparatory techniques to be followed by a
return to work, to polish and sharpen the crude verses resulting from
the induced inspiration. Suetonius has described him correcting and
improving, over and over again, poems written down in the first flush
of rapture. Besides, the Emperor had a task of a higher order and more
onerous than that of any artist; there was the world to reshape as well
as creative work to do; he had to set the example to his subjects, as well
as using his authority, to put them on the way to happiness and beauty.

This heroic aspect of the Neronian conception was expressed,
through the mythological symbolism of the time, by the Emperor's
assimilation with Hercules. There was no risk of Nero being accused of
some new sacrilege—Hercules was one of the most ancient gods of
Rome; his great altar, which stood in front of the Circus, was believed
to date from before the time of Romulus, and to commemorate Hercules' defeat of the monster Cacus. The god's reputation had been a
little damaged, though, by Antony's claim to be descended from one
of his sons; Augustus had consequently looked coldly upon Hercules.
It was Agrippina who had first established a connection in the mind of
the public between the son of Alcmene and her own. During her
rivalry with Messalina she had spread one of those wonderful stories
that always delighted the Romans—and which were cleverly used by
the imperial propaganda, and by that of the religious sects too, in order
to increase the prestige of the princes and the prophets. Agrippina's
story was that Messalina had hired some thugs to strangle her rival's
baby in his cradle; but as they entered the bedroom a large serpent
emerged from under the baby's pillow and frightened them away. The
reptile—obviously sent by some god—had then vanished, but first
changed its skin and left the old one behind, as a kind of visiting-card.
Agrippina made a bracelet of this skin, and told her son to wear it
always. Suetonius added the moral necessary to every fable: Nero cast
aside the bracelet after the murder of his mother, and when he saw his
own end approaching he searched for it frantically but never found it.
The story was greatly reminiscent of the celebrated mythical
exploit of Hercules as a baby in his cradle, strangling with his own
hands the two serpents that jealous Hera had sent to destroy him. So

the popularity of this theme in Pompeian paintings of the fourth style can hardly be explained away as a mere coincidence; it is repeated in four frescoes, based on the same prototype. These, moreover, are the only Pompeian paintings in which Hercules is shown struggling or fighting. That may seem surprising, but the classical 'Twelve Labours' did not inspire painters at all; though they were much attracted by the amorous adventures of Hercules, which show the least glorious side of him.

The Greeks had been representing the story of Hercules in that odd manner since the fourth century B.C., and it fitted the Neronian ideology. When the decorator of Lucretius Fronto's villa painted Hercules staggering drunkenly, a hand round the neck of Priapus, and being teased by a bevy of young loves, with naked Omphale near by—had not the painter the 'inimitable' life of the Emperor in mind?

The museum of Aquileia has a pedestal from a statuette of Hercules which seems to have been dedicated to Apollo by Nero himself. Some verses can still be read on it—feeble verses, but in Nero's complicated style—in which the Emperor expressed his peculiar policy symbolized for him by these two gods: Hercules represented the struggle that he believed himself called upon to make for the betterment of a world still disordered and in the grip of evil; afterwards the god of light and the arts would preside over the paradise brought about by that struggle.

This dual conception that Nero had of his mission cannot be explained by separating the aesthete in him from the politician, the artist from the man of action, the voluptuous liver from the reformer. Everything about his conduct during the last years of his reign, when he was complete master and free to act as he liked, was determined by the deep conviction that we have been analysing. It remains to be seen how he tried to give effect to his ideas, transforming the very nature of the powers he had inherited in order to bring about the supreme revolution, that 'reign of Apollo' insufficiently prepared for by his predecessors, that peaceful era in which Beauty would reign and reconcile Man and Nature in a perfect harmony, eliminating bondage, pain and suffering.

≫≫≫ IV ≪≪≪

PRECURSORS OF THE REVOLUTION—THE JUVENALIA AND THE FOUNDING OF THE 'NERONIAN SOCIETY'

However absurd Nero's Utopia may seem, he must be credited with using method and perseverance in his endeavours to bring it about, working for ten years to reduce opposition by a gradual process, cleverly making use of the resources available through the official religion—of which he was high pontiff—and the political and psychological set-up instituted by Augustus. In 59, having performed in private as a singer and musician, Nero created the Juvenalia; these were games of the traditional kind and were placed under the patronage of the goddess of youth—who had been admitted to the Roman pantheon a long time previously, and was associated with Hercules. The Juvenalia were held on the north bank of the Tiber, round the lake that Augustus had caused to be made for a *naumachia*. The scene was more like a fair-ground, with booths kept by upper-class people and selling all kinds of luxury goods; there was, of course, much rivalry to spend the most money. And as at fêtes for charity today, amateur plays were performed. Nero encouraged young men and women of the aristocracy to act in them, though little urging was required, whatever Tacitus wrote about it later. It is not surprising that in such an atmosphere the young Emperor—he was just twenty-two—should have demonstrated his talent as a singer; and he drove chariots, too, in the private circus he had built not far from where St Peter's now stands.

Tacitus took a severe view of these festivities, which were really little worse than modern fancy-dress balls. 'They gave opportunity for debauchery, and never were the already corrupt morals so submerged by wicked desires as in that overflow of filth.' As a consequence of the Juvenalia, however, the 'Neronian Society' was founded; this was court, academy and private club combined, and undoubtedly the most original organization of the reign. It had several different sections; one consisted of Roman knights chosen for their youth and good looks. These were called the *Augustani*, and their task was to applaud Nero and acclaim him as a god; this 'fan club' was later increased by the admission of young plebeians, and the number of members rose to more than five thousand. Another section was composed of young boys who were required to let their hair grow, have it scented and waved like a woman's, and were given a ring to wear on the left hand; they went on the stage with the Emperor as a mute chorus or acolytes. The society was legally constituted; all the members were registered, they wore uniforms and had to attend regular practice which included different kinds of acclamations, each having its degree of importance. The leaders received payment, in some cases as much as four hundred thousand *sesterces* a year—more than double the pay of procurators in the most important provinces. Moreover, some of the highest positions in the administrative services and in the army were reserved for them. At about the same time 'academies' of music, poetry and philosophy were founded, and can be regarded as part of the same society.

Nero thus obtained a well-organized body of supporters drawn from all ranks and classes, from the lowest to the very highest. It was an entirely new organization in its extent and, especially, in its close relationship with the theatre and the games. During Augustus's reign, though, there were many brotherhoods and similar groups which celebrated the imperial cult in its various forms; the best known was the *Augustales*, whose membership in each city consisted of the wealthy freedmen, and who held their meetings and ceremonies in specially arranged buildings.

Nero made another step in his programme the following year, 60, by introducing the Greek games to the Romans. The public festivals in Rome had always been influenced by Greece, but there were two major differences. Whereas the *agones* of Olympia, Delphi and Corinth were performances by amateurs belonging to the city's *élite*, the Roman *ludi* were shows given by professionals, mostly foreigners by birth and generally disdained. Secondly, the Greeks preferred artistic competitions, in poetry, music and eloquence, or sporting contests such as athletics or chariot-races; but the Romans had dances and pantomime, gladiator fights and animal hunts, and races too, with professional charioteers on whom the public betted. The basic difference between the Greek and Roman games was in fact akin to the division between amateur and professional sport today. The Greek conception was obviously the more noble. It is to Nero's credit, then, that he instituted the Quinquennial Games, which had three sections: one for music, poetry and eloquence; another for athletics; and only the third consisting of races. Traditionalists were not lacking with bitter complaints, which Tacitus deemed worthy of a whole chapter; but he had to admit that the great majority of people approved Nero's action.

The Emperor's efforts were still more praiseworthy in a matter that Suetonius alone has mentioned. The so-called monster of cruelty tried to have the gladiator fights, which were a disgrace to Roman civilization, reduced to harmless fencing matches in which representatives of all social classes would take part. Four hundred senators and six hundred knights did in fact go into the arena, delighted at being able to indulge their fighting instincts without running any risk. But Nero's humane and intelligent reform was regarded by the conservative opposition as a move to degrade the upper classes and destroy ancient customs. A more enlightened age can but deplore that Nero's attempts failed, and that the Greeks soon became contaminated by the sadistic cruelty of the Romans, instead of reforming them.

By giving great importance to 'amateurism' Nero was admittedly trying to facilitate his own performances. He entered the competitions for eloquence, Latin poetry and the zither, and of course carried off all three prizes. Yet it should not be forgotten that these victories had an official character, that measures were taken to assimilate them with the exploits whereby an Emperor justified his *auctoritas* by the *virtus*. The jury was composed not of experts but of the most respectable consuls. When Nero received the crown for the music contest he kissed it and then dedicated it to Augustus, at the foot of the deified Emperor's statue. This was intended to show that the practice of his talents, far from lowering his dignity, proved him a worthy successor to the founder of the dynasty. Besides, the Neronian games were a revival of those held during Augustus's reign, at similar intervals, in most of the cities of the Empire. As André Piganiol points out, their object was to assure the survival of the Emperor, by an association with ancient magical conceptions. And Nero associated the athletic contests with the ceremony of his first shave; under the old Roman religion this was a sacred occasion that marked a young man's majority.

The religious character of the ancient games should not be forgotten. In Greece the victorious contestants were covered with more than the brief glory of champions; their triumphs in contests instituted by the gods, and held at famous sanctuaries, elevated them above common mortals. Previous to the fourth century B.C. they were even accorded honours greater than those granted to victorious generals. They were privileged—obviously because of the sacred character of the *agones*—

to escape the jealousy of the Immortals, that dreaded Nemesis who visited with disaster all others having too many gifts of fortune. They returned home in great triumph, on horseback or riding in a chariot; sometimes a victor at the Games was brought into his native town through a breach in the walls, just like a conqueror. These primitive conceptions had become rationalized; though now that Greece had lost her political power but had grown aware of her spiritual values, these peaceful contests drawing upon physical and moral qualities and exalting the Hellenic genius consoled her for her military decline. The 'hieronics', as the victors at the Games were called, were honoured more than ever as demi-gods; and it was even thought that their triumphs gave them the right to immortality in the celestial paradise.

These noble concepts had spread to the Roman *élite* by the first century B.C., as Franz Cumont and Henri-Irénée Marrou have explained. Texts of philosophers and rhetoricians indicate—and epitaphs and sculptured decorations on tombs are even more precise—that throughout the Empire the *mousicos aner* could expect the blessed immortality which the civic religion of Rome reserved first and foremost for the faithful servants of the country. Now the ideology upon which the imperial power was based justified the supreme *auctoritas* of the *princeps* through the same virtues as permitted individuals to accede to official immortality. Nero was therefore not violating any accepted ideas by vindicating his position through his artistic talents, by wishing to be acclaimed first of all as the best of the hieronics. However, there was a greater possibility of this being accepted by the Greeks than by the Romans, many of whom still regarded the arts and athletics as mere relaxations, and considered them detrimental, moreover, to warlike spirit and manly qualities. This explains Nero's increasing favours towards his Greek-speaking subjects during the last years of his reign, towards the inhabitants of 'Achaea' and the old-established colonies in southern Italy, or—for want of any better—Eastern emigrants who had settled in Rome. The resistance of conservative elements also explains, though does not justify, Nero's furious and indeed crazed attack at this time on the narrow outdated ideas of traditional discipline, and indeed on all that the old Roman morality had in common with universal ethics.

ᗑᗑᗑ V ᗐᗐᗐ

CARRYING OUT THE GRAND DESIGN

Nero's projects were delayed by serious troubles in 61 and 62, both at home and abroad. Corbulo was victorious in Armenia, but revolt had spread in Britain, there was social agitation in Rome, and a conspiracy to dethrone the Emperor was suspected. But Nero was particularly occupied in ridding himself of all those who had restrained him in the early years. He had not dared do anything while Burrhus lived; but the death of the Praetorian prefect was at once followed by the dismissal of Seneca and the divorce of Octavia, whom Nero had been forced by Claudius to marry when he was sixteen and had always detested. Twelve days after the divorce he married Poppaea. Tigellinus succeeded Burrhus at the head of the Praetorian Guard. Nero was now free to act as he wished, and at the beginning of the year 63 he decided to perform for the first time in a public theatre. He chose Naples for this *début*, as it was still essentially a Greek city due to considerable immigration from Alexandria. Tacitus, in this instance, must have faithfully interpreted his thoughts. 'It is a first step,' Nero was quoted as saying. 'Then I shall go to Greece, and after having won illustrious crowns that have been sacred throughout antiquity I shall compel the interests of citizens because of my increased glory.' So the final object was to be achieved by a gradual process—the Romans were to be won over by his artistic talents, in the manner of Apollo and Orpheus.

Nero was so pleased by the applause of the Neapolitans—who even in those days were exceedingly demonstrative—that he took measures to aid Alexandrians wishing to settle in Campania. All the members of the 'Neronian Society' had accompanied the Emperor to Naples, and they too were in the theatre, seated according to their functions. Soldiers were also present, not so much to keep watch on the public as because the army owed allegiance and devotion to the Emperor and had to be represented at all ceremonies of the imperial cult. Unfortunately the Praetorians did not possess sufficient culture to appreciate their General's talents. At one moment a guard became scared when seeing Nero playing the part of Oedipus, and dashed to his rescue.

The spectators had only just left the theatre when it collapsed, probably weakened by the unusually high attendance. Nero's opponents tried to make out this was a sign of the wrath of the gods; but Nero pointed out, with some reason, that it was miraculous no one had been hurt by the accident, and he composed some thanksgiving hymns. He was still fearful, though, which shows how much the matter was on his mind; and, in spite of his great desire to go to Greece or Egypt immediately, to add to his reputation, he postponed both voyages consequent upon some inauspicious omens.

This state of alternating enthusiasm and uneasiness may well explain his strange conduct during the last months of 63. Superstitious as he was, he felt a need to mark his success and also to avert the threats overhanging his future. And that called for rites commensurate with the immense importance he attached to his work, for acts of unheard-of audacity and sacrifices capable of rousing the forces controlling the universe. It was then that he resorted to sexual perversions and debaucheries similar to the Dionysiac initiation rites, but on a scale and with an ostentation that the boldest Bacchants would never have dared. The Tigellinus orgy and the 'wedding' with Pythagoras were propitiatory rites whose outrageousness was proportionate to the vastness of his revolutionary undertaking. And the great fire of Rome, which occurred shortly afterwards, may have been a deliberate climax; for the wild ritual had on occasion turned the worshippers of Bacchus into fire-raisers, and was possibly the reason why Alexander and his companions, together with Thaïs and her Bacchantic women, destroyed the palace at Persepolis. Nero was an admirer of Alexander, which makes the supposition all the more disturbing. In any case the accusation that the Christians were responsible for the fire takes on a deeper significance and becomes more understandable—the crime retained its sacred character, as another sect was made responsible.

A change in the iconography of Nero during 64 is noted by P. L'Orange. Previously the Emperor had been shown with his hair short and flattened like Augustus; but then it began to appear raised by a band round the head and arranged crown-shape, often with a long-pointed crown on top—the solar emblem that was on the head of the Colossus in front of the Golden House. L'Orange suggests that Nero's new hair-style was taken from the Hellenistic *basileis*: 'From the time of Alexander, arranging the hair in an upward sweep became an effective means of suggesting the nature of the divinity, like the

F

"glory" at the end of the Roman epoch.' The change in the representation of the Emperor on coins thus bears out the contrast between the 'constitutional prince' of the early years of the reign and the Easternizing tyrant towards the end. However, L'Orange's interpretation is challenged by scholars in England. Miss J. Toynbee argues that the high hair-style was copied from charioteers and musicians. Support for this theory can be found in Suetonius:

'As for his dress and appearance, he took so little care over it that during his visit to Greece he let his hair, which had always been wavy, hang down over his neck; and he appeared in public on most occasions wearing a large flowing gown, a scarf round his neck, and without belt or sandals.'

Tacitus, too, wrote that the spectators at the Juvenalia and the Quinquennial Games had to wear the Greek pallium. Once again Nero acted against the policy of Augustus, who had insisted on the toga being worn by all Romans and had set the example himself.

Dress had a deeper significance in the ancient world than in modern times; it was the outward sign of a person's membership of a social community, so much so that a change of dress was often the equivalent of a real apostasy. The importance of such an act can be judged by considering, for instance, the gravity of the measures taken by Kemal Atatürk to modernize Muslim dress; Eastern peoples still retained the old sacred value of the form of dress, which in the West only lingers on with the priest's cassock and the soldier's uniform. It is therefore most important to be able to give the exact date of Nero's change of hairstyle as 64, which was the year of his initiation into the aesthetic sect he had founded. Members of religious societies often recognized each other by a particular hair-style, which had a symbolic meaning and a sacred significance too—the tonsure is the one surviving instance of this today. Bacchants used to dedicate a large curl of their hair to their god. And by adopting the wavy hair-style usually given to Apollo and Dionysus, Nero was emphasizing in his provocative and showy way that he had definitely adopted a pattern and a way of life for the world to take as an example.

The Piso conspiracy seems to have spurred the Emperor on, instead of making him prudent. It revealed to him how he was hated by the great majority of the senators, including several among his intimate circle, such as Petronius and Lucan. Even more serious was that the loyalty of the army officers, if not the troops, had wavered dangerously;

for a few hours only the German bodyguard was reliable. Nero concluded that he could no longer count on the organization created by Augustus. It had become absolutely necessary to awaken in the masses a love and admiration for his talents, to protect him against plots and the ungrateful nobility.

The Quinquennial Games were about to be held again; the Senate made a fresh attempt to prevent the Emperor from taking part by awarding him the prizes for singing and eloquence in advance. This, of course, showed complete misunderstanding of Nero's mind and character. The Emperor was determined to subject himself to the strict rules imposed on the competing musicians, and did not avoid making the humble gestures with which the artists asked for the public's approval; he knelt on the stage and held an imploring hand towards the crowded tiers of seats, while giving every sign of anxiety. The public displayed its pleasure with an enthusiasm that Tacitus, in a few bitter phrases, admitted to be sincere. But the applause was led by soldiers and the *Augustani*, and was hardly voluntary; it took the form of rhythmic clapping and chanted acclamations, not unlike canticles. This liturgy of praise—which still has echoes in some hymns of the Roman Catholic and Orthodox churches—had previously been heard during Augustus's reign, the reader will remember. There were other obligations, of a graver nature, which call to mind some aspects of modern totalitarian régimes: people holding official positions had to be present in the theatre; municipalities in the provinces as well as in Italy were obliged to send delegations—whose awkwardness was remarked upon; and no one was allowed to leave his or her seat, not even for the most pressing reasons. Tacitus and Suetonius both maintained, with some exaggeration no doubt, that women gave birth while a performance was taking place and that some spectators caught diseases from which they later died. Finally, and most important, anyone who showed signs of boredom was guilty of the crime of lese-majesty; though no one appears to have been a victim on that account. Vespasian fell asleep and was rudely awakened by the freedman Phoebus, but no other action was taken. According to Tacitus, the incident occurred during the Games, but Suetonius connected it with Nero's visit to Greece.

⊰⊰⊰ VI ⊱⊱⊱

THE VISIT TO GREECE AND NERO'S MADNESS

The encouragement of the Roman crowds decided Nero to go and take part in the Greek Games. Realizing the advantages to be obtained from the Emperor's visit, the shrewd Greeks had enticed him by awarding him the crowns of all the music competitions in advance, and sent ambassadors to present them to him. An unpleasant surprise awaited the ambassadors, though: Nero demanded the money prizes that went with the crowns. The imperial coffers were empty, and no opportunity could be neglected. Then there were complications over the organization of the voyage and the Emperor's programme. Nero wanted to take part in all the Games; but their dates had been fixed throughout antiquity, and each was held in a different year of an Olympiad to avoid clashing. Nero decided that one or two would be brought forward, that the others were to take place again, and that the contests were to be adapted to his tastes. For instance, a singing contest had to be included in the Olympic Games, which were only for athletes. This urge for change was not just a whim of the Emperor; his intention was to monopolize the Games to his own advantage. He therefore decided to wipe out the memory of all the 'hieronics' of the past—and their statues (many of them works of a high order) were cast down, dragged away and thrown into the latrines, in other words treated like corpses of people executed for lese-majesty. And these victors had in fact been found guilty of that—for having usurped a glory of which Nero alone was worthy!

The Emperor was so convinced that he was giving his power the merit which would make it more stable that, when Helius—the freedman in charge at Rome during Nero's absence—warned him to return as soon as possible, his reply was: 'Whatever your advice and desire for me to hasten back, you ought to be encouraging me and hoping to see me return worthy of Nero.' The Emperor's great mistake was not so much in disregarding Helius's warnings—agents in the provinces had noticed signs of unrest, soon to break into the open revolt led by Vindex—as in imagining that he would be able to restore order and crush his enemies through the prestige obtained by victories at the Games.

Since the time of Marius, the generals returning victorious from foreign campaigns had always held political power in Rome. As Nero believed his artistic triumphs were superior to military successes, it was reasonable on his part to think they made him as powerful as Caesar or Augustus. His behaviour and actions in the last months of 67 were therefore inspired by those of the *imperatores* of the Republic: by granting Greece her 'liberty' at the Isthmian Games, Nero was repeating Falmininus's gesture in 196 B.C. of proclaiming the Greek states free.

Nero's return to Italy was like the homecoming of a Greek victor at the Games and of a successful Roman general. He entered Naples through a breach in the walls, in a chariot drawn by white horses—an equipage that Camillus was believed to have been the first to employ, and which assimilated the rider to the Sun-god. The same ceremonious entry took place at Antium, Nero's birthplace, and also at Alba Longa, the traditional capital of the Latins. But Nero entered Rome in the chariot used by Augustus for his triumph, clad in purple and a *chlamus* (the Greek military cloak) embroidered with golden stars; on his head was the Olympic crown, and in his right hand was the Pythic; he was preceded by a *cortège* carrying written announcements that told of his other victories and where and over whom he had triumphed, and the subject of his songs and acting; and behind his chariot came an applauding procession of people shouting that they were the *Augustani* and the soldiers of his triumph.

Nero's chariot passed through an opening specially made in an arcade of the Circus Maximus, crossed the Forum, and so arrived at the temple of Apollo on the Palatine. All along the way there were sacrificial victims, saffron strewn on the ground, flocks of birds being released. Nero placed his sacred crowns in his bedrooms, above the beds; and similarly disposed the statues of him in the dress of a zither-player. He also had coins struck showing him in like guise.

There were clearly three ideas behind this strange ceremony, the first to copy a classical triumph, but for victories at the Games instead of for military successes. This was the reason for the parading of the victor's 'spoils', for his appearance dressed and crowned like an *imperator*, and for the 'army' of *Augustani*. The route taken was a variant of the traditional one, which followed the Sacred Way; the procession ended at the temple of Apollo, instead of at the Capitol. But some of Jupiter's prerogatives had already been transferred by

Augustus to the Actium god. The second characteristic was the imitation of Augustus himself, by the use of his chariot and by dedicating the 'trophies' to his protector. This could be taken to mean that Nero was still something of a traditionalist. Each of his predecessors, except Caligula, had tried to follow in the path of Augustus; and when Seneca and Burrhus had controlled the young Nero they had guided him in that direction. One would have expected Nero to have cast this model aside with the rest of the principles of his education. But it is highly probable that in 67 he regarded Augustus more as an imperfect predecessor whose actions he repeated in order to improve on them.

History was then considered by Roman philosophers, partly influenced by Messianism, as a gradual development towards another 'Golden Age', which would be brought about by some predestined hero. Virgil had represented Augustus as that saviour of mankind for whom the way had been prepared by Aeneas, Romulus and the heroes of the Republic. Nero's followers adapted the theme to his advantage, as the passage already quoted from the prelude to the *Pharsalia* has shown; Augustus became merely the last of the precursors, the founder of the Empire of Strength which his great-grandson was converting into a reign of beauty. Apollo, who had protected the victor at Actium in his capacity as a warrior, now returned to his true role of god of the arts to crown the artist-sovereign. Augustus had closed the doors of Janus on three occasions, and each time war had broken out again, so that they had to be reopened. Nero had them closed before leaving for Greece, convinced they would remain shut this time. It would soon be possible to disband the legions; and, with men of the sword no longer needed, their honours would go to artists. The zither-player Menecrates and the gladiator Speculus had already been given the houses and possessions of victorious generals.

The whole world was going to obey the new Apollo; indeed, the third idea behind the 'triumph' was the control of nature. Instead of a general's *paludamentum*, Nero had worn the star-spangled cloak symbolizing the heavens, like the awning for the homage of Tiridates and the revolving dome in the Golden House. The animal world would help the ruler of the world without any bidding: a ship with some of the imperial jewels on board had sunk on the way back from Greece, and Nero told his friends quite seriously that the fishes would return them to him. A large expeditionary force would still be needed to subdue the East—though it would be more like a military parade than a war; and training was begun to revive the phalanx formation of Alexander's armies.

These dreams were brutally shattered by news of the revolt in Gaul. But so single-minded was Nero's madness that he considered he could put down the insurrection with intellectual weapons. He said he would present himself unarmed before the rebellious troops, and just weep; his sadness would cause them to repent, and the following day he would sing a hymn of victory—which he was about to compose. In place of artillery he had carts made to carry the organs whose music would accompany his singing. For a bodyguard he wanted to take his concubines dressed as Amazons; and a start was made by cutting their hair and issuing them with crescent-shaped bucklers and double-edged axes, as used by that fabulous race of women warriors.

Such inconsequence was obviously pathological; Nero was so convinced of holding magical powers strong enough to change the natural order to suit his dream-world that he was incapable of taking action in the real world into which he had been suddenly plunged. It was beyond him to grasp any of the opportunities afforded by division among his enemies, by Vindex's defeat at the hands of the German legions, or by the support he still had among the people of Rome and from his procurators in the provinces. This apathy shows the depth and gravity of his mental illness and the delusions to which he was subject.

Chapter Six

THE FALL AND RESURRECTION
OF NERONISM

⤜⤜ I ⤛⤛

SETTING THE PROBLEM

NERO's course of conduct during the last years of his reign has appeared so scandalous and infamous, and absurd too, that one is almost bound to conclude there was madness behind it—a madness which had been coming on for a long time, due to heredity, physical defects, his early upbringing and the influence of his social environment. But if so, a new and more difficult problem presents itself. The case of a mad sovereign is not unknown; Rome had suffered one twenty years earlier, in the person of Caligula. But Caligula had soon been got rid of, and nobody had regretted him; whereas less than three months after Nero's death a revolutionary movement, supported by a large proportion of the public, both in Rome and the provinces, successively brought to power two emperors who each based his policy on Nero's and officially honoured Nero's memory. This resurrection of Neronism was admittedly short-lived; nevertheless, not until thirty years after his death was Nero first denounced as the worst kind of criminal tyrant, a charge repeated throughout history.

It is not unknown for a people to be drawn into the lunatic policy of its leader, and for some of his misguided followers to remain obstinately faithful to him after his downfall and death. If such was the case in the present instance, it must at least be admitted that, in spite of all that was detestable in Neronism, there was something positive about it, something capable of arousing enthusiasm. In any case, before pronouncing judgment, a close scrutiny should be made of historical tradition concerning the events of 68–9.

All the data about Nero given by second-century historians must be treated with caution; particularly the details concerning his downfall. Tacitus and Suetonius both wrote about the revolution which brought to an end the Julio-Claudian dynasty while it was still present in men's minds; some of those deeply involved in it still held highly responsible positions. Modern scholars are agreed that one of the writers was an influential politician and the other a high official in the civil service, and that both were chiefly concerned to influence their contemporaries. Their accounts cannot therefore be accepted as impartial.

It is precisely the most gifted and intelligent of the two, Tacitus, whose account is most biased. His hostility to Nero is evident in the *Histories*, written between 106 and 109, even though the account begins with Galba and Otho. But while he presents the facts from his own point of view, none is suppressed; and he gives a fair account of the posthumous popularity of the Emperor he obviously detested. The *Annales*, on the other hand, remain silent on everything that might disprove the author's thesis. Even from a literary point of view, Books XV and XVI (dealing with Nero) seem inferior to the earlier parts; the detached view in face of awful events, which makes the early books so moving, gives way to a wearisome declamation; the psychology is less penetrating, the good are too heroic and the bad too abnormal. This deterioration may have been due to the author's age, although he was little more than sixty-five at the time. Ronald Syme, in his biography of Tacitus, has probably revealed the true reason—Tacitus was conservative, and feared a revival of some aspects of Neronism in the policy of Hadrian. The summary execution of the four consulars who conspired against the new Emperor was some justification for Tacitus's anxiety. The final part of the *Annales* is a dramatic warning, the anguished cry of an old man who saw threats to the political ideal to which he had dedicated his life.

It is known through the works of Josephus that some historians defended Nero. Suetonius provides a few instances of their work, but combined with that of their opponents. He makes no secret, moreover, of his personal sympathy with Otho, under whom his father had served as a centurion.

⇛ II ⇚

THE DIVISIONS AMONG THE OPPOSITION TO NERO

The works of the times thus give a distorted picture of the political situation in the spring of 68, when Nero had just returned from Greece and his enemies were plotting his downfall. Tacitus's account—of

which the parts covering the last eight months of the reign are lost—
was concerned only with justifying the conspirators and the end of
Nero. He deliberately omitted the events—even the most important—
which might be interpreted in the Emperor's favour. The homage of
Tiridates was dismissed in a few lines; whereas the trials, sentences and
exemplary deaths of Nero's enemies were described with a wealth of
touching detail, intermingled with accounts of natural disasters. While
adopting such a partial attitude, Tacitus's only scruple was the literary
one of not wishing to weary the public with a monotonous series of
deaths. But in spite of his somewhat hypocritical excuses for arousing
such distaste, it was done intentionally so that the reader should feel
too satiated to query the rightfulness of the revolt, and should think
only of blaming its leaders for submitting with 'servile patience' for
so long. In fact, the situation was not nearly so clear-cut.

Right to the end Nero was supported by senators and others who
were later considered to be the most respectable members of their class.
Piso's plot was suppressed by the praetor Cocceius Nerva, aided by
Tigellinus, with an energy that earned him a rare honour—a statue on
the Palatine; and thirty years later this senator was unanimously chosen
to succeed Domitian and inaugurated the régime which, according to
Tacitus, would reconcile the principate with liberty. When Vindex and
his makeshift forces were wiped out under the walls of Besançon, the
commander of the victorious army was Verginius Rufus; he subsequently refused supreme power on several occasions, and ended his
long career laden with honours and sharing the consulate with Trajan.

As for the opposition to Nero, a major cause of its weakness was the
diverse elements. Among them were doctrinaire republicans whose
intransigence resulted from their philosophic creed. The lax Stoicism
of Seneca did not suit everybody; there was a move to revive the
austerity and uncompromising purity of the sect, led by Musonius
Rufus and later by Epictetus. These puritans appear as the very opposite of Nero, and indeed Tacitus emphasized the contrast in the touching chapters he devoted to the trials of Thrasea and Barea Soranus.
Their deaths were presented as the supreme crime of the demon
tyrant; they were not just political victims of a cruel régime, but the
incarnation of virtue crushed by vice personified. . . . Tacitus's account
of the last moments of Thrasea was obviously inspired by the *Phedon*,
a pagan hagiography that surely influenced the writing of the lives of
Christian martyrs.

But the hatred between Nero and those uncompromising Stoic philosophers was all the more intense because their opposing attitudes were both derived from reaction to the ambiguities of the Augustan society. Nero intended to bring harmony to the world by giving aesthetics the place held by morality. Thrasea and his supporters would have sacrificed politics for ethics. More by defiance than tradition, they proclaimed themselves republicans; but restoration of government by the Senate, which had disgraced itself by covering up the exploitation of the provincial populations, was scarcely less fanciful than the 'reign of Beauty' that was the dream of Nero. In fact Thrasea does not appear to have had a political programme. The philosophers of the Porch were unable to supply him with one to his satisfaction. For lack of anything better Thrasea seems to have turned to the Cynics; their anarchic view was that the family, the city and political life in its entirety were all equally illusions. Demetrius, who was Thrasea's 'confessor' in his last moments, belonged to that school. But such self-sufficiency, such rejection of all social relationships, was even more contrary to the traditional Roman morality than the Neronian humanism. This was fully realized by Cossutianus and Marcellus, the men who accused Thrasea of failing in his civic duties.

To what extent was this accusation just? According to Tacitus, the virtuous senator had merely absented himself when a motion of approval after the murder of Agrippina was being voted; had defended the praetor Antistius, who had written a satirical poem directed against the Emperor, and managed to save him from the death sentence; and, finally, had refused to be associated with the apotheosis of Poppaea. In point of fact, Thrasea had been leading a sort of political strike since 63, directed against the régime as well as the Emperor. Thrasea's son-in-law, Helvidius Priscus, whom Nero only exiled, later continued the same opposition policy against Vespasian, but with more violence; and Vespasian, although wishing to avoid conflict with the Senate, found it necessary to have him put to death. The 'republican' sympathies of Stoics and Cynics again found expression against Domitian, and he banished all 'philosophers' from Italy. These theorists were considered by the 'liberals' of Trajan's time—according to Tacitus and Pliny—as being instrumental to the rebellion of 96.

It is quite true that in the second century the principate was based upon an ideology different from that of the previous century, and owing much to the Stoic philosophy. Instead of the Emperor's authority reposing on an irrational divine right, it was justified by the virtuous example he set his subjects. Trajan even let his régime be presented for a time as a restoration of the Republic; but the concessions he granted were pure form, and in no way diminished the imperial omnipotence. Much goodwill was needed by theorists for them to be taken in by the theme of 'the best of the republics'. The man chiefly responsible was the Greek sophist, Dio Chrysostom (*Chrusostomos*, the golden-mouthed—a sufficient indication of his eloquent ways). While pretending to be influenced by the Cynics and proclaiming his deep respect for Diogenes, he brought the Stoic doctrine of a righteous monarchy back into favour—the very doctrine that Thrasea had opposed. This *volte-face* would probably have been less acceptable had it not corresponded with a social evolution that eased the task of the emperors; the old aristocracy with republican traditions had been superseded at the head of affairs by an upper middle class whose interests corresponded with those of the régime. More or less unwittingly, all the intellectuals—Tacitus and Pliny in Latin, Plutarch in Greek—supported this questionable presentation of political events; all that was necessary was to make scapegoats of the emperors of the first century and to exaggerate the part played by the opposition. It was cleverly done, and for a long time was accepted without question by posterity.

There were other elements, less radical than Thrasea and his group, who by the year 68 were partisans of a solution midway between a republic and the Neronian principate. They consisted of three distinct groups—Galba and his supporters in the Senate, the army leaders and the provincials who were preparing the insurrection led by Vindex.

Servius Sulpicius Galba was born in 3 B.C., grew up during the reign of Augustus and had his first official position under Tiberius. He was one of the last of that generation of the nobility who had faithfully backed up Augustus and supported his principles; as an able general and a strict administrator he had a brilliant career, notably in southern Gaul and Germany, and became finally proconsul in Africa. He was living in retirement when, in 60, Nero appointed him governor of Hispania Tarraconensis. This post would normally have gone to a younger senator, less charged with honours; but there was widespread discontent in the province, due to heavy taxation and an uprising of the mountain tribes in the north-west. Galba was a specialist in dealing with such matters. Moreover Nero was pleased to have a legitimate pretext for sending a possible leader of the opposition far from Rome. For a man of Galba's mettle and background the solution to the political crisis was quite simple—all that was needed was a return to the principles laid down by Augustus. All the emperors had of course based their *auctoritas* on a kind of divine right due to descent from the founder of the dynasty, and Galba had no blood of the Caesars in his veins. He did, however, belong to a noble and ancient family, the Sulpicii. His great-grandfather, Q. Catulus Capitolinus, had been a prominent politician in the time of Cicero and Caesar. There was no law of devolution keeping the Empire in the hands of a dynasty; it was enough for the prince to belong to the nobility and to justify his accession by his talents and service to the country. According to Tacitus, when Galba thought of deciding upon his eventual successor, he wanted it to be a rule for the reigning sovereign to appoint his heir, thus permitting the most worthy candidate to be designated. But the speech attributed to him by Tacitus was actually an outline of the ideas prevailing in the Senate under Trajan. Galba's political creed, such as can be discovered from literary sources and symbols on coins, was inspired by theories having much in common with Cicero's *De Republica*; but in practice he followed the examples set by Tiberius. While the outcome of his struggle to hold power was uncertain he contented himself with the title of 'Legate of the Senate and the Roman People', which could be taken as republican. But before long he gave himself the names of Caesar and Augustus, honoured the first Emperor's memory in every way, and governed with a privy council consisting of his close friends, senators and freedmen.

This 'Augustan' party found little support outside Rome, and even in the capital it came almost entirely from men of the older generation. There were newer and more active movements in the provinces and among the armies. The great revelation of the upheavals in 68, said Tacitus, was that emperors could be made elsewhere than in Rome. His surprise is, to us, unexpected; for during the civil wars armies and provincial governments had been the means by which generals had seized power. But the vanity of the Romans prevented their accepting the fact that their future could be determined by descendants of people they had conquered. Nero suffered from this illusion like the rest; he decimated the Roman nobility but turned too late on the army faction, and he thought he was reducing his enemies by sending them to govern provinces—where they found the military support they needed to bring him down.

Yet Nero's confidence in the discipline of the legions and in the personal bond, of a religious character, that united the troops with the *Imperator* was not altogether unjustified. Their generals, who all belonged to the senatorial order, were certainly not completely loyal, but they had doubts as to whether the troops would follow them against the Emperor. There was the example of Corbulo, who had a more brilliant record than most generals; during the reign of Claudius he had pacified Lower Germany, and since 57 he had been in command of the Armenian campaign. A fundamental difference of opinion soon opposed this 'Field Marshal', who believed in the traditional imperialism founded on conquest and annexations, to Nero and his policy of diplomacy based upon economic and cultural prestige. Events in 62 seemed to prove Corbulo to be right; Paetus, whom Nero had sent to maintain the Roman nominee Tigranes on the Armenian throne, suffered an overwhelming defeat. Corbulo succeeded in restoring the situation. But then Nero obliged him to adopt a compromise and accept the Parthian Tiridates as King of Armenia on condition that he went to Rome to receive the crown from Nero. Corbulo was furious, and sent his son-in-law Vinicius to contact the opposition party in the Senate. The plot was discovered, and the victorious general was summoned to Greece by the Emperor and ordered to commit suicide. Now the legions in Asia Minor made no demonstration at the news of his death, nor did the troops on other fronts. Neither the army in Britain, which had just quelled the revolt led by Boudicca, nor the legions on the Danube commanded by Plautius, responded to Vindex's call to revolt; and the legions in Lower Germany crushed his insurrection.

Nero had given command of the army in Palestine to Vespasian. When the latter became Emperor he tried very hard to prove that he had always been a 'resistant', but could only bring up two rather inglorious incidents. He had fallen asleep at the theatre while Nero was singing (but so little notice had been taken that nobody was quite sure where it had occurred), and a member of the imperial secretariat whom Vespasian asked to use his influence to obtain a post for him had told him to go and hang himself. Such slight incidents could equally well be interpreted as showing that the wily general, whose brother was prefect of Rome, had done everything to keep in Nero's good books, and that his appointment to army commander was the result of long intrigues.

The loyalty of the armies contrasted with the ferment in some of the provinces, and these were not all in the West. While Greece and Egypt applauded Nero's daring conduct, Asia—which included western Anatolia—made no secret of sympathy for his opponents. Nero had blundered when, in 60, he had banished Rubellius Plautus (who was a descendant of Augustus and a likely pretender) to those parts. The exile had become the centre of intrigues which were openly backed by the proconsul Barea Soranus, one of the leading Stoics; and the movement was joined by members of wealthy and important local families, such as the Bithynian Cassius Asclepiodotus, and by leading citizens of the chief towns, notably Ephesus and Pergamum. It was in this manner that the provincial aristocracy and the Roman nobility combined to form the cosmopolitan class which governed the Empire in the second century. But that time most of the high officials came from Asia, while Greece and Egypt had lost much of their influence.

The legate commanding the legion in Africa, Clodius Macer, was one of the first to support the revolt in 68. He quickly obtained control of the whole of the proconsulate (Tunisia, Tripolitania and eastern Algeria), and was able to prevent the shipment of wheat to Rome. Coins struck by Macer show that he was in favour of a republic, either from conviction or, what was more probable, through opposition to Galba, whom he refused to recognize. But he does not appear to have had much support locally; in fact, according to Plutarch, it was fear of being punished for his cruelty and dishonesty as legate that caused him to revolt. His unpopularity in the province is confirmed by the ease with which he was put to death by the procurator of Carthage, acting under Galba's orders. The population only showed some enthusiasm for events when rallying to the cause of Otho, at the appeal of a freedman of Nero. Everything seems to show that Nero had retained much popularity in North Africa, in spite of having greatly increased the contribution that had to be made to Rome's food supplies. But the mass of people had not been affected, for Nero had confiscated the chief *latifundia*, the large agricultural estates, and diverted to public stocks the farm-rents in kind that had been paid to the late owners; so the peasants had lost nothing by the change, and were in fact given more favourable conditions which were later embodied in the *lex Manciana*.

The seat of the revolt was in Spain and southern Gaul. It was a high-born Gaul, Vindex, who first raised the standard of liberty, demanding equality for his fellow countrymen with their Roman conquerors, if not independence. Nero was not altogether wrong in accusing Vindex and his compatriots of the deepest ingratitude. Peace and prosperity had never been so great in the provinces between the Pyrenees and the Rhine. Admittedly the increases in taxation following the great fire of Rome had been resented, but they did not seriously harm the economic development of the region. New industries were being set up in the north-east; Narbonne was a growing port, and cultivation of the vine— which paid well—had extended from the Rhône valley across to Bordeaux. In the political field Nero had placed restrictions on the liberal policy of Claudius which had made it possible for Gauls to enter the Senate. This was proved by the career of Vindex himself; when he had become a senator Nero made him governor of the people his ancestors had ruled over! His idea appears to have been to create a kind of federal empire, with the western provinces sharing the leadership with Italy. One of his coins symbolizing the 'concord of Gaul and Spain' shows the busts of the two nations on a globe and crowned by Victory. Unfortunately it was concord that was most lacking among the Gauls, even then; hostility to Nero had not eliminated old tribal rivalries. The capital of the three provinces, Lyons (Lugdunum), was ardently pro-Nero. In the year 66, when Vindex was planning the revolt, Mainz celebrated Tiridates' homage to Nero by erecting a triumphal column decorated with images of the protective gods of the Empire. German and Belgian tribes supported the legions in their area to put down Vindex. But two years later the Gauls refused to aid the Batavian Civilis in his attempt to establish a so-called *Imperium Galliarum*. In all this the Celts lost their chance of taking part in governing the world; for the next two hundred years their representatives were systematically excluded from high office—to which the way had been opened for them by emperors who were poorly rewarded for so doing.

Nero's imprudence over Gaul may be excusable, but he acted with sheer folly in his dealings with Spain. It should have been obvious that his proscription of Seneca's clan, the Annaei, would rouse the clients of this wealthy family in its homeland. Seneca's relatives were able to make almost feudal demands upon their Spanish dependants— a matter upon which Robert Étienne has recently thrown a new light.

And Nero was loading the scales against himself by sending Galba and Otho to govern those distant provinces, rich and militarily strong, because he feared their presence in Rome.

The revolt against Nero in the provinces—in some provinces—was not due, then, to tyranny on his part but was a result of placing too much confidence in his representatives; and that happened because he was so naïve, a characteristic often remarked upon in these pages and one which distinguishes him from the usual type of tyrant. He was so wrapped up in his dream-world, not realizing that others could not share it, that he failed to take the most elementary precautions against disgruntled or turbulent factions.

⫸ III ⫷

AMBIGUITIES OF THE COUNTER-REVOLUTION

This state of mind is revealing and explains much about a cause of Nero's downfall that the ancient historians kept in the dark—many of the most active participants came from his own inner circle, from the 'Society' he had founded to help him carry out his grand design. Our source for this, Suetonius, fortunately had personal reasons for being particularly interested in the chief of these discontented supporters who became opponents. By drawing a portrait of Salvius Otho, Suetonius supplied a key to the Neronian problem.

Otho belonged to an Etruscan family whose fortune had been made through Livia. His father was a close friend of Tiberius and a strict believer in the discipline recommended by Augustus. Young Otho therefore had a harsh upbringing, and reacted against it with a wildness that attracted Nero into his company. The young prince, who was five years junior to Otho, was delighted to join his band of youngsters of good family who roamed about the city at night; one of their favourite pranks was to throw a cloak over a drunk or a cripple in a deserted street and carry him off. Otho already had a mistress, a freedwoman who was rather ancient but very wealthy and influential in court circles. When Nero became Emperor his closest friend and confident was Otho, who helped him against his tutors and his mother. The Senate treated Otho with respect, because of his influence; he became an advocate and made a speciality of pleading—and winning—the most hopeless cases, for fantastically high fees. He aided Nero in planning the murder of Agrippina, and on the day of the crime invited the Emperor and his mother to dinner, offering succulent dishes that must have dispelled any suspicions in the victim's mind.

Like all the gilded youth of the time, Otho took great care of his appearance. But he had the misfortune to be short, knock-kneed and flat-footed; however, he shaved himself very close, rubbing his face with bread soaked in water—a novel means of softening the beard, shaving-soap being unknown. It was even said that he plucked the hairs from his arms and body as women did. And because the hair on his head was thin he wore a wig, so well made as to be unnoticeable. These personal attentions naturally set tongues wagging as to the nature of his intimacy with the Emperor.

A day arrived when Otho was asked to perform a service of a truly personal nature for the Emperor. Poppaea Sabina had been Nero's mistress for some time, and he was still afraid to divorce Octavia, for she was very popular. But Poppaea's husband, an ex-Praetorian prefect, refused to turn a blind eye on his misfortune; divorce was pending, and as her liaison with the Emperor could not be made public, someone was needed to deputize for Nero and marry the girl. And who better for this delicate task than the Emperor's best friend?

It is not known for certain whether Otho knew Poppaea before marrying her; but in any case a few days of close contact with this ravishing young woman of twenty-two were enough for him to fall passionately in love with her. He cast all ambition and prudence aside. When Caesar's envoys arrived to claim his mistress they found all doors closed. The Emperor, as one can guess, could hardly believe his ears when his messengers returned; boiling with rage, he hastened to the Salvii house. But it was a waste of time; he was left out in the street, and passers-by could hear the ruler of the world alternately entreating his friend to return the precious object entrusted to him and threatening him with the most dire consequences. What had Poppaea to say of all this? As she was not the kind of woman to let herself be held by force, one can assume she enjoyed it all. The news soon spread, and there were many popular ditties about Otho having the nerve to become his own wife's lover!

Nero must certainly have felt like dispatching some of his guard to seize Poppaea and to show Otho the cost of making Caesar look ridiculous. But—as already indicated—the Emperor greatly feared public opinion. In the event he acted like the head of a modern government who rids himself of some obstructive official by appointing him ambassador to a distant country. Otho was sent to govern Lusitania. It was rapid promotion, for at twenty-six he was only a quaestor, and would normally have had to serve in two higher positions before being eligible to govern a province. But Lusitania—corresponding very nearly to modern Portugal—was the most distant of the provinces in the West. And Nero had quite decided to leave his rival there indefinitely, instead of limiting his appointment to the usual two, or at the most three, years.

Such was the version of the affair given by Suetonius. Tacitus followed it at first, but then favoured another which showed the three concerned in a worse light. According to Tacitus, Poppaea married Otho through ambition; and he, to increase his hold over the Emperor, pushed the latter into the arms of his wife and only rebelled when he found himself being eliminated. But in that case it is difficult to see why he did not agree to a divorce, which would have been quite normal and enabled him to obtain payment for being so obliging. However, neither of the two versions is free of improbabilities.

Suetonius at least gave the better explanation for the surprising moral change in Otho, who appears to have had a real love for Poppaea. It was the shock of losing her that probably led to his reformed character. The dissolute young man became an excellent administrator, scrupulous and thoughtful for the betterment of those he governed. He turned to religion, perhaps to seek consolation for his troubles; to the cult of Isis, who demanded strict discipline of her worshippers and gave them hopes of a better life in the other world.

As the year 65 was drawing to a close the post from Rome brought Otho the news of his beloved's death; and soon afterwards he heard rumours that Nero was responsible for the fatal accident. Perhaps he had already begun plotting against Nero, but in any case his urge for revenge must have been strong for him to have formed an alliance with a man so different from himself as Galba—an alliance brought about with the assistance of leading provincials already hostile to the Emperor.

The causes of Otho's revolt are clear enough; but the uncompromising conservatives supporting it must have found difficulty in accepting a man whose principles were not in line with their own, and whose past history did not exactly inspire confidence. However, the leading Italian and provincial families had no control or influence over the army and administrative services, in spite of their wealth and large numbers of clients. The only way of assuring military support or at least neutrality was through people like Otho, many of them 'Neronians'. There was Calvia Crispinilla (she had been in charge of the palace pleasures), who acted as go-between with Macer; and in particular Nymphidius Sabinus, the Praetorian prefect. He really entered the conspiracy with the intention of betraying his accomplices and seizing power himself; this was ignoring the unwritten law—but which had always held—that only senators could be made emperors.

The insurrectional movement of 68 lost its original motive through these tardy supporters; it was no longer directed against Nero's policy but against Nero himself. This was further emphasized by the leading part that Nymphidius Sabinus played in the actual revolt. The defeat of Vindex had revealed the real weakness of the conservatives; Galba thought of committing suicide; the armies continued in the main to support the Emperor. However, the prefect cunningly played on Nero's naïve and nervous character. It was essential that the Emperor should be prevented from showing himself in public, from rallying his many supporters among the troops in the capital and among the people. Nymphidius could count on active help from the senior officers of the Praetorian Guard and from the freedmen in charge of the imperial administration; his colleague, Tigellinus, assisted him by remaining passive. Nymphidius controlled the postal services, and began to demoralize the Emperor by feeding him with false reports, notably that there had been a general defection among the legions. Nero shut himself up in the palace. Nymphidius then made the bold move of announcing to the Praetorians that the Emperor had fled from Rome. At the news of this abandon, and the suggestion of better times under Galba, the Guard acclaimed the usurper. But all could still be lost, if Nero became aware of the deceit and treachery going on around him. He had to be persuaded to leave Rome, yet prevented from taking refuge on a ship and so reaching an army still loyal to him. Phaon and Epaphrodites, who had remained with Nero in the deserted palace, got him to flee to a villa in the northern outskirts of Rome; and there, completing his mad despair by telling him that the Senate had condemned him, they compelled him by moral—and perhaps physical—pressure to commit suicide by thrusting a dagger into his throat.

Nero's death, then, was brought about by a devilish plot and trickery; public support for the deed was not stirred up by the conservatives until after the event, and then without success. In fact there was soon evidence of opposing movements: Nero's tomb was covered with flowers; images of him and the texts of his edicts were placed at night on the Rostra. These indications led Nymphidius to change his coat again; he pretended to have been deceived himself, and proposed taking power to continue Nero's work. But the move was too clumsy to convince anyone; Tigellinus dissociated himself from it, and the Praetorians abandoned the leader who had betrayed their confidence. Galba then marched on Rome and was proclaimed Emperor.

Tacitus summed up Galba in a cutting phrase that defies translation: 'Ipsi medium ingenium, magis extra vitia quam cum virtutibus' (*Histories*, I. 9). The general sense is—he had an average intelligence, free of vice rather than endowed with virtue. Galba's success was in fact due more to his insignificance than his talent. A moderate conservative, he was acceptable to reactionaries and reformers alike. Both parties were hoping that the childless old man would reign for only a short transitional period, after which each expected to regain power.

The state of the two parties was given in some detail by Tacitus in the opening chapters of his *Histories*. The conservatives consisted of most of the senators, the more influential members of the equestrian order and 'the sound elements among the people, those attached to the great houses, clients and freedmen of the condemned and the banished [by Nero]'. Opposed to them were 'the base people, regulars at the circus and theatre, with the worst kind of slaves, and those who had squandered their fortune and lived on the infamies of Nero'. These expressions—similar to those used by Sallust to describe Catiline's accomplices—confirm that the Neronians came from the old rebellious classes which for more than a century had obstinately remained outside the Roman social order. Tacitus also made several references to the *aula Neronis*, which has here been called the 'Neronian Society', containing men of all classes united in the desire to bring about a new order. There had been many divisions in its ranks after the events of 66; but now opposition to the conservatives was drawing them together again.

Tacitus gave a revealing account, too, of the reactions and feelings among the troops. The formations stationed in Rome, which included the cohorts of the Praetorian Guard, the First Adjutrix legion and units raised for the war in the Caucasus, were still deeply loyal to Nero's memory, indignant over the part they had been made to play and suspicious of their officers who had deceived them. This under-current of insubordination naturally drew the troops towards the lower classes, creating a dangerous solidarity that could lead to social revolution. On the frontiers of the Empire the legions along the Rhine were Neronians at heart too. The attitude of the commander in Upper Germany, Verginius Rufus, was still ambiguous; his colleague in Lower Germany, Fonteius Capito, refused to acknowledge Galba and was killed by the legates of the legions under his command. The troops in Illyria had let Verginius Rufus know that he could count on them. The other generals—including Mucian and Vespasian in the East—were playing a waiting game, but had taken the oath to Galba.

The new Emperor was trying hard to maintain his delicate balance of power. One of his three chief counsellors, the senator Vinicius, was in contact with the Neronian party through Otho; the other two, Laco the Praetorian prefect and the freedman Icelus, were connected with the conservatives. But Galba proved incapable of subtlety. He made the troops in Rome more embittered by taking harsh reprisals against the supporters of Nymphidius, by attempting to disband the First Adjutrix legion and having it decimated. He recalled Verginius, but did not appoint a successor to the command straight away; his choice ultimately fell upon a consul with Neronian sympathies, Vitellius. Towns along the Rhine suspected of regretting the late régime were heavily fined, while supporters of Vindex were given political and fiscal advantages—just the way to drive civilian and military leaders into a common hostility. At the same time the members of the *aula Neronis* came under attack from a commission of inquiry set up to recover the donations that they had received.

All these measures tended to make a fresh revolt inevitable. The first move was taken by the legions of Lower Germany early in January 69, when they withdrew their allegiance to Galba and called upon the Senate and the Roman people to choose another Emperor. So now it was Vitellius, who had certainly initiated the movement, who was conjuring up the ghost of the Republic against Galba!

It was high time for the Emperor to put an end to half-measures and manœuvres. The decisive act was the designation of a successor, or rather the naming of a co-regent. The choice of Vitellius or Verginius Rufus would have probably appeased the Rhine legions; some years later, in 97, Nerva escaped from a similar difficulty by taking Trajan as an associate, under pressure from the legions in Germany. But there was still too much hatred and bad feeling over Verginius's crushing of the Vindex revolt for him to be a suitable choice. Vinicius was in favour of Otho, who would have satisfied the Neronian party in Rome at least. In the end, on the insistence of Laco and Icelus, the Emperor chose a conservative by adopting Piso Licinianus; he was descended from Pompey and from Crassus, and was one of the last representatives of the republican patricians. His beliefs and character were in keeping with his origins and background. One of his brothers had been put to death by Claudius and the other by Nero; he himself had just returned from exile. By this choice Galba was more or less proclaiming his future policy—the Empire was to be the common property of the nobility, managed by the most worthy of its members. This extremist solution only angered the masses, and the crisis which had been simmering since Nero's death finally broke.

⫸⫸⫸ IV ⫷⫷⫷

OTHO AND VITELLIUS: NERONISM WITHOUT NERO

Tacitus and Suetonius are agreed that Otho's seizure of power was a military *coup d'état* of no significance. He was believed to have acted entirely through motives of self-interest—by financial difficulties and fear of being murdered by Piso if he did not take the initiative.

Galba's downfall was in fact the logical outcome of the misunder-standings and treacheries of the revolt in the previous year. The con-servatives had used the Neronians to bring down Nero, but the great majority of the military and civilian leaders refused to accept a reaction-ary régime. Rome had probably never been so near to a popular revolu-tion; the proletariat—Tacitus's 'base people'—and the angry soldiers were ready to wipe out the upper classes. This is clearly shown by an incident which took place a short time after Galba's death. Otho had ordered arms to be issued to one of the newly recruited cohorts from the store of the Praetorian Guard. The tribune responsible thought it best to keep the matter secret and make the distribution at night. But the Praetorians, already highly suspicious of their officers, got wind of the affair and thought some senators' slaves were being armed in order to get rid of Otho. The Praetorians mutinied, massacred their officers and rushed off to the palace, calling for the Emperor and threatening death to the whole Senate. Otho happened to be entertaining a number of senators and their wives to dinner, and his guests had an unpleasant minute or two, thinking they had fallen into a trap. Tacitus gave a vivid account of the scene, which Racine drew upon for his description of the death of Britannicus. Otho's coolness saved the situation. The guards received a bribe, though the two mainly responsible for the uprising were executed.

In overthrowing Nero the conservatives had let loose the destructive potential of the crowds that he had enthralled. The senators were aware of being powerless in the face of this danger, which explains why they did nothing to save Galba or oppose Otho. The latter had no illusions about the reasons for his success; the people and the troops saw him as Nero's friend, the man most likely to bring about the transformation of the world which had been interrupted by the revolt in 68. They even acclaimed him by the name of Nero, which he did not refuse and may even have used for some official acts.

The memory of the June victim began to be honoured; his statues were set up again, and his officials dismissed by Galba were reinstated. This was somewhat embarrassing for Otho, who found himself obliged to continue the policy of the man he had helped to overthrow. That was probably why, apart from a desire to treat the Senate with caution, he did not ask that assembly to repeal the condemnation of Nero, though he had Poppaea's annulled. The most significant action he took was to have work begun again on the Golden House, to which he apportioned a credit of fifty million *sesterces*. This hasty decision, taken at a time when civil war and social revolution were threatening, would have been sheer folly if the palace were no more than a luxury. Even Otho's enemies admitted that he had sound sense, so his decision was proof of the essentially political nature of Nero's great project; the Golden House was more than a symbol of the revolution: it was the first step in changing the order of the world. Far from spurning the poverty of the masses, Otho was showing his desire to fulfil Nero's idealism by ordering a resumption of the work.

Otho's reign was so short that it is impossible to discern the lines he would have followed, but at least it is evident that he had no more intention than Nero of blindly unleashing revolutionary forces. He protected the senators on the night of the mutiny. The speech ascribed to him by Tacitus on that occasion contained the writer's own ideas; but the execution of the leaders of the mutineers is sufficiently significant.

There was, too, the reorganization of the 'Neronian Society', whose part in the revolution was similar—*mutatis mutandis*—to that of totalitarian parties in modern times. The main cause of the crisis in 68 had been dissension within this group. Otho tried to restore unity by eliminating those members whose treachery had been most evident. Galba had protected Tigellinus, who had a reciprocal arrangement with Vinicius for their personal safety—an arrangement customary in times of revolution between leaders on opposite sides. According to Tacitus, the people demanded the death of Tigellinus, who was the only one remaining of the men immediately responsible for Nero's death, and Otho was obliged to give way to this demand—which was stirred up by Neronian extremists who considered Otho too moderate.

Whether this 'militant wing' contributed to the success of Vitellius, who had played no part in Nero's downfall, is a matter that remains complex and obscure. Vitellius was proclaimed Emperor at the beginning of January 69—against Galba, and just before Otho seized power —by the legions in Germany and the towns of north-east Gaul, all pro-Nero and incensed against the late supporters of Vindex.

'The legions who had been thrown against Vindex, and were aware of their might and that of Gaul, were eager for further combats, another civil war; they no longer considered them [the Gauls of central France] as allies, but as defeated enemies. They could rely on the Rhineland towns, which held the same views and were at that time the most wrathful with the Galbians—the name given by the legions through hatred of Vindex' (*Histories*, 1. 51).

Tacitus also stated that Lyons was still wholly for the Neronians ('infensa Lugdunensis colonia et pertinaci pro Nerone fide'); while the main Galbian towns were those of the Aedui, the Helvetii and the Sequani (in present-day Burgundy and the Franche-Comté) and Vienne.

So that while the tendency of Neronism in Rome was towards a popular revolution, in Gaul it was becoming a kind of Belgica-Rhineland nationalist movement. Tacitus noted that the Galbian towns were the richest; and, it may be presumed, the places where the wealth had remained concentrated in the hands of the old Celtic nobility, by then Romanized. In a recent history of Roman Gaul, Jean-Jacques Hatt has shown that in the second century this class was supplanted, partially at least, by an industrial and commercial middle class, well entrenched in the north-east. Economic rivalry and class warfare thus gave rise to 'geopolitical' conflicts; and these went very deep, for they continued until the end of the Middle Ages in the struggle between the Capetian kingdom and the great Burgundian duchy.

So it was not just personal ambition that prevented Otho or Vitellius from withdrawing in favour of the other, although both claimed to represent Nero's party. Otho's position was the more difficult, being the more moderate, and also because of his great part in the conspiracy of 68, which made him suspect to the ultra-Neronians. The noble but strange indifference which marked the last months of his life thus becomes understandable. His suicide, at a time when all was not entirely lost, could hardly have sprung from Stoicism—which was quite foreign to his character. Tacitus and Suetonius are certainly right in seeing it as the consequence of a kind of sentimental pacifism, a tendency to non-violence; Nero, too, had gone through such a phase, which was a logical outcome of his aesthetic ideals. But Otho differed from his predecessor by inclining towards mysticism; and his worship of Isis, with the hope of salvation in another world, probably aided him in making his sacrifice. The basic reason, though, was more likely a realization of his false position; of the fact that he could only have consolidated it by again associating himself with the most determined opponents of his own ideals.

The senators were completely at a loss, and showed a lack of vision that was fairly common among conservatives; they thought at first that they could persuade Vitellius to join them, and their clients—whose fidelity merited better leadership—tried to organize a public manifestation in honour of Galba. This was showing complete misunderstanding of the new Emperor and his supporters. Vitellius, to his credit, soon cleared away any doubts as to his position:

'In order to make quite clear the political aims that he intended to pursue, he assembled all the priests of the different public cults in the Field of Mars, and sacrificed to the shades of Nero; at an official banquet he called on a favourite zither-player to sing one of the "master's" compositions; whereupon he chanted one of Nero's poems, and the delighted Emperor gave the sign for applause' (Suetonius, *Vitellius*, 11).

One of Vitellius's first acts was to revive the 'Neronian Society', of which he had been a keen member. Suetonius accused him of giving actors and charioteers a political role. And Tacitus wrote:

'The nearer he drew to Rome, the more his retinue became tainted by an admixture of actors, bands of eunuchs, and everything which characterized the "Neronian Society" (*aula Neronis*); for Vitellius voiced his admiration for Nero, whom he used to follow round to hear sing, not because—like so many honest men—he had been obliged to, but because he was enslaved by the immorality and indulgence' (*Histories*, II. 61).

Tacitus also wrote of the notorious banquets, made famous by Vitellius's gluttony, and compared them with Dionysiac revelries: 'Pervigilis ac Bacchanalibus quam disciplinae et castris propiora' (*Histories*, II. 68). This was not just for stylistic effect; the Neronian ritual was based on Bacchism, as we know.

But civil war had been a fatal blow to the unity of a party whose internal differences had not been solved even by the founder himself. The extremists thought it time for an agrarian revolution, and obtained the support of Rhineland troops. In the Po valley peasants disguised as soldiers urged on the Germans to plunder the great estates and murder the owners (*Histories*, XVI. 56). But such violence was distasteful to the legionaries, whose officers were drawn from the Italian lower middle classes. At Aosta the regular soldiers supported the landowners against the auxiliaries; at Ticinum two cohorts from Gaul were massacred. The situation was all the more serious for Vitellius because the Italian troops had been loyal to Nero. The Praetorians and the First Adjutrix legion—which had many freedmen in its ranks, so was socially 'advanced'—had not forgiven him for overthrowing Otho; and the fleet, too, which had supported Otho and effected a landing in Provence in the rear of Caecina (the commander of part of Vitellius's forces), was awaiting an opportunity for revenge. Vitellius feared his party would go too far; he decided to disband the Batavian units and send them back home, where they readily joined Civilis in the great revolt against Rome. Then Vitellius turned on the freedmen in charge of the Chancellery, replacing them by knights; and the senators exiled by Nero were allowed to re-establish their authority over their old clients. In the political field the Emperor made a few formal concessions to the Senate, allowing criticism of his proposals and pretending to respect freedom of election; he refused the title of Caesar and only later accepted that of Augustus. He also made himself perpetual consul, but this may have been to restore some lustre to the highest magisterial office of the Republic, or perhaps to give the supreme authority another basis than the tribunician power.

⤜⤜ V ⤛⤛

VESPASIAN AND THE END OF NERONISM

Barely a year had passed since Nero's death. The conservative party had realized how powerless it was, and the most reactionary of the *patres* knew that any attempt to restore the Republic or even an Augustan régime would lead to revolution and the massacre from which Otho had with difficulty saved them; while the Neronians were divided and without a leader, and felt themselves to be dominated by the anarchist elements in their party. The terrible devastation of civil war had again made an appearance, disrupting the Italian economy, which had already been adversely affected by competition from the provinces. The time had come for a reconciliation, under a man independent of all factions and whose neutral position would allow both sides to save face.

Tacitus prided himself (*Histories*, II. 10) on having refuted the historians of the Flavian period, who accounted for Vespasian being proclaimed emperor as a move for peace and the public good. Tacitus, through his hatred of Domitian, could see only ambition as the motive; one therefore looks in vain for any political ideas in the speeches he put into the mouths of Antonius Primus and Mucian, who were waging civil war while Vespasian was taking Jerusalem. This makes it difficult to understand the unusual disinterestedness of the two generals after their successful march on Rome. Modern historians on the whole believe that Primus's ambition was curbed by his consciousness of a somewhat doubtful past, and that the childless Mucian feared Galba's fate; both these theories seem rather weak.

Tacitus gave a glimpse of what might be the truth of the matter: there was a third party—the Flavian. The backbone of this party were the centurions, who hated Vitellius for the execution of their fellow officers loyal to Otho. These junior officers swayed the legions of Dalmatia and Pannonia, and forced the hand of the commanders in those provinces (*Histories*, II. 86); it was they, too, who supported Primus's offensive and made sure that he became Commander-in-Chief, assisted by Arrius Varus, who had been a senior centurion. The other militants in the party were procurators belonging to the equestrian order—notably Cornelius Fuscus, who administered Dalmatia and Pannonia and was the civilian head of the party in the Danube region, and the Prefect of Egypt, Tiberius Alexander, who was the first to take the oath to Vespasian. Tiberius Alexander then organized the religious propaganda, rallying the cults of Isis and Serapis to the cause and giving the sceptical Vespasian all the prestige of a Pharaoh. The procurator of Syria was put in charge of the party's finances; he imposed special taxes and issued moneys from Antioch. For the first time the military and administrative structure created by Augustus was used for political ends. Its officers and officials, who belonged to the lower middle classes, chose as their leader a man whose father and grandfather had been respectively a tax-collector and a centurion, and who had not a drop of aristocratic blood in his veins.

Nero had not feared these middle-class civil servants and officers, who were almost all Italian; on the contrary, he had given many of them important positions, at the expense of the nobility. Procurators and centurions had remained loyal to him to the very end, but it was loyalty to the descendant of Augustus rather than to the ideological innovator. And any attraction that Neronism may have had for them was ended by the excesses that followed on Galba's death, by the slackness in military discipline and the loose social behaviour. They were consequently drawn closer to the conservatives. When Antonius Primus defeated the forces of Vitellius and marched into Italy he had the statues of Galba set up again. Nevertheless, except for Mucian and Primus himself, the senators were still excluded from responsible positions. As soon as Vespasian had established himself in power he made sure of controlling the Senate by 'packing' it with nominees drawn from the equestrian order and the Italian municipalities. Of the 176 senators of known origin during his reign, 93 were Italians who already had seats when he came to power, 55 were Italians chosen by him, 14 were provincials nominated by previous emperors, and another 14 provincials were Vespasian's men, almost all from the West.[1]

The origins of Vespasian's rise to power were a cause of the principate undergoing a radical change during his reign. The 'state secret' revealed by the 68–9 crisis was the strong association between the imperial authority and the body of officers and civil servants; they had ceased to be mere instruments of the prince, and had become the basis and foundation of his authority—which thus took on a more institutional and a less mystical aspect. Almost the whole of mankind had

[1] Mason Hammond, *J.R.S.*, 47 (1957), pp. 78-9.

sanctified Augustus as a Messiah; both Caligula and Nero had suc-
cumbed through trying to assume the same role; Tiberius and Claudius
had, more modestly, been satisfied to act as a kind of curate-in-charge
for the *Divus Augustus*. In spite of the propaganda of Tiberius Alexander, Vespasian's authority remained of a purely human character.
It is probably not just through chance that the first law we know of
which actually conferred powers on the Emperor dates from this reign.
Although law historians are not agreed on the differences between this
procedure and that prevailing in the reigns of the Julio-Claudians, it
does seem to correspond to a change in the nature of the monarchy.

Relations between the Emperor and his subjects were indeed from
that time founded on a purely human and political structure. Nothing
exemplifies this better than a comparison between the plan of the
Flavian palace, built by Domitian on the western heights of the Palatine, and the residences of Augustus and Nero. The modest house of
Augustus, with its ramparts of sanctuaries, served as a refuge where the
Emperor could escape from his official role and become a human being
again. The Golden House was a theatre where Nero displayed his ideas
of the perfect life, a cosmic sanctuary where daily incidents were surrounded with magical mystery. Different though they seem, both
conceptions allowed the Emperor to move in a supernatural realm. But
the Flavian palace, with its large audience-halls, had something of the
character of a public building; the private apartments were reminiscent
of official quarters adjacent to the public part of a government building,
and indeed the whole idea was probably modelled on the *praetoria* of
provincial governors. It was, then, an indication of the desanctifying
of the person of the Emperor, a lessening of his superhuman nature.

The small part played by the supernatural in the Flavian conception
of the Empire is apparent in the reliefs discovered under the Papal
Chancellery in 1938; one of them appears to represent Vespasian's
official entry into Rome in 70, and the other the departure of Domitian
for one of his campaigns. The work is obviously in the tradition of the
Ara Pacis, but differing by its lack of realism. Apart from the imperial
figures and their supernumeraries (vestals, priests, lictors), the others
are either allegorical (Rome, and the genii of the Senate and the People,
Virtue and Victory) or the traditional gods (Mars and Minerva).
Similar symbolic groups have already been noted on the breastplate of
the Primaporta statue and the large cameos; they bear witness to the
secularization of official religion, which Augustus wanted to bring

about after he had shaken off the influence of the Pythagoreans. But the Flavian reliefs are more conventional; the groups have less life to them, less sincerity, than the earlier works. The paintings in the basilica of Herculaneum, where Hercules with a boxer's head symbolizes 'the royal virtues', are lacking in mystical inspiration too. From the point of view of style, the Chancellery reliefs are indicative of a return to classicism, such as Karl Schefold noted in the Pompeian paintings of the decade preceding the catastrophe of 79. This, then, was another general reaction against the unreality which had dominated Neronian art. In this respect Vespasian conformed to Augustan tradition.

In the social sphere, however, the Flavians followed a policy the reverse of that of Augustus. The latter had tried to put new life into the republican nobility and to obtain its co-operation; but he had not been able to prevent its members reacting against the old traditional values. Vespasian put power into the hands of the Italian and provincial middle classes; as in Europe in the eighteenth century, these classes continued to uphold the values which the aristocracy considered outmoded. The ferment among the 'progressive' nobility was, moreover, spreading to elements of the lower classes—freedmen and *plebs sordida*, and the degenerates and slaves mentioned by Tacitus. These sections had been dangerously ripe for social revolt during Nero's reign. But in the latter part of the century the middle classes—having supplanted the aristocracy—established firm control over the proletariat. In addition, as a result of the economic evolution, great differences in wealth began to disappear and so class hatred abated. On the other hand, the economic decline of Italy and the growing prosperity of the provinces affected the freedmen whose fortunes depended on economic concentration; luxury trades—a most fruitful source of speculation—were declining and their place was being taken by less rewarding commerce. So towards the end of the first century and at the beginning of the second there was a lessening of the moral and social instability which had weakened the sound policy established by Augustus, and it did not increase again until the reign of Marcus Aurelius and the menace from the Germanic tribes.

Thus the general conditions which had provided a fertile soil for the doctrines issuing from Nero's fantastic mind disappeared in the twenty-five years after his death. So there could not be another Nero. Domitian and then Hadrian showed an interest in Greek culture which led their enemies to compare them with Agrippina's son; but neither would ever have conceived the amazing idea of a society wholly ruled by aesthetic standards. Nero was not the harbinger, born before his time, of a possible new form of society. He was the champion of a Utopia, and the strangest thing was that it captivated such a large section of mankind.

CONCLUSION

Every Roman emperor bore, among others, the name of Augustus, and in that name reincarnated the person of the founder and attached himself to his descendants in the spirit by a sort of fictional adoption. (Adoption played a more significant part in the Roman social system than it does in ours.) Furthermore, 'the policy of Augustus in all its branches had been sufficiently flexible and complex for each one of his successors, or nearly each one, to proclaim himself, on assuming the purple, as his faithful continuator, even if he happened to succeed a prince, who in his time had given himself out as the new Augustus but had been committed to a quite contrary policy' (Jean Beaujeu).

Historically considered, the imperial function may then appear either profoundly stable, or on the other hand essentially variable according to the temperament of those who in turn assumed it.

In the century which followed the battle of Actium it is the variability which comes to the fore: each Caesar in his own way trying to imitate, to perfect or to resume the work of the founder.

After A.D. 68, on the contrary, the burden begins to settle; the Augustan tradition is maintained, although time and again certain princes or certain groups of senators may have tried to interrupt it. But the position of the Flavian and Antonine monarchs, henceforward defined as much by law as by custom, presents a totally different appearance from that of the Julio-Claudian emperors.

This difference is not, however, apparent in the political power of the Emperor: juridically it still combines the same offices: ordinary and extraordinary magisterial offices, the same sacerdotal offices, the same administrative functions which had been grouped under the person of Augustus; and its title (*auctoritas*) remained quite as absolute in its vagueness as it had ever been under the founder. We cannot trace any constitutional evolution of the principate, either by the wasting away of an original 'diarchy', or by the progress of a relative liberalization. Only the perfecting of the administrative organs at his disposal effectively makes the second-century Emperor more omnipresent than his predecessors.

The transformation is even more apparent at the level of ideology. The mission of Augustus was essentially justified by a sort of supernatural favour, irrational and manifest above all in the undeniable fortune that crowned his military enterprises. This fortune had continued to protect the members of his dynasty; shortly before the death of Nero, says Suetonius, the laurel tree planted by Livia at her villa 'Ad Gallinas' was observed to wither: this was a sign of the celestial mandate of the Caesars. The emperors of the second century justified their power by Virtue, which rendered them worthy to serve as guides of humanity, shepherds of the flock of whom Zeus is the master. Certainly Augustus had already officially adhered to this Stoic doctrine by accepting the dedication of the Shield of Virtue, but the historians Dio Chrysostom, Plutarch, and even Pliny, clearly marked the inferiority of this corrupt Stoicism which still grants a large part to the irrational and immoral notion of chance entrusted to the true 'royal wisdom' which Marcus Aurelius demonstrates effectively in so far as this is permitted to man. In fact the notion of imperial 'Virtue' quickly takes on a mystical sense, which deprives it of the greater part of its ethical value. But it would be unfair and inaccurate to deny the effort they made to clothe in morality the power which Nero had striven to divest of every tribute save aesthetic ones.

It is above all in their relations with society that Vespasian, Trajan, Antonius or Marcus Aurelius behave very differently from Augustus or his descendants: the Julio-Claudians, including their founder, are at pains to isolate themselves willy-nilly and by various means from their subjects of all classes. The Flavians all save Domitian, and the Antonines except for Commodus, strive on the other hand to identify themselves with organized humanity of which they are the leaders.

This solidarity of the head with the limbs of the Empire is manifest in various ways; it would need another whole book to examine them all. The *Panegyric* of Pliny is well known as the manifesto of the 'liberal' Empire established by the revolution of 96; but it tells us that the *Patres* were content with a purely formal liberalism; they were delighted with the spectacle of the prince conforming in the exercise of his magisterial functions with the old republican ceremonial, and sometimes yielding precedence to the consul.

Modern commentators have had a great time denouncing the childish sham of these appearances, which left the reality of autocratic rule intact; but for all that they had a very great psychological importance, re-establishing, between the Senate and the prince, a climate of sympathy which had before existed only for short terms under Augustus and at the beginning of Nero's reign. Domitian has been accused of needlessly accumulating triumphal monuments, and those of Trajan are no less numerous, but they do express a feeling of comradeship between the *Imperator* and his troops who served together in hardship and glory: Trajan himself and his successors also showed their cordiality to the people as well at Rome as in the provinces where they toured regularly. Imperial humour thus takes on a new form, e.g. in the epigrams of Hadrian or in the anecdote of the bathers: Hadrian, on his way to bathe in the public baths, questions an old soldier who is scratching his back on the stone rim of the bath, and the veteran explains to him that he has not the means to afford a slave to scratch his back for him, whereupon the Emperor makes him a present out of his private purse. The next day swarms of bathers are to be seen scratching their backs on the rim of the bath and the Emperor forms them up in a circle one behind the other and bids them scratch each others'. Now the jokes of Augustus and his family, as we have seen, all tended to intimidate or to embarrass those to whom they were addressed, whereas those of Vespasian or Hadrian tended to put them at their ease.

This 'new style' had not only its trivial aspects. The administrative activity of the second-century princes attempted some practical betterment of the mode of life as it was lived by the Empire's inhabitants, by means of a whole series of economic or social or cultural measures, such as grants for children, loans to farmers, the protection of slaves, the provision of schools and medical services, etc.; and sometimes these were successful.

At the root of this attitude of fatherly care we find, on the one hand, the Hellenistic philosophical concept of philanthropy and, on the other hand, the old Roman institution of clienthood. But now these venerable ideas take on a practical force they never had before. They give rise to a relationship between the prince and his subjects which is expressed again and again in town after town and village after village, in monuments and in literary works which we may find repetitious to the point of monotony but which are nevertheless real and sincere.

Certainly Augustus in the hour of his death had been consoled for the sadness of his old age by the gratitude of Alexandrine sailors. The love of these poor people, however, served only to remind him of the

great gulf which separated him from his nearest of kin, his hate-intoxi-
cated family and his senators constrained to a conventional loyalty
which for the most part they detested. This sentimental setback which
the old emperor felt so painfully was not the lot of his second-century
successors. This is demonstrated by a particular fact which allows us to
pinpoint the difference which we have just observed.

Augustus, it will be remembered, had tried to invest his family with
the prestige of his own person; the *Ara Pacis* and the altar dedicated at
Carthage to the *gens Augusta* bear witness to that attempt. Now the
cult—and let us take the word in the very secular down-to-earth
context which fits the whole imperial religion—the cult of the reigning
family comes to a sudden end with the first century: there are no later
monuments of the kind which we have just noted. But the cult does
reappear in the course of the second century when it enjoys a remarkable success; the dedications of the *Domus Augusta* are duplicated
many times throughout the Empire, and the private life of the Emperor
and his family becomes the subject of official veneration, sometimes in
a form which strikes us as familiar to the point of indiscretion, as for
instance in the coins proclaiming in so many words not only the
fecundity but the chastity of the Empress! With us good taste would
demand that we take this for granted and pass it over in silence as the
older Greek and Roman tradition would also have done, since for the
ancients the perfect woman was she of whom men spoke as little as
possible of good or ill.

At first the historian is tempted to see in these facts proof that the
régime was evolving in the direction of hereditary monarchy; and
indeed it would be true to say that in the second century the dynastic
idea assumes a greater importance just at the moment when the succession of father to son is frustrated by a series of chances. But the imperial
family is not the sole object of public attention; private monuments,
both funerary and religious, and even public monuments concerning
the upper and middle classes, all reflect the importance of private life.
Towards the middle of the century, for instance, there appear those
pathetic sculptured tombs showing the child being brought up under
the tender eye of the parents; as well as those in which marriage
occupies the central place of honour in a man's career. This is a phenomenon comparable with that to which Philippe Ariès has recently
called attention in Europe of the sixteenth and seventeenth centuries,

that is the open avowal of family feeling which previously either did not exist or was considered unsuitable for public expression, at least in the medium of art.

The cult of the *Domus Augusta* thus appears at first sight as a special instance of a general social phenomenon which would explain its success; the princely family interests people, not by its unique status—the principal source of that constant interest which the masses in all ages have taken in dynasties—but by its resemblance to private families, for whom it serves as a pattern. If one were to venture a somewhat inaccurate comparison, one could say that the popularity of the *Domus Augusta* in the second century is more like the interest taken in the family of Louis-Philippe than in that of Louis XIV.

This ascendancy of the social element is strong enough to insulate any interior disorders of the royal house from the wider repercussions which such affairs in the first century had caused in the political scene. Not that they have disappeared however: between Trajan and Plotina, between Hadrian and Sabina and between Marcus Aurelius and Faustina there was never any such thing as conjugal accord either physically or morally. But their quarrels and their adventures were kept, if not secret, at least purely private. Even Hadrian's passion for Antinous, which manifested the queerest forms, did not lead to a crisis; on the contrary the astonishing tide of mystical sympathy which followed the death of his favourite shows the personal affection which the inhabitants of the Empire felt for a master whom his intimate friends knew to be neurotic, and whose personality suggested to Fronto those most unpleasant deities, Mars the Furious and Pluto.

If individual failings of character were thus without significance it is only because the fundamental ethical problem, insolubly presented by Augustus, was no longer an issue.

The scandalous conduct of many aristocrats at the end of the Republic and at the beginning of the Empire resulted, as we have seen, in the need for liberation from the traditional norms, as we see both in the literature and in the art of the time. In the second century this revolt has disappeared, and those who will not conform practise a particularly austere system of morality, especially the Christians. In the aesthetic field neo-classicism, which begins to reappear under the Flavians and triumphs under Hadrian, once more blocks off any escape by way of dreams. The essential cause of this spiritual evolution is certainly the complete turnover in personnel among the upper strata of society. Under Augustus 16 per cent of senators still belonged to patrician families, which were then some four or five centuries old: whereas under the Flavians the Curia contained not more than a dozen of these noble descendants of the founders of Rome, and by the time of Trajan's death there were only two of them left. The plebeian clans, who formed part of the nobility of the Republic, disappeared just as quickly. In A.D. 65 only a dozen clans survived, represented by nineteen individuals. Of all the plebeian families having a member in the Senate which are known to us for the Julio-Claudian period, about thirty-five had died out by the time Vespasian came to the throne and a hundred and twelve others perished during the reign of the Flavians (Mason Hammond).

The reigns of terror which Tiberius, Nero and Domitian let loose against the senators would not of themselves be sufficient to explain the death of a class. For the antique moralists such as Juvenal the explanation was divine punishment for their abandonment of those moral values which had constituted the great strength of Rome. But the moral reforms of the second century were not sufficient to modify the popular pattern: the families brought into the senatorial order by the Flavians and Antonines proved no more durable than their predecessors: in fact social promotion itself almost invariably brought about the extinction of a family.

In a world where medicine remained primitive and infantile mortality enormous the perpetuity of the race could be assured only by a fecundity which was exhausting for wives, the more refined of whom naturally blenched before this exacting duty. Paradoxically, the improvement in marital fidelity and in the stability of the family, which seems to be well attested by inscriptions, had the effect of reducing the upper-class birth-rate.

The higher offices continued to be filled by an influx of 'new men'. Now these newcomers still practised what one might call a provincial code of morals, more strict than the metropolitan one: funeral inscriptions prove that middle-class virtues continued to be honoured in the innumerable small cities which formed the political backbone of the Empire. Thus Nature herself brought about by a pitiless process of selection that moral reform which Augustus had been impotent to impose by law.

This biological transformation of society is on the other hand inseparable from the political evolution which gave the Empire its characteristic institutions. The rights of the middle classes would certainly not have been accomplished without a general increase in wealth due principally to the bringing under the plough of marginal land and better husbandry of impoverished soils: we have stated this phenomenon in another work on the civilization of Roman Africa, but from the very moment when they parted from their place of origin, the provincials began to climb the social ladder by promotion in the hierarchy of those civil and military services which the emperors had set up as the instrument of their own power: the small landed proprietor becomes a municipal official and the son of the urban magistrate graduates to the equestrian order, while the son of the procurator puts on the broad-striped gown of the senator. Thus one can say that the monarchy gives rise progressively to classes on which it leans for support just as later the absolute monarchy of France created the administrative middle class and drew from it an aristocracy of higher officials (*noblesse de robe*).

All this evolution existed in embryo in the organization founded by Augustus, but the latter cannot possibly have foreseen the distant consequences of his action. For example, in reserving to the 'knights' certain appointments as procurator, his intention was to avoid conferring major responsibility on freedmen; perhaps also he was careful to afford a new field of activity to members of the equestrian order and to compensate the guilds of *publicani* for their loss of the contract for tax collection. The idea of creating a new aristocracy of essentially Italic stock was far from his mind and he would have rejected it if he had been conscious of such a thing. In his plan the aristocracy recognized by the Republic, to which he was very conscious of belonging himself, was to remain in control of the Empire: all it had to do was to accept a reasonable measure of discipline equally essential to its own survival as for the good ordering of the universal society.

But Augustus, whose mind was essentially a political one, failed to assess the gravity of the spiritual revolt which was bringing the majority of these aristocrats into conflict with the traditional order. Because this revolt manifested itself above all in scandals, many modern historians in their turn have refused to recognize how serious it was. We hope we have demonstrated that the shocks to public opinion caused by the behaviour of Julia or Messalina are a symptom of the need for liberation which was shared by most people at this time.

By turning away from the teaching of Pythagoras, and in refusing to understand the message of Virgil, Augustus himself rejected the only power which would have led him to turn this striving towards emancipation into more noble forms and in compensation to make more acceptable the re-establishment of a discipline which would not have been a mere hypocritical conformity.

Thus the founder of the most rational material order, and moreover the least unjust one known to the Mediterranean world throughout its history, became the cause of the rift which separates the Emperor from his subject and condemns him to that isolation which Plato called the 'punishment of tyrants'. This loneliness at the summit was given form by Tiberius when he withdrew to Capri, and in accentuating its spiritual aspect Caligula lost his reason. Nero too went out of his mind in his attempt to take the revolt against traditional forms on himself and make a better order emerge from it. In the last analysis Augustus is responsible for all these sufferings, and only for lack of magnanimity and spiritual initiative. The conflict which tore apart the whole of the first century only came to an end by a sort of natural selection and biological evolution, thanks to which the supreme function was finally reintegrated into the social framework instead of opposing it. The political success undoubtedly enjoyed by the Empire of the Antonines rested only on a fragile material prosperity. When the first attacks of the barbarians broke down the frontiers and brought financial equilibrium to ruin, the metaphysical unrest which up to now had worried only a limited *élite* was shatteringly extended to the mass of the people. Henceforward the first task of the emperors, besides a welter of military, political and economic difficulties, will be to find the right doctrine to cure this agony, to which the only remedy offered by Augustus had been the rites of a 'religion' which was utterly secular and materialistic.

SIMPLIFIED GENEALOGICAL TABLE

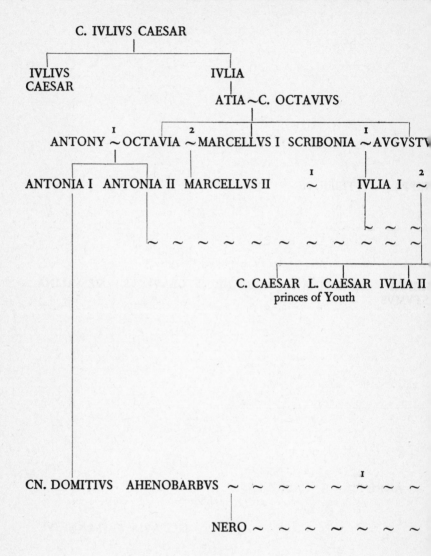

Principal persons omitted: (1) Julia, only daughter of Julius Caesar and wife of
was Messalina's grandmother; (3) the descendants of Tiberius through an earlier
Drusus, married Claudia Livilla, daughter of his uncle Drusus, and by her had three

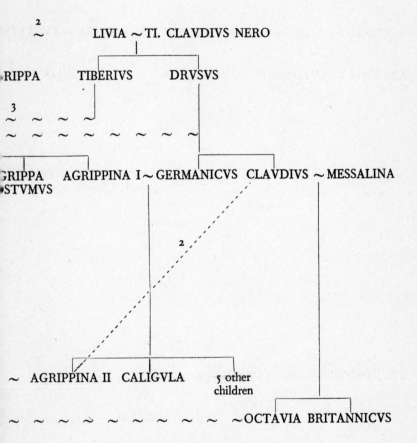

ompey, died childless; (2) two daughters of Marcellus and Octavia, one of whom
narriage with Vipsania, daughter of Agrippa by his first wife: the son of this union,
hildren.

INDEX

187

This is the story of the first and last emperors of an illustrious line—the Julio-Claudian House synonymous with the creation of the Empire of Rome. It spans the crucial century from 31 B.C., when Augustus came to power, to A.D. 68, when Nero committed suicide. An analysis of the imperial Roman mentality, it illuminates an epoch whose effects can still be felt in the modern world.

To the extraordinarily complex personalities of Augustus and Nero, and the courts which surrounded them, the author brings profound insights and dramatic powers of storytelling. The result is an unforgettable gallery of portraits, full-fleshed human beings whose makeup and motives are revealed with such clarity that the reader is forced to remind himself that these people lived almost two millennia ago.

Here, for example, is a sharply etched study of the man Augustus who lurked behind the mask of the Emperor Augustus. In it, we learn the real nature of Augustus' strange double life. The author makes clear why this politician and general whose immense talents remade the Roman state chose to refuse the title of monarch—and why Augustus died asking his intimates if he had been "a good actor in the comedy of life."